AF674852

DATA SCIENCE AND DATA ANALYTICS

USING PYTHON PROGRAMMING

Dr. Munesh Chandra Trivedi
Dr. Anil Kumar Dubey

KHANNA BOOK PUBLISHING CO. (P) LTD.
Publisher of Engineering and Computer Books
4C/4344, Ansari Road, Darya Ganj, New Delhi-110002
Phone : 011-23244447-48 **Mobile:** +91-9910909320
E-mail : contact@khannabooks.com
Website : www.khannabooks.com

Dear Readers,

To prevent the piracy, this book is secured with HIGH SECURITY HOLOGRAM on the front title cover. In case you don't find the hologram on the front cover title, please write us to at contact@khannabooks.com or whatsapp us at +91-99109 09320 and avail special gift voucher for yourself.

Specimen of Hologram on front Cover title:

Moreover, there is a SPECIAL DISCOUNT COUPON for you with EVERY HOLOGRAM.

How to avail this SPECIAL DISCOUNT:

Step 1: Scratch the hologram
Step 2: Under the scratch area, your "coupon code" is available
Step 3: Logon to www.khannabooks.com
Step 4: Use your "coupon code" in the shopping cart and get your copy at a special discount
Step 5: Enjoy your reading!

Thanks,
Khanna Publishing House

Price: ₹ 395.00

ISBN: 978-93-5538-426-3

Data Science and Data Analytics Using Python Programming
by Dr. Munesh Chandra Trivedi,
Dr. Anil Kumar Dubey

First Edition: 2025

To view complete list of books, please scan the QR Code:

Published by:
Khanna Book Publishing Co. (P) Ltd.
CIN: U22110DL1998PTC095547

Visit us at: www.khannabooks.com
Write us at: contact@khannabooks.com

Printed in Bharat.

Copyright © Publisher

No part of this publication may be reproduced, stored in a retrieval system or transmitted, in any form or by any means, electronic, mechanical, photocopying, recording or otherwise without prior permission of the publisher.

This book is sold subject to the condition that it shall not, by way of trade, be lent, re-sold, hired out or otherwise disposed of without the publisher's consent, in any form of binding or cover other than that in which it is published.

Disclaimer: The website links provided by the author in this book are placed for informational, educational & reference purpose only. The Publisher do not endorse these website links or the views of the speaker/ content of the said weblinks. In case of any dispute, all legal matters to be settled under Delhi Jurisdiction only.

Preface

The world of data science and analytics has revolutionized how we understand and utilize data in fields ranging from finance and healthcare to marketing and social sciences. As data volumes grow exponentially, so does the demand for skilled professionals who can interpret this wealth of information to drive decisions and foster innovation. "Data Science and Data Analytics Using Python Programming" isn't just a book—it's your gateway to mastering this dynamic field, packed with hands-on learning experiences and real-world examples that bring data science to life.

Whether you're a student diving into Python for the first time or a seasoned professional looking to enhance your data skills, this book is designed to make your journey engaging and rewarding. After introducing data science, we focus to Python basics, ensuring you build a solid foundation before exploring advanced techniques. From manipulating data to visualizing insights and conducting statistical analyses, each chapter builds upon the last, guiding you through the essential tools and methodologies of data science.

One of the most exciting parts of this journey is diving into machine learning. You'll uncover the power of algorithms that can predict trends, classify data, and even learn from new information—all using Python's powerful libraries. But it's not just about theory; we emphasize practicality. Throughout the book, you'll tackle real-world challenges through hands-on exercises. These exercises aren't just about memorizing syntax—they're about applying what you've learned to solve problems that data scientists face every day.

By the end of this book, you won't just know how to crunch numbers; you'll have the skills to extract meaningful insights and create impactful data-driven solutions. Whether you're analyzing customer behavior, predicting market trends, or optimizing healthcare outcomes, you'll be equipped to make a difference in your field.

Think of "Data Science and Data Analytics Using Python Programming" as your companion on the path to becoming a proficient data scientist or analyst. Whether you're starting fresh or aiming to elevate your expertise, this book provides the practical guidance and hands-on experience you need to thrive in the rapidly evolving world of data science. Let's embark on this journey together and unlock the endless possibilities that data has to offer.

—Author

Contents

1

INTRODUCTION OF DATA SCIENCE

BASICS OF DATA SCIENCE

Data science is a multidisciplinary field that involves extracting knowledge and insights from data through various processes, including data collection, cleaning, analysis, and interpretation. It combines expertise from computer science, mathematics, statistics, domain knowledge, and communication skills to make informed decisions and predictions.

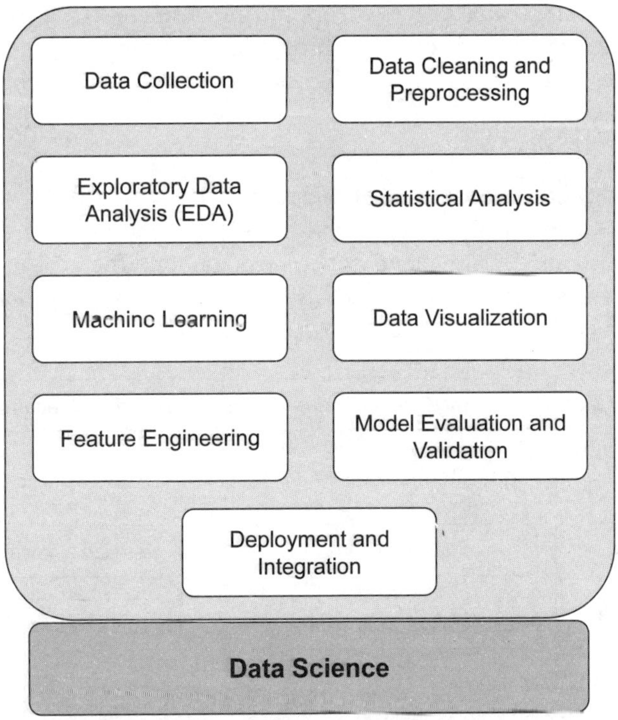

Fig. 1.1: Data Science Key Components

- **Data Collection**: Gathering relevant data from various sources, such as databases, APIs, web scraping, sensors, or surveys.

- **Data Cleaning and Preprocessing**: Processing and preparing the data to ensure it is accurate, consistent, and ready for analysis. This step often involves dealing with missing values, handling outliers, and transforming data into a suitable format.
- **Exploratory Data Analysis (EDA)**: Exploring and visualizing the data to gain insights, identify patterns, and understand the underlying relationships between variables.
- **Statistical Analysis and Machine Learning**: Applying statistical methods and machine learning algorithms to build predictive models and make data-driven decisions. This involves tasks like regression, classification, clustering, and more.
- **Data Visualization**: Presenting the findings and insights in a visual and easily understandable format using graphs, charts, and other visual elements.
- **Feature Engineering**: Selecting or creating relevant features (input variables) for the machine learning models to improve their performance.
- **Model Evaluation and Validation**: Assessing the performance of the predictive models using metrics and cross-validation techniques to ensure they are accurate and generalize well to new data.
- **Deployment and Integration**: Implementing the developed models into production systems or applications to solve real-world problems.

Data science is widely used in various industries, such as finance, healthcare, marketing, e-commerce, and more, to extract valuable information from vast amounts of data and make data-driven decisions. It plays a critical role in improving processes, optimizing business strategies, and creating personalized user experiences. Python and R are common programming languages used in data science, and there are numerous libraries and frameworks available to facilitate data analysis and machine learning tasks.

DATA MINING

Data mining is a subset of the broader field of data science. It refers to the process of discovering patterns, relationships, insights, and valuable information from large datasets using various techniques, such as statistical analysis, machine learning, and pattern recognition. The goal of data mining is to extract useful knowledge from data, which can then be used for decision-making, prediction, and optimization.

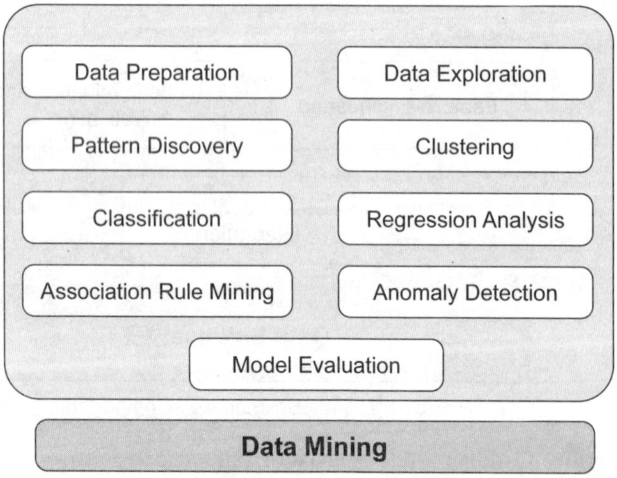

Fig. 1.2: Data Mining Key Components

- **Data Preparation**: Similar to data science, data mining starts with data collection and data cleaning. It involves gathering relevant data from various sources and ensuring that it is in a suitable format for analysis.
- **Data Exploration**: Exploring the data to gain an understanding of its structure, identifying important variables, and uncovering any initial patterns or trends.
- **Pattern Discovery**: This is the core of data mining, where different algorithms and techniques are applied to the data to identify meaningful patterns, associations, correlations, or anomalies.
- **Clustering**: Grouping similar data points together based on their characteristics to identify inherent structures or segments in the data.
- **Classification**: Assigning data points to predefined categories or classes based on their features, typically used for predictive modeling.
- **Regression Analysis**: Establishing relationships between variables to predict numerical values, such as sales or prices.
- **Association Rule Mining**: Identifying interesting relationships between variables that frequently co-occur in the data, often used in market basket analysis.
- **Anomaly Detection**: Identifying unusual or rare instances in the data that deviate significantly from the normal behavior.
- **Model Evaluation**: Assessing the performance and accuracy of the data mining models to ensure their reliability and generalization to new data.

Data mining has numerous applications across various industries, including marketing, finance, healthcare, customer relationship management, fraud detection, and more. It helps organizations uncover hidden insights and gain a competitive advantage by making data-driven decisions and improving business processes.

It's important to note that data mining should always be done ethically and with consideration for privacy and data protection regulations, as it involves working with potentially sensitive and personal information.

STATISTICS

Data collection, analysis, interpretation, presentation, and organization are all topics that fall under the purview of statistics, a subfield of mathematics. It offers strategies and procedures for interpreting numerical data so that readers can come to meaningful conclusions and take wise judgments. Numerous sectors, including science, social sciences, business, economics, engineering, healthcare, and others, heavily rely on statistics.

- **Descriptive Statistics**: Descriptive statistics involve the methods used to summarize and describe the main features of a dataset. Common descriptive statistics include measures such as mean, median, mode, standard deviation, variance, and percentiles.
- **Inferential Statistics**: Inferential statistics uses data from a sample to make inferences or draw conclusions about a larger population. This involves hypothesis testing, confidence intervals, and estimating population parameters based on sample data.
- **Probability**: Probability is the study of random events and the likelihood of their occurrence. It provides a mathematical framework to quantify uncertainty and randomness.
- **Sampling Techniques**: When dealing with large populations, it is often not feasible to collect data from everyone. Sampling techniques help select representative subsets (samples) from the population to draw valid statistical inferences.

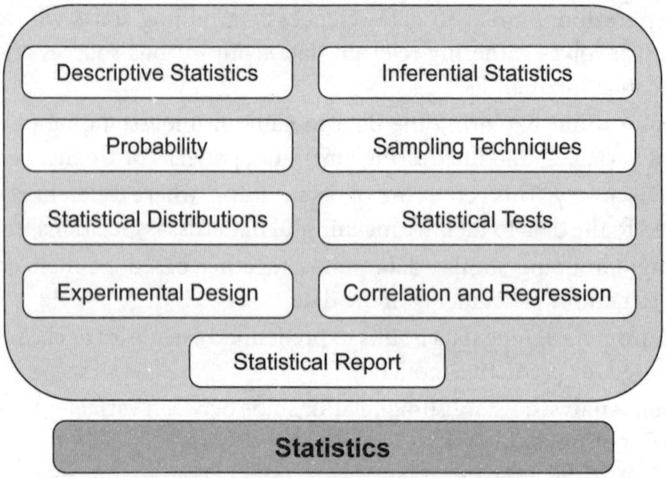

Fig. 1.3: Statistics Key Components

- **Statistical Distributions**: Different types of data follow specific distributions. Common distributions include normal (Gaussian), binomial, Poisson, exponential, and many others. Understanding these distributions is crucial for data analysis and modeling.
- **Statistical Tests**: Statistical tests are used to determine whether observed differences or relationships in data are statistically significant or due to random chance. Examples include t-tests, chi-square tests, ANOVA (Analysis of Variance), and regression analysis.
- **Experimental Design**: In experimental studies, proper design and control of experiments are essential to ensure reliable results. Randomized controlled trials (RCTs) are a common experimental design used in research.
- **Correlation and Regression**: The intensity and direction of the relationship between two variables are measured through correlation. The relationship between variables can be modeled and predicted with the use of regression analysis.

Statistics plays a crucial role in scientific research, business analytics, quality control, market research, public policy, and more. It enables professionals to extract valuable insights from data, identify patterns, make predictions, and evaluate the significance of findings. Additionally, it is also used to assess risks, test hypotheses, and support evidence-based decision-making.

MACHINE LEARNING

A subfield of artificial intelligence called "machine learning (ML)" focuses on developing statistical models and algorithms that enable computers to learn from data and improve at a given task without needing to be explicitly programmed. Computers can improve their performance on a task through experience (data) without human intervention thanks to machine learning, which aims to enable them to automatically learn from experience, find patterns, and make data-driven judgments.

- **Training Data**: For training, machine learning algorithms need a lot of data. This information is made up of input samples (features) and the labels or desired values which correspond alongside them. The algorithm analyzes this information to discover patterns and relationships.

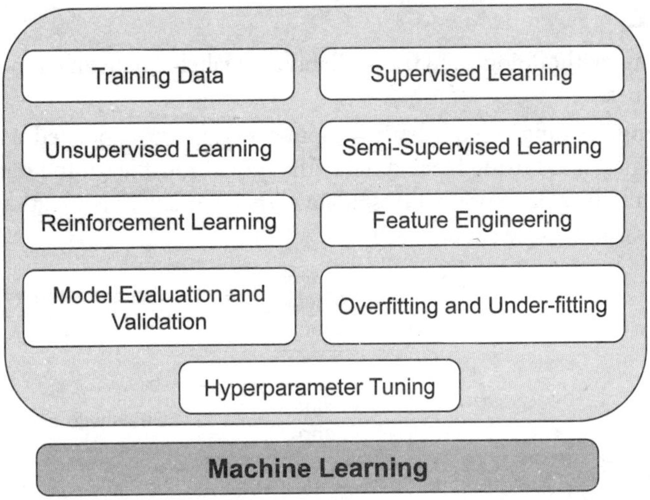

Fig. 1.4: Machine Learning Key Components

- **Supervised Learning**: In supervised learning, the algorithm is trained on data that has been labeled, where the input features and their appropriate outputs (labels) are given. The algorithm learns to map inputs to outputs by minimizing the error between predicted and actual labels. Common supervised learning tasks include classification (assigning labels to categories) and regression (predicting continuous values).
- **Unsupervised Learning**: In unsupervised learning, the algorithm is trained on unlabeled data in the absence of clear output labels. The algorithm learns to find patterns or groupings in the data without any specific guidance. In unsupervised learning, the algorithm is trained on unlabeled data in the absence of clear output labels.
- **Semi-Supervised Learning**: This is supervised and unsupervised learning combined. When there is a lack of labeled data, the algorithm's performance can be improved because it was trained on a dataset with both labeled and unlabeled data.
- **Reinforcement Learning**: Reinforcement learning involves training agents to interact with an environment and learn from the feedback they receive. The agent takes actions to maximize a reward signal over time, and the learning process is based on trial and error.
- **Feature Engineering**: Feature engineering is the process of selecting or creating the most relevant and informative input features for a machine learning model. It can significantly impact the model's performance.
- **Model Evaluation and Validation**: Assessing the performance of machine learning models is essential to ensure they generalize well to new, unseen data. Techniques such as cross-validation and metrics like accuracy, precision, recall, and F1 score are commonly used for evaluation.
- **Overfitting and Under-fitting**: When a model performs well on training data but poorly on fresh data, this is known as overfitting. On the other side, underfitting happens when a model is too straightforward to detect the underlying patterns in the data. Balancing these issues is crucial for building effective models.
- **Hyperparameter Tuning**: Machine learning models have hyperparameters that need to be set before training. Hyperparameter tuning involves finding.

TYPES OF ML

Based on the learning methodology and the availability of labeled data, machine learning may be roughly divided into four types.

Supervised Learning: In supervised learning, input samples are associated with corresponding output labels, and a model is trained using labeled data. The model must learn the relationship between inputs and outputs in order to be able to predict fresh data with accuracy. Classification and regression are a few of examples of tasks that require supervision.

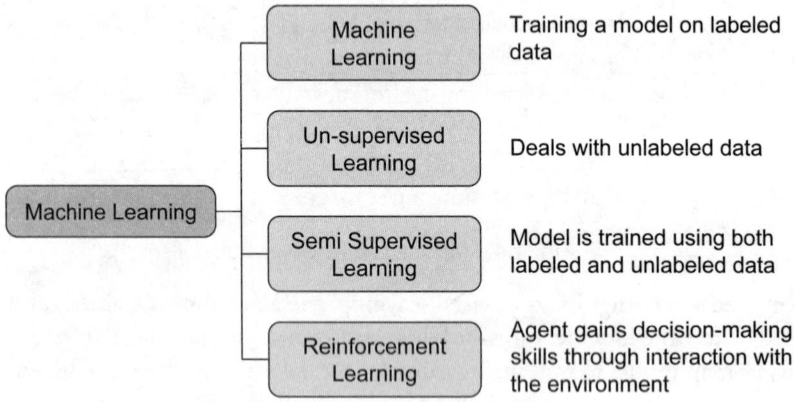

Fig. 1.5: Types of Machine Learning

- **Classification**: The model learns to categorize input data into specified categories or classes when performing classification tasks. For instance, spam email detection is a common example of a binary classification problem, when an email is classified as spam (class 1) or not (class 0) by the model. Multi-class classification involves categorizing data into more than two classes, like classifying animals into different species.
- **Regression**: Regression tasks involve predicting continuous numerical values based on input features. For example, Regression problems include estimating housing prices based on attributes like size, number of bedrooms, and location.

Unsupervised Learning: Unsupervised learning deals with unlabeled data, without explicit direction on the output, the model looks for patterns, correlations, or structures within the data. The algorithm explores the data to identify clusters of similar data points or to reduce the data's dimensionality.

- **Clustering**: Based on their characteristics or commonalities, clustering algorithms place related data points in clusters. K-means, hierarchical clustering, and DBSCAN are examples of common clustering techniques.
- **Dimensionality Reduction**: Utilizing dimensionality reduction techniques, it is possible to reduce the number of features in the data set while preserving essential information. Principal Component Analysis, or PCA, and t-distributed Stochastic Neighbor Embedding (t-SNE) are two common methods for dimensionality reduction.

Reinforcement Learning: In a different paradigm known as reinforcement learning, an agent learns to make decisions through interacting with its surroundings. Based on its behaviors, the agent receives feedback in the form of incentives or punishments. The objective is to teach the agent the correct course of behavior to accomplish a certain task or maximize a cumulative reward.

- **Agent**: The decision-maker or learner who engages with the environment.
- **Environment**: A system outside of the agent with which it communicates. According to the agent's behaviors, the environment gives it feedback.
- **Actions**: The decisions or moves made by the agent in response to the environment.
- **Rewards**: The feedback or reinforcement that the agent receives from the environment based on its actions.

Gaming (such as AlphaGo), robotics, autonomous vehicles, and resource management are a few applications that frequently use reinforcement learning. Each method of machine learning has advantages and disadvantages, and it is best suited for particular challenges. Depending on the specific task and the availability of labeled data, one may choose the most appropriate type of machine learning approach.

Semi-supervised learning: Machine learning techniques such as semi-supervised learning train the model utilizing both labeled and unlabeled input. In traditional supervised learning, the algorithm is provided with labeled examples, where each data point has a corresponding target or label. In unsupervised learning, there are no labeled examples, and the algorithm tries to find patterns or structures within the data on its own. Semi-supervised learning lies between these two approaches. It leverages the information present in both labeled and unlabeled data to improve the model's performance. The motivation behind using semi-supervised learning is that labeled data can be expensive and time-consuming to obtain, while unlabeled data is often more abundant and easier to acquire. The general idea behind semi-supervised learning can be summarized as follows:

- **Labeled Data**: The model is trained on a smaller set of labeled data, where each data point is associated with a known target value.
- **Unlabeled Data**: Additionally, the model is also exposed to a larger set of unlabeled data, where the target values are missing or unknown.
- **Learning from Both**: The model tries to find patterns and structures in the combined labeled and unlabeled data. By leveraging the information from the unlabeled data, it can learn a more generalized representation of the underlying data distribution.

There are several techniques used in semi-supervised learning, such as:

- **Self-training**: The labeled data is used to train the model initially. The unlabeled data is then used to generate predictions using the trained model. The model is retrained using this supplemented dataset, adding the predictions with the highest degree of confidence to the labeled dataset. This procedure is repeated iteratively.
- **Generative models**: Unlabeled data can be utilized to simulate the underlying data distribution using methods such as Generative Adversarial Networks with Variational Autoencoders. The generated data can then be combined with the labeled data to train a supervised model.
- **Graph-based methods**: These methods leverage the similarity between data points and create a graph using both labeled and unlabeled data. The labels propagate through the graph, allowing the model to make predictions on unlabeled data based on the information from neighboring labeled data points.

Semi-supervised learning can be particularly useful in scenarios where obtaining a large labeled dataset is challenging but acquiring a substantial amount of unlabeled data is feasible. By utilizing the unlabeled data, semi-supervised learning can potentially improve the model's performance and generalization abilities. However, it requires careful handling to prevent the propagation of noise from the unlabeled data to the model.

SUPERVISED V/S UNSUPERVISED LEARNING

Mainly machine learning is categorized in two parts as supervised and un supervised machine leaning.

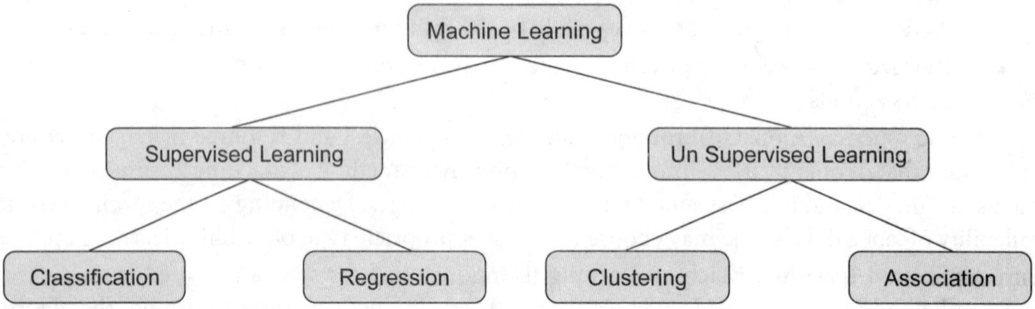

Fig. 1.6: Categorised Machine Learning

Supervised and unsupervised learning are the two main classifications of machine learning techniques. These two methods handle data and the learning process in different ways.

Table 1: Supervised V/s Un supervised Machine Learning

Key Differences	Supervised	Un supervised
Definition	By pairing input samples with associated output labels or goal values, supervised learning entails training a model using labeled data.	Unsupervised learning deals with unlabeled data, where the algorithm does not have access to corresponding output labels during training
Objective	Aims to make accurate predictions.	Focuses on finding patterns or structures in the data
Training Process	The algorithm learns the connection between input features and the appropriate target labels during training	The algorithm explores the data to identify patterns, similarities, or structures within the data without explicit guidance on the output
Data Availability	Requires labeled data for training.	Works with unlabeled data
Tasks	Includes tasks like classification and regression.	Includes tasks like clustering and dimensionality reduction
Performance Evaluation	The model's performance is assessed using metrics including accuracy, precision, recall, and mean squared error.	Evaluation is more subjective, often relying on visual inspection and cluster validity indices
Example Algorithms	Popular supervised learning techniques include Support Vector Machines, Decision Trees, Random Forests, Logistic Regression, and Neural Networks..	K-Means, DBSCAN, Gaussian Mixture Models (GMM), and Singular Value Decomposition (SVD) are popular unsupervised learning algorithms.

CLASSIFICATION ALGORITHM

The objective of supervised learning tasks that use classification algorithms is to group incoming data into predetermined categories or classes based on the properties of the data. These algorithms develop predictions on new, unlabeled data by learning from labeled training data.

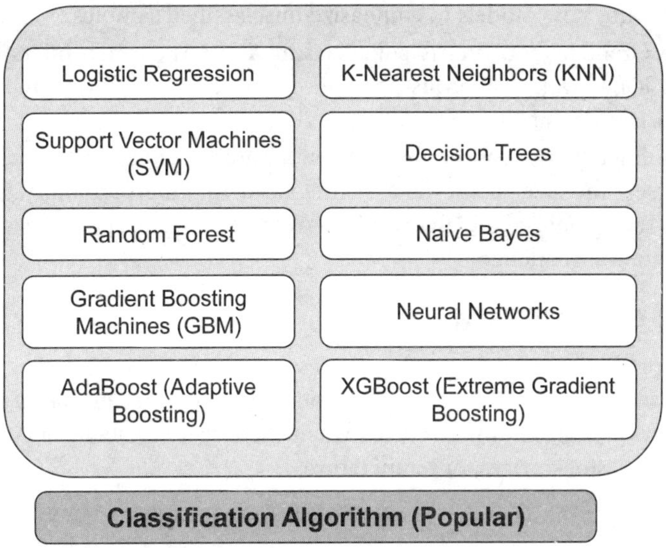

Fig. 1.7: Popular Classification Algorithm

- **Logistic Regression**: It is a classification algorithm that is utilized for binary classification applications, despite its name. Through the use of a logistic function, it simulates the likelihood that an input will fall into one of the two groups (0 or 1).
- **K-Nearest Neighbors (KNN)**: An easy-to-understand categorization algorithm is KNN. When given a new data point, it places it in the feature space's most prevalent class among its k closest neighbors, where k is a user-defined value.
- **Support Vector Machines**: For both binary and multi-class classification applications, SVM (Support Vector Machines) is a potent method. It determines the ideal hyperplane in the feature space for separating the data points from various classes.
- **Decision Trees**: To produce a tree-like structure, decision trees iteratively partition the data into subsets according to the features. Each leaf node corresponds to a class label, and each internal node reflects a judgment based on a feature.
- **Random Forest**: Multiple decision trees are combined in Random Forest, an ensemble learning technique, to increase accuracy and decrease overfitting. To reach a judgment, it combines the predictions of other trees.
- **Naive Bayes**: Based on Bayes' theorem, Naive Bayes is a probabilistic classification algorithm. Despite being straightforward, it frequently excels at jobs like text classification and other related ones.
- **Gradient Boosting Machines (GBM)**: Another ensemble learning technique is GBM, which successively constructs a number of weak learners, often decision trees, with each one aiming to fix the flaws of the preceding one.
- **Neural Networks**: A subset of deep learning techniques called neural networks is employed for challenging categorization tasks. They are made up of layers of interconnected nodes (neurons) that process and change the input data.
- **AdaBoost**: An ensemble learning technique called AdaBoost (Adaptive Boosting) combines weak learners to produce a strong learner. It increases the weights of misclassified samples and

iteratively trains new models to emphasize misclassified samples.

- **XGBoost**: Gradient boosting is enhanced in XGBoost, which offers high performance and efficiency. It has won numerous machine learning competitions and is frequently used for structured/tabular data.

The classification technique chosen depends on a number of variables, including the type of data, the number of classes, the size of the dataset, the need for interpretability, and the computational resources available. Trying out various algorithms is frequently necessary to see which one best addresses a particular categorization challenge.

REGRESSION ALGORITHM

When performing predictive modeling tasks, regression algorithms are a type of supervised learning technique that are used to forecast a continuous numerical output variable based on input characteristics. In other words, regression algorithms are used when the target variable is a continuous value, such as predicting house prices, stock prices, or temperature.

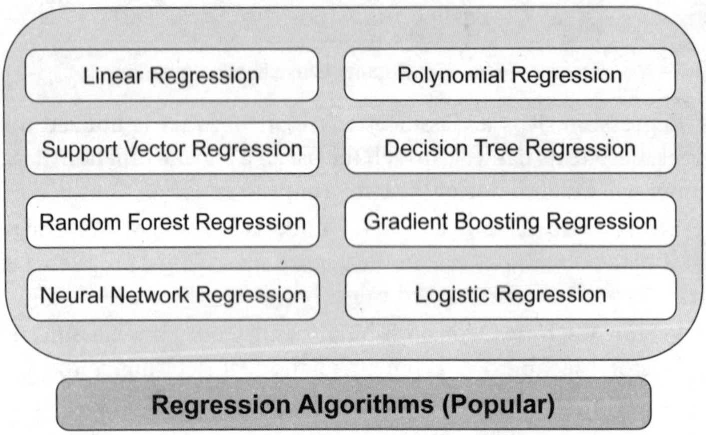

Fig. 1.8: Popular Regression Algorithm

- **Linear Regression**: One of the simplest and most popular regression approaches is linear regression. It attempts to minimize the sum of squared discrepancies between the predicted and actual values by fitting a straight line to the data points.
- **Polynomial Regression**: The relationship between the characteristics and the target variable is described as an nth-degree polynomial rather than a straight line in polynomial regression, which is an extension of linear regression.
- **Support Vector Regression** (SVR): SVR is based on SVM and is used for regression tasks. It tries to find a hyperplane that best fits the data points within a certain margin of error.
- **Decision Tree Regression**: Regression tasks can also use decision trees. The average target value of the samples within each leaf node is used as the anticipated value after they iteratively divide the data into subgroups based on feature thresholds.
- **Random Forest Regression**: An ensemble learning technique called Random Forest mixes various decision trees to produce predictions that are more precise. The final prediction is the average of all individual predictions made by each tree in the forest.
- **Gradient Boosting Regression**: Another strategy for building several weak learners (often decision trees) consecutively is gradient boosting. Each subsequent tree corrects the mistakes

produced by the prior ones, resulting in a prediction that is more accurate.

- **Neural Network Regression**: Regression tasks can also be performed using neural networks. The network is trained to map input features to the continuous output target, and they are made up of interconnected nodes grouped into layers.
- **Logistic regression**: Binary classification challenges are handled using the statistical and machine learning technique known as logistic regression. It is mostly used to forecast the likelihood that an instance falls inside a certain class or category. Contrary to what its name implies, logistic regression is a classification algorithm. The output variable, often referred to as the dependent variable or goal, is binary (i.e., it can take on one of two potential values, commonly represented as 0 and 1) in logistic regression. Both continuous and categorical input variables, often known as independent variables or predictors, may be used.

The selection of a regression technique is influenced by a number of variables, including the type of data, the relationship between features and the target variable, the size of the dataset, and the availability of processing resources. It is customary to test out various algorithms and choose the one that works the best for a certain task.

CLUSTERING ALGORITHM

Unsupervised ML algorithms known as clustering algorithms are used to cluster together comparable data points based on their characteristics or similarities. Instead of using predetermined classifications or labels like classification does, the algorithm for clustering looks for innate structures or patterns in the data.

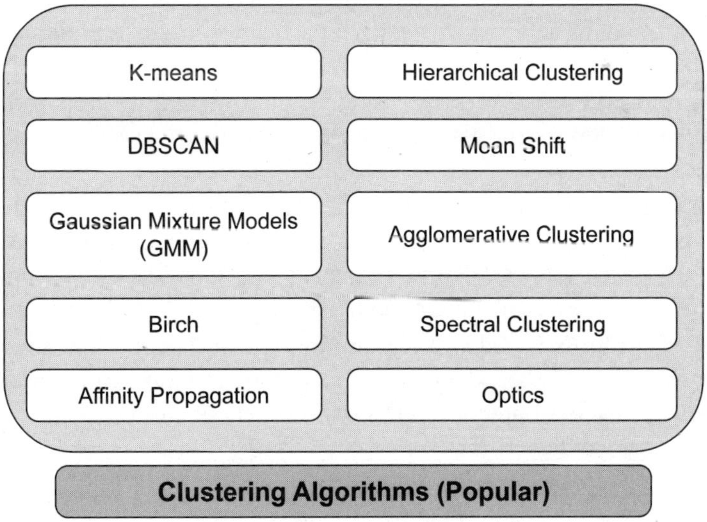

Fig. 1.9: Popular Clustering Algorithm

- **K-Means**: One of the most used clustering algorithms is K-Means. With K being a user-defined parameter, it divides the data into K clusters. The algorithm updates the centroids based on the newly assigned data points after iteratively assigning each data point to the closest centroid (cluster center).
- **Hierarchical Clustering**: A dendrogram, created through hierarchical clustering, resembles a

tree and is made up of layered clusters. It can be agglomerative, where individual data points are first clustered separately and are then combined into bigger clusters, or divisive, where all of the data points are first clustered together and are then successively divided into smaller clusters.

- **Density-Based Spatial Clustering of Applications with Noise**: A density-based clustering algorithm is DBSCAN. It classifies data points according to their density and recognizes clusters as high-density regions divided by low-density regions. It can also identify noise spots, or outliers.
- **Mean Shift**: Mean Shift is another density-based algorithm that iteratively moves data points towards the mode (peak) of the data distribution. It identifies cluster centers as points where data converges.
- **Gaussian Mixture Models (GMM)**: GMM makes the assumption that the data points were produced using a combination of different Gaussian distributions. It identifies the Gaussian distributions that match the data the best and allocates data points to the clusters corresponding to those distributions.
- **Agglomerative Clustering**: Agglomerative clustering is a bottom-up method that begins with each data point as a separate cluster and then repeatedly merges the closest clusters until all of the data points are members of a single cluster or a certain number of clusters are attained.
- **Birch (Balanced Iterative Reducing and Clustering using Hierarchies)**: Birch is a hierarchical clustering approach that creates a structure that resembles a tree by combining centroids and clustering features.
- **Spectral Clustering**: Spectral clustering uses the eigenvalues and eigenvectors of a similarity graph to partition the data into clusters. It is particularly useful for finding non-linear structures in the data.
- **Affinity Propagation**: The message-passing algorithm affinity propagation selects a subset of data points as exemplars and associates further data points with these exemplars based on their similarity.
- **OPTICS:** Ordering Points To Identify the Clustering Structure is what it stands for. It is an unsupervised machine learning approach used to cluster data points in a dataset according to density. The well-known DBSCAN (Density-Based Spatial Clustering of Applications with Noise) algorithm is expanded upon in OPTICS.

The clustering algorithm selected will rely on the type of data, the intended number of clusters, the density of the clusters, and the requirements for interpretability. To choose the optimal strategy for a particular dataset, it is usual practice to test out a variety of clustering algorithms and assess their effectiveness using cluster validity criteria.

ASSOCIATION

Association rule learning is a type of machine learning technique used to discover interesting relationships or patterns in large datasets. It is particularly useful for analyzing transactional data, such as customer shopping baskets or itemsets in a database. The most famous algorithm for association rule learning is the Apriori algorithm.

The goal of association rule learning is to identify strong associations between items in the dataset. These associations are represented as "if-then" rules, where the presence of certain items (antecedents) implies the presence of other items (consequents) with a certain level of confidence.

Here's an example of an association rule:

IF {Milk, Bread} = {Eggs}

This rule states that if a customer buys both "Milk" and "Bread" together (antecedent), then there is a high likelihood that the customer will also buy "Eggs" (consequent).

In association rule learning, the two main measures are:

- **Support**: It is the proportion of transactions in the dataset that contain both the antecedent and the consequent items. High support means the itemsets occur frequently in the dataset.
- **Confidence**: It measures the conditional probability that the consequent item appears in a transaction given that the antecedent item is present. High confidence indicates a strong relationship between the antecedent and consequent.

Additionally, there is another metric called "lift," which quantifies the degree to which the presence of the antecedent influences the presence of the consequent beyond what would be expected by chance.

Association rule learning is widely used in various applications, including market basket analysis, recommendation systems, customer behavior analysis, and web usage mining. It helps businesses and organizations identify cross-selling opportunities, optimize product placement, and gain insights into customer preferences and habits.

REVIEW QUESTIONS

Q.1. What are the main types of machine learning?

Ans. Machine learning can be broadly categorized into four types, based on the learning approach and the availability of labeled data.

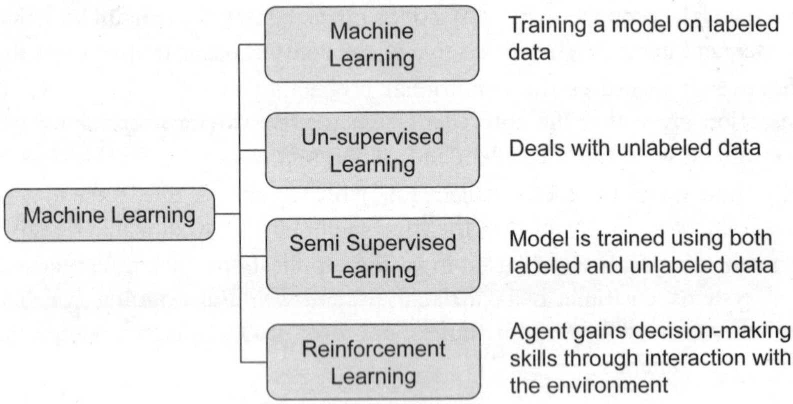

Fig. 1. Types of Machine Learning

Supervised Learning: Supervised learning involves training a model on labeled data, where the input samples are paired with their corresponding output labels. The goal is for the model to learn the mapping between inputs and outputs so that it can make accurate predictions on new, unseen data.

Unsupervised Learning: Unsupervised learning deals with unlabeled data, where the model seeks to find patterns, relationships, or structures within the data without explicit guidance on the output. The algorithm explores the data to identify clusters of similar data points or to reduce the data's dimensionality.

Reinforcement Learning: Reinforcement learning is a different paradigm where an agent learns to make decisions by interacting with an environment. The agent receives feedback in the form of rewards or penalties based on its actions. The goal is for the agent to learn the best sequence of actions to achieve a specific goal or maximize a cumulative reward.

Semi-supervised learning: Semi-supervised learning is a type of machine learning where the model is trained using both labeled and unlabeled data. In traditional supervised learning, the algorithm is provided with labeled examples, where each data point has a corresponding target or label. In unsupervised learning, there are no labeled examples, and the algorithm tries to find patterns or structures within the data on its own. Semi-supervised learning lies between these two approaches. It leverages the information present in both labeled and unlabeled data to improve the model's performance. The motivation behind using semi-supervised learning is that labeled data can be expensive and time-consuming to obtain, while unlabeled data is often more abundant and easier to acquire.

Q.2. What are the main differences between supervised and unsupervised learning?

Ans.

Table 1. Supervised V/s Un supervised Machine Learning

Key Differences	Supervised	Un supervised
Definition	Supervised learning involves training a model on labeled data, where the input samples are paired with their corresponding output labels or target values	Unsupervised learning deals with unlabeled data, where the algorithm does not have access to corresponding output labels during training
Objective	Aims to make accurate predictions.	Focuses on finding patterns or structures in the data
Training Process	During training, the algorithm learns the relationship between input features and the corresponding target labels	The algorithm explores the data to identify patterns, similarities, or structures within the data without explicit guidance on the output
Data Availability	Requires labeled data for training.	Works with unlabeled data
Tasks	Includes tasks like classification and regression.	Includes tasks like clustering and dimensionality reduction
Performance Evaluation	Model's performance is assessed using metrics like accuracy, precision, recall, and Mean Squared Error (MSE).	Evaluation is more subjective, often relying on visual inspection and cluster validity indices
Example Algorithms	Support Vector Machines (SVM), Decision Trees, Random Forests, Logistic Regression, and Neural Networks are popular supervised learning algorithms.	K-Means, DBSCAN, Gaussian Mixture Models (GMM), and Singular Value Decomposition (SVD) are popular unsupervised learning algorithms.

Multiple Choice Questions

Q.1. Which of the following statements best describes the role of data science?

(*a*) Data science involves extracting insights and knowledge from structured and unstructured data through various techniques and algorithms.

(*b*) Data science focuses on analyzing historical data exclusively.

(*c*) Data science is primarily concerned with the physical storage and retrieval of data.

(*d*) Data science is solely focused on building predictive models without interpreting the results.

Q.2. Which of the following tasks is an example of supervised learning in data science?

(*a*) Clustering customer segments based on purchase history.

(*b*) Identifying anomalies in network traffic.

(*c*) Predicting stock prices based on historical data.

(*d*) Extracting topics from a collection of news articles.

Q.3. Which type of machine learning involves training algorithms on data without labeled responses?

(*a*) Supervised Learning (*b*) Unsupervised Learning

(*c*) Reinforcement Learning (*d*) Semi-supervised Learning

Q.4. In which type of machine learning does the algorithm learn to make decisions by interacting with an environment and receiving feedback in the form of rewards or penalties?

(*a*) Supervised Learning (*b*) Unsupervised Learning
(*c*) Reinforcement Learning (*d*) Semi-supervised Learning

Q.5. What is the primary goal of supervised learning in machine learning?

(*a*) To discover hidden patterns in unlabeled data.
(*b*) To reduce the dimensionality of the dataset.
(*c*) To optimize decisions based on interactions with an environment.
(*d*) To predict or classify new data based on labeled examples.

Q.6. In classification, what is the primary task of a machine learning algorithm?

(*a*) Assigning labels or categories to input data. (*b*) Predicting continuous values.
(*c*) Reducing the dimensionality of the dataset. (*d*) Clustering similar data points together.

Q.7. Which of the following algorithms is commonly used for binary classification tasks?

(*a*) K-means clustering (*b*) Decision Trees
(*c*) Principal Component Analysis (PCA) (*d*) Linear Regression

Q.8. In multi-class classification, how many classes are there?

(*a*) Two (*b*) Three
(*c*) More than three (*d*) It depends on the dataset

Q.9. What is the main evaluation metric used for assessing the performance of classification algorithms?

(*a*) Mean Absolute Error (MAE) (*b*) Root Mean Squared Error (RMSE)
(*c*) Accuracy (*d*) R-squared

Q.10. Which of the following best describes the goal of regression in machine learning?

(*a*) Assigning labels or categories to input data.
(*b*) Predicting continuous values based on input features.
(*c*) Clustering similar data points together.
(*d*) Extracting principal components from the dataset.

Q.11. Which evaluation metric is commonly used to assess the performance of regression algorithms?

(*a*) Accuracy (*b*) Mean Absolute Error (MAE)
(*c*) Precision (*d*) F1 Score

Answer to Multiple Choice Questions

1. (*a*) **2.** (*c*) **3.** (*b*) **4.** (*c*) **5.** (*d*) **6.** (*a*) **7.** (*b*) **8.** (*c*) **9.** (*c*)
10. (*b*) **11.** (*b*)

❑❑❑

2

PYTHON PROGRAMMING

BASIC PROGRAMMING AND DATA STRUCTURES

Python is a versatile and widely used programming language, known for its simplicity and readability. It offers a vast range of libraries and frameworks, making it a popular choice for various applications, including data analysis and machine learning.

Jupyter Notebooks: Jupyter Notebooks are interactive computing environments that allow you to combine code, output, and rich-text documentation in a single interface. Matplotlib works seamlessly with Jupyter Notebooks, allowing you to create, display, and interact with plots directly in the notebook cells.

IPython: IPython is an interactive command-line shell for Python. It enhances the standard Python shell with features like tab-completion, history, and object introspection. When used with Matplotlib, you can create plots and view them interactively within the IPython environment.

Here's an introduction to basic Python programming and common data structures:

(*a*) **Variables and Data Types**: Variables are used to hold data values in Python. Every variable has a name that is used to refer to the value of the data it stores. Python is a dynamically typed language, thus when you declare a variable, you don't have to specify its data type directly. Instead, based on the value supplied to the variable, the data type is automatically deduced. Declaring variables and giving them values are both possible in Python. Python includes a number of built-in data types, like as:

Numbers: int (integer), float (floating-point numbers), complex (complex numbers).

int: Integer data type represents whole numbers, such as 10, -20, 100, etc.

float: Floating-point data type represents decimal numbers, such as 3.14, -0.5, 2.0, etc.

complex: Complex data type represents numbers in the form of a + bj, where a and b are floating-point numbers, and j represents the square root of -1.

Strings: enclosing text data in single or double quotations.

str: String data type represents sequences of characters enclosed in single quotes (' '), double quotes (" "), or triple quotes (''' ''' or """ """).

Boolean:

bool: Boolean data type represents True or False values. These are used in conditional statements and logical operations.

Sequence:

list: List is an ordered, mutable collection of elements. Elements can be of different data types and can be changed after creation.

tuple: Tuple is an ordered, immutable collection of elements. Once created, elements cannot be changed.

range: Range represents an immutable sequence of numbers and is commonly used in loops.

Set:

set: Set is an unordered, mutable collection of unique elements. It does not allow duplicate values.

frozenset: Frozenset is an unordered, immutable set, similar to a set, but its elements cannot be changed.

Mapping:

dict: Dictionary is an unordered, mutable collection that stores data in key-value pairs. Keys are unique, and they are used to access the corresponding values.

None:

None: None represents a null value or absence of data. It is often used to initialize variables or indicate that a value is missing.

You can create variables and assign values to them using the assignment operator '='. For example:

```
# Numeric Types
age = 25
salary = 35000.50
complex_num = 3 + 4j

# String
name = "John Doe"

# Boolean
is_author = True

# List
numbers = [1, 2, 3, 4, 5]

# Tuple
coordinates = (10, 20)

# Set
fruits = {'apple', 'banana', 'orange'}

# Dictionary
person = {'name': 'Alice', 'age': 30}

# None Type
no_data = None
```

```
In [1]: # Numeric Types
        age = 25
        salary = 35000.50
        complex_num = 3 + 4j

In [2]: # String
        name = "Anil"

In [3]: #Boolean
        is_author = True

In [4]: # List
        numbers = [1, 2, 3, 4, 5]

In [5]: # Tuple
        coordinates = (10, 20)

In [6]: # Set
        fruits = {'apple', 'banana', 'orange'}

In [7]: # Dictionary
        person = {'name' : "Alice", 'age' : 30}

In [8]: # None Type
        no_data = None
```

Python's flexibility in data types and variables allows you to work with different kinds of data and perform various operations efficiently.

(*b*) **Control Flow:** Control flow in Python describes the order in which the code is executed based on specific circumstances or loops. Python has a number of control flow structures to manage how a program is executed. Python offers control flow statements to manage the execution of programs.

Conditional Statements:

if: If a specific condition is met, a block of code is run using the if statement.

elif: If the previous if or elif conditions are false, the elif (short for "else if") statement is used to test additional conditions.

else: If neither of the if nor elif conditions are true, a block of code is run using the else expression.

Example of if-elif-else:

```
x = 10

if x > 0:
    print("Positive")
elif x < 0:
    print("Negative")
```

```
else:
    print("Zero")
```

```
In [9]: x = 10

    if x > 0:
        print("Positive")
    elif x < 0:
        print("Negative")
    else:
        print("Zero")
    Positive
```

Loops:

- **for**: A sequence (such as a list, tuple, string, set, or dictionary) or an iterable object can be iterated over using the for loop. It repeatedly runs a code block for each component of the sequence.
- **while**: While a certain condition is true, a while loop is used to run a block of code.

Example of for loop:

```
fruits = ['apple', 'banana', 'orange']

for fruit in fruits:
    print(fruit)
```

```
In [10]: fruits = ['apple', 'banana', 'orange']

    for fruit in fruits:
        print(fruit)

    apple
    banana
    orange
```

Example of while loop:

```
count = 0

while count < 5:
    print("Count:", count)
    count += 1
```

```
In [11]: count = 0
    while count < 5:
        print("Count:", count)
        count += 1
```

```
Count: 0
Count: 1
Count: 2
Count: 3
Count: 4
```

Break and Continue:

break: Regardless of the loop condition, a loop can be broken with the break statement.

continue: To go to the next iteration and skip the remaining portions of the loop body, use the continue statement.

Example of break and continue:

```
numbers = [1, 2, 3, 4, 5]

for num in numbers:
    if num == 3:
        break
    print(num)

for num in numbers:
    if num == 3:
        continue
    print(num)
```

```
In [12]: numbers = [1, 2, 3, 4, 5]

         for num in numbers:
             if num == 3:
                 break
             print(num)

         for num in numbers:
             if num == 3:
                 continue
             print(num)

         1
         2
         3
         4
         5
```

Pass:

pass: The pass statement performs no action and is a null operation. When a statement is syntactically necessary but you don't want to run any code, you use it as a placeholder.

Example of pass:

```
x = 10

if x > 5:
    pass  # No code here yet, but it won't raise an error
else:
    print("x is less than or equal to 5")
```

```
In [13]: x = 10

    if x > 5
        pass # No code here yet, but it won't raise an error
    else:
        print("x is less than or equal to 5")
```

(*c*) **Functions:** Blocks of code known as functions carry out particular responsibilities. They let you make your code modular and reuse it. A function in Python is a segment of code that can be reused to carry out a single operation or group of related actions. With the use of functions, complicated programs can be divided up into smaller, easier-to-manage chunks, improving the organization, modularity, and maintainability of the code. The general Python syntax for defining a function is shown below:

```
def function_name(parameters):
    """
    Docstring: Description of the function (optional but recommended).
    """
    # Function body: Code to perform the task(s)
    # ...
    return result  # (optional) Return statement to send back a value/result
```

Let's go through the important components of a function:

def: The def keyword is used to start the function definition.

function_name: This is the name of the function. It should follow Python's naming conventions (lowercase with underscores for multi-word names).

parameters: These are the input values passed to the function when it is called. They are optional and can be multiple if needed. You can define default values for parameters.

Docstring: An optional, multi-line string placed as the first statement in the function body. It serves as documentation for the function, describing what it does and providing information about parameters, return values, etc.

Function body: This is where you write the actual code that defines the behavior of the function.

return: The value that the function should return after finishing its tasks is specified by the return statement. The method returns None if it is omitted.

Here is an illustration of a straightforward function that computes the square of an integer:

```
def square(num):
    """"This function calculates the square of a number.""""
    result = num ** 2
    return result

# Calling the function
print(square(5))
```

Output: 25

```
In [15]: def square(num):
             """"This function calculates the square of a number.""""
             result = num ** 2
             return result

         # Calling the function
         print(square(5))
         25
```

Functions can be called from other functions, within loops, and anywhere in the code where their scope allows them to be accessible.

(*d*) **File Handling:** You can read and write data to external files stored on your computer's storage using Python's file handling functionality. It is simple to do operations like reading text from a file, writing data to a file, or modifying file content with Python's built-in functions and methods for working with files.

There are three main steps involved in file handling in Python:

Opening a File: The open() function is used to open files. It accepts two arguments: the file name (or file path) and the mode (read, write, append, etc.) in which the file should be opened.

File handling is essential data from files, saving program output, and working with external data sources. It is a fundamental part of many real-world applications in Python.

Save this file in your system drive like example.txt file is saved in D drive D folder.

```
# Opening a file in read mode
file = open("D:\D\example.txt", "r")
```

Here, "example.txt" is the name of the file you want to open, and "r" specifies that the file should be opened in read mode.

Common file modes:

"r": Read mode (default). Open the file for reading.

"w": Write mode. Open the file for writing. If the file exists, it truncates it (deletes the content). If the file doesn't exist, it creates a new file.

"a": Append mode. Open the file for writing, but append data to the end of the file instead of overwriting it.

"x": Exclusive creation mode. Create a new file, but raise an error if the file already exists.

Reading from a File: After opening a file in read mode, you can read its content using various methods like read(), readline(), or readlines().

```
# Reading the entire content of the file
content = file.read()
print(content)
```

```
In [19]: # Opening  a file in read mode
         file = open("D:\D|example.txt", "r")
```

```
In [20]: Reading the entire content of the file
         content = file.read()
         print(content)
```

File handling is essential for reading data from files, saving program output, and working with external data sources. It is a fundamental part of many real-world applications in Python.

```
# Reading one line at a time
line = file.readline()
print(line)
```

```
# Reading all lines into a list
lines = file.readlines()
print(lines)
```

Keep in mind to use the close() method to close the file after reading.

```
In [21]: # Reading one line at a time
         line = file.readline()
         print(line)
```

```
In [22]: # Reading all lines into a list
         lines = file.readlines()
         print(lines)
         []
```

Writing to a File: You must open a file in write or append mode in order to add data to it. After that, you can write data to the file using the write() method.

```
# Opening a file in write mode
file = open("D:\D\example.txt", "w")
```

```
# Writing data to the file
file.write("Hello, this is some data.")
```

```
In [23]: # Opening a file in write mode
         file = open("D:\D\example.txt", "w")

In [24]: # Writing data to the file
         file.write("Hello, this some data add in file.")
Out[24]: 37

# Closing the file
file.close()

In [25]: # Closing the file
         file.close()
```

If you use the write mode ("w"), the file's existing content will be overwritten. If you want to append data without overwriting, use append mode ("a").

Remember to always close the file after working with it to free up system resources. Alternatively, you can use the with statement to automatically close the file after its suite is executed, even if an exception occurs:

```
with open("example.txt", "r") as file:
    content = file.read()
    # Do something with the content
```

The file is automatically closed here, outside the `with` block.

File handling is essential for reading data from files, saving program output, and working with external data sources. It is a fundamental part of many real-world applications in Python.

(*e*) **Lists and List Comprehensions:** A list is a data structure in Python that can hold a group of elements. Lists can include components of many data types and are ordered. They are also mutable (changeable). Elements are enclosed in square brackets [] and separated by commas to form lists. List comprehensions are quick ways to build lists from iterables or already-existing lists.

Here's an example of creating a list:

```
# Creating a list
fruits = ["apple", "banana", "orange", "grape"]
```

A list's individual elements can be accessed using indexing. The first element in Python has an index of 0, the second element has an index of 1, and so forth.

```
# Accessing elements in the list
print(fruits[0]) # Output: "apple"
print(fruits[2]) # Output: "orange"

In [26]: # Creating a list
         fruits = ["apple", "banana", "orange", "grape"]
```

```
In [27]: # Accessing elements in the list
         print(fruits[0])
         print(fruits[2])
         apple
         orange
```

Because lists are mutable, you can alter their content by assigning new values to particular indexes.

```
# Changing an element in the list
fruits[1] = "mango"
print(fruits)
```

Output: ["apple", "mango", "orange", "grape"]

```
In [26]: # Creating a list
         fruits = ["apple", "banana", "orange", "grape"]

In [27]: # Accessing elements in the list
         print(fruits[0])
         print(fruits[2])
         apple
         orange

In [28]: # Changing an element in the list
         fruits[1] = "mango"
         print(fruits)
         ['apple', 'mango', 'orange', 'grape']
```

Lists in Python also support negative indexing, where -1 refers to the last element, -2 to the second last element, and so on.

```
# Negative indexing
print(fruits[-1]) # Output: "grape"
print(fruits[-2]) # Output: "orange"

In [29]: # Negative indexing
         print(fruits[−1])
         print(fruits[−2])
         grape
         orange
```

List slicing allows you to extract a portion of a list by specifying start and end indexes.

```
# List slicing
print(fruits[1:3]) # Output: ["mango", "orange"]

In [30]: # List slicing
         print(fruits[1:3])
         ['mango', 'orange']
```

Python's list comprehensions offer a clear and elegant approach to build lists. By specifying an expression to generate items based on pre-existing lists or sequences, they enable you to create new lists. Here is an illustration of a list comprehension that generates a new list of 0 to 9-digit squares of numbers:

```
# To make a list of squares, use list comprehension
squares = [x**2 for x in range(10)]
print(squares)
```

Output: [0, 1, 4, 9, 16, 25, 36, 49, 64, 81]

```
In [31]: # List comprehension to create a list of squares
         squares = [x**2 for x in range(10)]
         print(squares)
         [0, 1, 4, 9, 16, 25, 36, 49, 64, 81]
```

List comprehensions can include conditional expressions as well. For example, you can create a new list with only even numbers from an existing list:

```
# List comprehension with conditional expression
numbers = [1, 2, 3, 4, 5, 6, 7, 8, 9, 10]
even_numbers = [x for x in numbers if x % 2 == 0]
print(even_numbers)
```

Output: [2, 4, 6, 8, 10]

```
In [32]: # List comprehension with conditional expression
         numbers = [1, 2, 3, 4, 5, 6, 7, 8, 9, 10]
         even_numbers = [x, for x in numbers if x % 2 == 0]
         print(even_numbers)
         [2, 4, 6, 8, 10]
```

List comprehensions are a powerful feature in Python that makes list creation and transformation concise and readable. They are widely used for filtering and mapping operations on lists and other iterables

(*f*) **Tuples:** Lists and tuples are both collection data types, although tuples differ significantly in certain important ways. Tuples can include items of many data kinds, are ordered, and are immutable (cannot be modified). Elements are enclosed in parenthesis () and separated by commas to form tuples.

Here's an illustration of how to make a tuple:

```
# Creating a tuple
fruits = ("apple", "banana", "orange", "grape")
```

```
In [33]: # Creating a tuple
         fruits = ("apple", "banana", "orange", "grape")
```

A tuple's constituent elements can be accessed individually just like lists using indexing. Tuple indexing also begins at 0.

```
# Accessing elements in the tuple
print(fruits[0]) # Output: "apple"
print(fruits[2]) # Output: "orange"
```

```
In [33]: # Creating a tuple
         fruits = ("apple", "banana", "orange", "grape")

In [34]: # Accessing elements in the tuple
         print(fruits[0])
         print(fruits[2])
         apple
         orange
```

Tuples, on the other hand, cannot have their contents changed once they are created since they are immutable. Contrary other lists, which permit you to change their elements, this one does not.

```
# Trying to change an element in the tuple (This will raise an error)
fruits[1] = "mango"
```

```
In [36]:  # Trying to change an element in the tuple (This will raise an error)
          fruits[1] = "mango"
          ---------------------------------------------------------------------
          TypeError                                 Traceback (most recent call last)
          Input In [36], in <cell line: 2>()
          1 # Trying to change an element in the tuple (This will raise an error)
          2 fruits[1] = "mango"

          TypeError: 'tuple' object does not support item assignment
```

Tuples also support negative indexing and slicing, just like lists.

```
# Negative indexing
print(fruits[-1]) # Output: "grape"
print(fruits[-2]) # Output: "orange"
```

```
In [37]: # Negative indexing
         print(fruits[-1])
         print(fruits[-2])
         grape
         orange
```

```
# Tuple slicing
    print(fruits[1:3]) # Output: ("banana", "orange")
```

```
In [38]: # Tuple slicing
         print(fruits[1:3])
         ('banana', 'orange')
```

When you want to create a group of elements that shouldn't be changed while the program is running, you frequently utilize tuples. For instance, you could use a tuple to represent the x, y coordinates of a point or the R, G, and B values of a color. Python's convenient triple packing and unpacking features are useful. A tuple can be unpacked into distinct variables or you can add several values to it in a single line.

```
# Tuple packing and unpacking
point = 10, 20  # Packing
x, y = point    # Unpacking
print(x, y)     # Output: 10 20
```

```
In [39]: # Tuple packing and unpacking
         point = 10, 20
         x, y = point
         print(x, y)
         10  20
```

As opposed to lists, which cannot be hashed, tuples can be used as keys in dictionaries.

```
# Using a dictionary's key as a tuple
student = ("John", 25, "Male")
grades = {student: 90}
print(grades) # Output: {('John', 25, 'Male'): 90}
```

```
In [40]: # Using a tuple as a key in a dictionary
         student = ("John", 25, "Male")
         grades = {student: 90}
         print(grades)
         {('John', 25, 'Male'): 90}
```

(g) **Dictionaries:** A collection data type called a dictionary stores data as key-value pairs. Dictionaries can include components of several data types, are unordered, and are changeable (can be altered). Key-value pairs are encased in curly braces and separated by colons to form dictionaries. Here is an illustration of how to make a dictionary:

```
# Creating a dictionary
student = {"name": "John", "age": 25, "gender": "Male"}
```

```
In [41]: # Creating a dictionary
         student = {"name": "John", "age": 25, "gender": "Male"}
```

In this example, "name", "age", and "gender" are the keys, and "John", 25, and "Male" are the corresponding values. Each key-value pair represents a piece of data associated with a particular key. You can use a key as an index to obtain the value linked to that key:

```
# Accessing values in the dictionary
print(student["name"])   # Output: "John"
print(student["age"])    # Output: 25
print(student["gender"]) # Output: "Male"
```

```
In [41]: # Creating a dictionary
         student = {"name": "John", "age": 25, "gender": "Male"}
```

```
In [42]: # Accessing values in the dictionary
         print(student["name"])
         print(student["age"])
         print(student["gender"])
         John
         25
         Male
```

Dictionaries are mutable, which means you can change, add, or delete key-value pairs after they are created.

```
# Modifying a value in the dictionary
student["age"] = 26
print(student["age"]) # Output: 26
```

```
In [43]: # Modifying a value in the dictionary
         student["age"] = 26
         print(student["age"])
         26
```

```
# Adding a new key-value pair
student["city"] = "New York"
print(student) # Output: {'name': 'John', 'age': 26, 'gender': 'Male', 'city': 'New York'}
```

```
In [44]: # Adding a new key-value pair
         student["city"] = "New York"
         print(student)
         {'name': 'John', 'age': 26, 'gender': 'Male', 'city': 'New York'}
```

```
# Deleting a key-value pair
del student["gender"]
print(student) # Output: {'name': 'John', 'age': 26, 'city': 'New York'}
```

```
In [45]: # Deleting a key-value pair
         del student["gender"]
         print(student)
         {'name': 'John', 'age': 26, 'gender': 'Male', 'city': 'New York'}
```

Using the in keyword, you may determine whether a key is present in the dictionary:

```
# Checking if a key exists in the dictionary
if "name" in student:
    print("Name is present in the dictionary.")
```

```
In [46]: # Checking if a key exists in the dictionary
         if "name" in student:
             print("Name is present in the dictionary.")
         Name is present in the dictionary.
```

A person's profile or a product's specifications are two examples of real-world objects having various qualities that are frequently represented by dictionaries. For managing setups, mappings, and look-up tables, they are also helpful. Dictionaries are adaptable for managing complicated data relationships because they can contain nested dictionaries or other data structures.

```
# Nested dictionary
person = {
    "name": "Alice",
    "age": 30,
    "address": {
        "city": "New York",
        "zipcode": "10001"
    }
}
print(person["address"]["city"]) # Output: "New York"
```

```
In [47]: # Nested dictionary
         person = {
             "name": "Alice",
             "age": 30,
             "address": {
                 "city": "New York",
                 "zipcode": "10001"
             }
         }
         print(person["address"]["city"])
         New York
```

(*h*) **Sets:** Sets is an unordered collection data type that resembles a list or a tuple but differs significantly in certain important ways. Curly brackets are used to enclose elements in sets, alternatively the set() constructor function can be used. Due to sets' restriction on unique elements, duplicate values are immediately eliminated. Here is a sample of how to make a set:

```
# Creating a set using curly braces
fruits = {"apple", "banana", "orange"}

# Creating a set using the set() constructor function
numbers = set([1, 2, 3, 4, 5])
```

```
In [2]:  # Creating a set using curly braces
         fruits = {"apple", "banana", "orange"}

In [3]:  # Creating a set using the set() constructor function
         numbers = set([1, 2, 3, 4, 5])
```

In the example above, fruits is a set containing three unique elements: "apple", "banana", and "orange". numbers is a set containing the unique integers from 1 to 5.

Sets do not support indexing because they are unordered collections. You cannot access elements using index positions as you would with lists or tuples. You can perform various set operations, such as union, intersection, difference, and more, using set methods or set operators.

```
set1 = {1, 2, 3, 4}
set2 = {3, 4, 5, 6}

# Union of two sets
union_set = set1.union(set2)
print(union_set) # Output: {1, 2, 3, 4, 5, 6}
```

```
In [4]:  set1 = {1, 2, 3, 4}
         set2 = {3, 4, 5, 6}

In [5]:  @ Union of two sets
         union_set = set1.union(set2)
         print(union_set)
         {1, 2, 3, 4, 5, 6}
```

```
# Intersection of two sets
intersection_set = set1.intersection(set2)
print(intersection_set) # Output: {3, 4}
```

```
In [6]:  # Intersection of two sets
         intersection_set = set1.intersection(set2)
         print(intersection_set)
         {3, 4}
```

```
# Difference between two sets
difference_set = set1.difference(set2)
print(difference_set) # Output: {1, 2}
```

```
In [7]:  # Difference between two sets
         difference_set = set1.difference(set2)
         print(difference_set)
         {1, 2}
```

Sets also have useful methods like add(), remove(), and discard() for adding and removing elements from a set.

```
# Adding elements to a set
fruits.add("grape")
print(fruits) # Output: {"apple", "banana", "orange", "grape"}
```

```
In [9]:  # Creating a set using curly braces
          fruits = {"apple", "banana", "orange"}

In [10]: # Adding elements to a set
          fruits.add("grape")
          print(fruits)
          ['orange', 'banana', 'grape, 'apple'}

# Removing elements from a set
fruits.remove("banana")
print(fruits) # Output: {"apple", "orange", "grape"}

In [11]: # Removing elements from a set
          fruits.remove("banana")
          print(fruits)
          {'orange', 'grape', 'apple'}

# Discarding elements from a set (no error if element not found)
fruits.discard("pear")

In [12]: # Discarding elements from a set (no error if element not fount)
          fruits.discard("pear")
```

(*i*) **Classes and Objects:** An object-oriented programming language is Python. To build objects that encapsulate data and action, classes can be defined

Class: A class is a blueprint for creating objects. It defines a set of attributes (variables) and methods (functions) that will be associated with the objects created from it. A class is like a template that encapsulates data and behavior.

Syntax for creating a class:

```
class ClassName:
    # class variables and methods
```

Example of a simple class:

```
class Dog:
    def __init__(self, name, age):
        self.name = name
        self.age = age

    def bark(self):
        print(f"{self.name} is barking.")
```

```
In [17]: class Dog:
             def_init_(self, name, age):
                 self.name = name
                 self.age = age

             def bark(self):
                 print(f"{self.name} is barking.")
```

Object: A class's instances are objects. It represents a particular entity that adheres to the class's stated structure and behaviors. Each object derived from a class has a unique set of instance variables and is capable of using the class's methods.

Syntax for creating an object:

```
object_name = ClassName(arguments)
```

Example of creating an object from the Dog class:

```
dog1 = Dog("Buddy", 3)
dog2 = Dog("Max", 5)
```

```
In [17]: class Dog:
             def_init_(self, name, age):
                 self.name = name
                 self.age = age
             def bark(self):
                 print(f"{self.name} is barking.")
```

```
In [18]: dog1 = Dog("Buddy", 3)
         dog2 = Dog("Max", 5)
```

In this example, dog1 and dog2 are two different objects of the Dog class. They have their own names and ages, even though they share the same class definition.

To access the attributes and methods of an object, you use the dot notation:

```
print(dog1.name) # Output: "Buddy"
print(dog2.age)  # Output: 5
dog1.bark() # Output: "Buddy is barking."
dog2.bark() # Output: "Max is barking."
```

```
In [18]: dog1 = Dog("Buddy", 3)
         dog2 = Dog("Max", 5)
```

```
In [19]: pring(dog1.name)
         Buddy
```

```
In [20]: pring(dog2.age)
         5
```

```
In [21]: dog1.bark()
         Buddy is barking.

In [22]: dog2.bark()
         Max is barking.
```

Constructor (__init__ method): When an object is formed, the Python classes' particular __init__ method is invoked. It is utilized to set the object's instance variables.

```
def __init__(self, parameter1, parameter2, ...):
    # initialization code here
```

Class Variables and Instance Variables: All instances (objects) of the class share class variables. Though not included in any methods, they are declared within the class. Each object's instance variables are distinct, and the self keyword is used to declare them in the __init__ method.All instances (objects) of the class share class variables. Though not included in any methods, they are declared within the class. Each object's instance variables are distinct, and the self keyword is used to declare them in the __init__ method.

Example of class and instance variables:

```
class MyClass:
    class_variable = 0  # Class variable shared by all instances

    def __init__(self, value):
        self.instance_variable = value  # Instance variable specific to each object
```

```
In [23]: class MyClass:
             class_variable = 0 # Class variable shared by all ınstances

             def_init_(self, value):
                 self.instance_variable = value # Instance variable specific to each object
```

Methods: Methods are functions defined within a class that operate on the object's data and perform actions related to the class.

```
class MyClass:
    def my_method(self):
        # method code here
```

(*j*) **Exception Handling:** Exception handling in Python allows you to deal with errors or exceptional situations that might occur during the execution of a program. It helps you write robust code by catching and handling errors gracefully, preventing the program from crashing. The key components of exception handling in Python are try, except, else, finally, and raise. Let's go through each of them:

try, except: The try block is used to enclose the code that might raise an exception. If an exception occurs within the try block, the program jumps to the corresponding except block that handles that specific type of exception.

```
try:
    # code that might raise an exception
except ExceptionType:
    # code to handle the exception
```

Example:

```
try:
    x = 10 / 0  # This will raise a ZeroDivisionError
except ZeroDivisionError:
    print("Error: Division by zero")
```

```
In [24]: try:
             x = 10/0 # This will raise a ZeroDivisionError
         except ZeroDivisionError:
             print("Error: Division by zero")
         Error: Division by zero
```

else: The else block is optional and follows the except block. It gets executed if no exception is raised in the try block. It is typically used for code that should run only when no exceptions occur.

```
try:
    # code that might raise an exception
except ExceptionType:
    # code to handle the exception
else:
    # if no exception is raised, run this code
```

Example:

```
try:
    x = 10 / 2  # This will not raise an exception
except ZeroDivisionError:
    print("Error: Division by zero")
else:
    print("Division successful")
```

```
In [25]: try
             x = 10/2 # This will not raise an exception
         except ZeroDivisionError:
             print("Error: Division by zero")
         else:
             print("Division successful")
         Division successful
```

finally: The finally block is optional and comes after the except or else block. It will always be executed, whether an exception occurred or not. It is commonly used to clean up resources, such as closing files or network connections.

```
try:
    # code that might raise an exception
except ExceptionType:
    # code to handle the exception
else:
    # code to run if no exception occurs
finally:
    # code that will always be executed
```

Example:

```
try:
    x = 10 / 0
except ZeroDivisionError:
    print("Error: Division by zero")
else:
    print("Division successful")
finally:
    print("Cleanup code here")
```

```
In [26]: try:
             x = 10/0
         except ZeroDivisionError:
             print("Error: Division by zero")
         else:
             print("Division successful")
         finally:
             print("Cleanup code here")
         Error: Division by zero
         Cleanup code here
```

raise: You can manually raise exceptions using the raise statement. It allows you to generate your custom exceptions when certain conditions are met.

```
raise ExceptionType("Error message")
```

Example:

```
try:
    age – int(input("Enter your age: "))
    if age < 0:
        raise ValueError("Age cannot be negative")
```

```
except ValueError as e:
    print("Error:", e)
```

```
In [*]:  try:
             age = int(input("Enter you age: "))
             if age < 0:
                 raise ValueError("Age cannot be negative")
         except ValueError as e:
             print("Error:", e)
         Enter your age:
```

(k) Libraries for Data Structures and Data Analysis: Python provides a number of potent packages for manipulating, analyzing, and visualizing data, including:

NumPy: for arrays and numerical computing. The foundational Python library for numerical computing is called NumPy. Large, multidimensional arrays and matrices are supported, and a selection of sophisticated mathematical operations are provided to work effectively on these arrays. Numerous other Python data analysis packages are built on the foundation of NumPy.

Website: https://numpy.org/

Pandas: for using dataframes to manipulate and analyze data. Pandas is a strong library for data analysis and manipulation. It offers data structures like DataFrame and Series that make it simple to work with organized data. Data cleansing, filtering, aggregation, and merging are frequent uses of the pandas tool.

Website: https://pandas.pydata.org/

Matplotlib: A well-liked Python charting library is Matplotlib. You may make a huge selection of static, interactive, and animated plots, charts, and visualizations using it. To successfully visualize data, NumPy and pandas work well together with Matplotlib.

Website: https://matplotlib.org/

SciPy: Built on top of NumPy, SciPy offers further features for technical and scientific computing. It has components for signal processing, interpolation, optimization, integration, and more.

Website: https://www.scipy.org/

scikit-learn: Python's scikit-learn library for machine learning is used. It provides straightforward and effective tools for data analysis and mining. For applications like classification, regression, clustering, and others, the library offers a variety of machine learning methods.

Website: https://scikit-learn.org/

Seaborn: A high-level visualization library built on Matplotlib is called Seaborn. It offers a simple interface for producing visually appealing and educational statistical visuals. Seaborn is a popular tool for statistical data visualization and works well with pandas DataFrames.

Website: https://seaborn.pydata.org/

TensorFlow and PyTorch: Many people use the deep learning libraries TensorFlow and PyTorch. For applications like image identification, natural language processing, and more, they enable you to construct, train, and use neural networks and other machine learning models.

TensorFlow website: https://www.tensorflow.org/

PyTorch website: https://pytorch.org/

Dask: Dask is a library for out-of-core and parallel processing. It enables parallelizing computations across numerous cores or machines and working with datasets that are greater than what is currently in memory. Scaling data analysis tasks to address massive data is possible with Dask.

Website: https://dask.org/

PYTHON ENVIRONMENT SETUP AND ESSENTIALS

Setting up a Python environment and understanding its essentials are crucial steps before starting any Python programming. Below is a step-by-step guide to help you get started:

- **Install Python:** Download the most recent stable version of Python from the official website (https://www.python.org/).
- Follow the installation instructions for your operating system.
- **Verify Python Installation:** Open a terminal or command prompt and type python --version to check if Python is installed correctly. It should display the installed Python version.
- **Installing a Code Editor or IDE:** For writing and running Python code, you can use a code editor or an Integrated Development Environment (IDE).

Some popular code editors for Python include Visual Studio Code (VSCode), Sublime Text, Atom, and PyCharm (IDE).

- **Create a Virtual Environment (Optional but Recommended):** You can construct separate Python environments for various projects in a virtual environment to prevent dependency problems.

To create a virtual environment, run python -m venv env_name in the terminal, where env_name is the name of your virtual environment.

- **Activate the Virtual Environment:** On Windows: env_name\Scripts\activate

  On macOS and Linux: source env_name/bin/activate
- **Install Python Packages:** Use pip (Python package manager) to install Python packages. For example, to install NumPy, run pip install numpy.
- **Basic Python Essentials:**

Variables and Data Types: Learn about data types (int, float, str, etc.) and how to assign values to variables.

Control Flow: Understand conditional statements (if, elif, else) and loops (for, while).

Functions: Learn how to define and call functions.

Data Structures: Familiarize yourself with lists, tuples, dictionaries, and sets.

File Handling: Explore how to read and write data to files.

- **Importing Modules and Packages:** Learn how to import modules (e.g., import math) and use functions from external packages.
- **Exception Handling**: Understand how to handle errors and exceptions using try, except, and finally.
- **Practice and Explore:** The best way to learn Python is to practice writing code regularly.
- Explore Python's standard library and third-party packages to find tools that suit your needs.
- **Online Resources:** There are many online resources, tutorials, and courses available for learning Python, such as Python's official documentation, tutorials on websites like w3schools, and video courses on platforms like Udemy and Coursera.

By following these steps and mastering the essential concepts, you will be well on your way to becoming proficient in Python programming. Remember that practice, patience, and a willingness to explore are key to becoming a successful Python developer.

ANACONDA - DOWNLOAD & SETUP

A well-liked Python distribution called Anaconda includes a lot of helpful libraries and machine learning, scientific computing, and data science applications. Setting up a Python environment for data analysis is made simpler, and managing packages and dependencies is made simple. The procedures to download and install Anaconda are listed below:

- **Download Anaconda:** Click here to see the Anaconda website: https://www.anaconda.com/products/individual

  Depending on your operating system (Windows, macOS, or Linux), pick the proper installation. Download Python 3.x's most recent Anaconda version.
- **Install Anaconda:** Windows:

  Double-click the downloaded .exe file.

  Follow the installation wizard instructions.

  Select the option to add Anaconda to your system PATH during installation (recommended).

  macOS: Double-click the.pkg file you just downloaded.

  Observe the wizard's installation instructions.

  Copy code

  bash Anaconda3-x.x.x-Linux-x86_64.sh

  Follow the installation prompts.
- **Set up Anaconda Environment (Optional but Recommended):** After installing Anaconda, you can set up and manage separate environments for different projects.

  To create a new environment, open a terminal (or Anaconda Prompt on Windows) and run:

  conda create --name myenv

  Replace myenv with the desired environment name.
- **Activate the Anaconda Environment:** To activate the environment, use the following command:

  conda activate myenv

  Replace myenv with the name of your created environment.
- **Install Packages with conda:** Conda can be used to install packages. Using NumPy as an illustration, utilize:

  conda install numpy
- **Install Packages with pip:** Anaconda also supports pip for package installation. To install a package using pip, simply run:

  pip install package_name
- **Launch Jupyter Notebook:** Anaconda comes with Jupyter Notebook, an interactive web-based computational environment for Python.

Use the following command to launch Jupyter Notebook in the terminal or Anaconda Prompt:
jupyter notebook

You can create new notebooks or edit ones that already exist once Jupyter Notebook has opened in your web browser as a result.

IDES - JUPYTER, SPYDER, PYCHARM

IDEs (Integrated Development Environments) are software applications that provide comprehensive tools and features to aid developers in writing, debugging, and testing their code. Here's an overview of the three popular Python IDEs: Jupyter, Spyder, and PyCharm:

- **Jupyter:** Using the interactive computing environment Jupyter, which is web-based, you may create and share documents with live code, graphics, and illustrative text. It supports interactive data analysis, data visualization, and machine learning experiments. Jupyter uses notebooks (.ipynb files) where you can write and execute code cells. Code cells can be executed individually, allowing you to see the output interactively. Jupyter is well-suited for exploratory data analysis, data visualization, and interactive presentations.

You can install Jupyter using Anaconda or directly via pip: pip install jupyterlab.

- **Spyder:** Spyder is an open-source IDE designed explicitly for scientific computing, data analysis, and data visualization. It provides an integrated environment with a code editor, a variable explorer, a debugger, and support for plotting and visualization. Spyder comes with NumPy, Pandas, Matplotlib, and other scientific libraries pre-installed. It is well-suited for data analysis, machine learning, and scientific computing tasks. Spyder can be installed alone or as part of the Anaconda distribution:

  pip install spyder.

- **PyCharm:** PyCharm is a popular and powerful IDE developed by JetBrains. It is available in both community (free) and professional (paid) editions. PyCharm provides extensive features for Python development, including code navigation, code completion, refactoring, debugging, testing, and version control integration. It is suitable for all types of Python development, from small scripts to large-scale projects. PyCharm has advanced support for web development with Django and Flask frameworks. The professional edition includes additional support for scientific tools and databases.

You can download PyCharm from the JetBrains website: https://www.jetbrains.com/pycharm/download/

- Use Jupyter for interactive data analysis, visualization, and sharing of notebooks with code, visualizations, and explanations.
- Use Spyder for scientific computing, data analysis, and data visualization with built-in support for scientific libraries.
- Use PyCharm for general Python development, web development, and large-scale projects with advanced features and a more traditional IDE experience.

GIT - SETUP AND CONFIGURATION WITH IDES

Git is a version control system used to track changes in code and collaborate with other developers effectively. Setting up Git and configuring it with Integrated Development Environments (IDEs) can streamline your development workflow. Below are the steps to set up Git and configure it with popular Python IDEs like Visual Studio Code (VSCode), PyCharm, and Spyder:

- **Install Git**: Download and install Git from the official website: https://git-scm.com/downloads

Follow the installation wizard instructions for your operating system.

- **Configure Git:** Open a terminal or command prompt and run the following commands to set your username and email, which will be used to identify your commits:

  git config --global user.name "Your Name"

  git config --global user.email "your.email@example.com"

- **Using Git with Visual Studio Code (VSCode):** If you haven't already, install Visual Studio Code from the official website: https://code.visualstudio.com/download

  Launch VSCode and open the Extensions view by clicking on the Extensions icon in the Activity Bar on the side of the window.

  Search for "Git" and install the official Git extension by Microsoft.

  After installation, you should see Git-related features in the Source Control view (Ctrl+Shift+G) and the command palette.

- **Using Git with PyCharm:** If you haven't already, download and install PyCharm from the JetBrains website: https://www.jetbrains.com/pycharm/download

  During the installation, you may have the option to install Git integration. If not, make sure Git is installed on your system.

  Open PyCharm and go to File -> Settings (or PyCharm -> Preferences on macOS).

  In the Settings dialog, navigate to Version Control -> Git.

  Set the path to the Git executable (if not automatically detected) and configure your Git username and email.

  Click "Test" to ensure that PyCharm can communicate with Git.

- **Using Git with Spyder:** If you haven't already, install Spyder using Anaconda or separately:

  pip install spyder

  Spyder comes with built-in Git integration, so there's no separate setup required. To use Git with Spyder, you can open the integrated Git plugin from the main menu: View -> Plugins -> Git.

  With Git set up and configured in your preferred IDE, you can now create repositories, commit changes, push, and pull code from remote repositories directly within your development environment. This makes version control seamless and allows for efficient collaboration with other developers on your projects. Remember to use descriptive commit messages to track changes effectively.

MATHEMATICAL COMPUTING WITH PYTHON

Mathematical computing with Python is made easy and powerful thanks to various libraries and tools available in the Python ecosystem. Below are some of the essential libraries and techniques for mathematical computing in Python:

- **NumPy:** The core Python package for numerical computing is called NumPy. Large, multidimensional arrays and matrices can be supported, and a variety of mathematical operations can be performed effectively on these arrays. Numerous more scientific computing libraries are built on the foundation of NumPy.

- **SciPy:** SciPy adds more capabilities for scientific computing and is built on top of NumPy. It has modules for statistics, linear algebra, interpolation, optimization, and more.
- **SymPy:** A Python library for symbolic mathematics is called SymPy. It enables you to solve equations, compute derivatives and integrals, work with algebraic expressions symbolically, and engage in a variety of symbolic operations.
- **Matplotlib and Seaborn:** A potent plotting library for making static, interactive, and publishable-quality visuals is called Matplotlib. Seaborn offers a more advanced interface for the viewing of statistical data on top of Matplotlib. For the purpose of plotting and displaying mathematical data, these libraries are crucial.
- **Pandas**: Pandas is a library made specifically for analyzing and manipulating data. For working with structured data, such as time series data or tabular data, it offers data structures like DataFrames. Pandas is frequently used in mathematical and statistical analysis for data pretreatment and exploration.
- **Scikit-learn:** Python's Scikit-learn is a well-liked machine learning library. For classification, regression, clustering, and other machine learning applications, it offers a large variety of techniques. Applying mathematical and statistical models to actual data with Scikit-learn is helpful.
- **SympyCAS (Computer Algebra System):** SympyCAS is a library that allows for symbolic computation and algebraic manipulations similar to SymPy but with an interface closer to traditional Computer Algebra Systems.
- **Fourier Transform and Signal Processing:** For Fourier transforms and signal processing tasks, you can use libraries like scipy.fft, numpy.fft, and scipy.signal.
- **Optimization:** For numerical optimization problems, you can use libraries like scipy.optimize or specialized optimization libraries like cvxpy for convex optimization.
- **Linear Algebra and Matrix Operations:** NumPy provides powerful linear algebra capabilities, such as matrix operations, eigenvalues, singular value decomposition, and more.

MANAGING AND MANIPULATING DATA

Python provides several powerful libraries for managing and manipulating data efficiently. Here are some of the key libraries and techniques you can use for data management and manipulation:

- **NumPy:** The core Python package for numerical computing is called NumPy. Large, multidimensional arrays and matrices can be supported, and a variety of mathematical operations can be performed effectively on these arrays. NumPy is a core library for data management since it uses arrays for data storage and processing.
- **Pandas:** Built on top of NumPy, Pandas is a strong library for data manipulation and analysis. It offers optimal data structures for managing structured data, such as spreadsheets and SQL tables, like DataFrame and Series. You can read data from a variety of sources, clean and prepare the data, filter, group, pivot, and carry out other data manipulation activities with Pandas.
- **Data Input/Output:** Python comes with a number of libraries that may be used to read and write data from a variety of file formats, including CSV, Excel, JSON, and databases. For instance, Pandas offers built-in routines to effectively read and write data from/to these formats.

- **Data Cleaning and Preprocessing:** Before analysis, data often requires cleaning and preprocessing to handle missing values, outliers, and inconsistencies. Libraries like Pandas and NumPy provide functions to handle missing data, filtering, and transforming data.
- **Data Aggregation and Grouping:** Pandas provides powerful tools for grouping data based on specific criteria and performing aggregation operations like sum, mean, count, etc.
- **Data Visualization:** Popular Python libraries for data visualization include Matplotlib and Seaborn. To view and analyze your data, you can use these libraries to generate a variety of charts, plots, and graphs.
- **Data Merging and Joining:** Pandas allows you to merge and join datasets based on common columns or indices.
- **Data Reshaping:** Pandas provides functions to reshape data, such as pivot(), melt(), and stack().
- **Data Indexing and Selection:** Pandas supports advanced indexing techniques to extract, filter, and manipulate specific portions of the data.
- **Date and Time Handling:** Python's datetime module and Pandas provide tools for handling date and time data, such as parsing dates and performing time-based operations.

These libraries and techniques are essential for effective data management and manipulation in Python. By combining their capabilities, you can efficiently handle data preprocessing, analysis, and visualization, making Python a popular choice for data science and data analysis tasks.

SCIENTIFIC COMPUTING WITH PYTHON

Scientific computing with Python involves using the language and its libraries for solving scientific and engineering problems. Python, with its rich ecosystem of scientific libraries, has become a popular choice for researchers, scientists, engineers, and data scientists. Below are some key aspects of scientific computing with Python and the libraries that make it possible:

- **NumPy:** Python's scientific computing is built on NumPy. Large, multidimensional arrays and matrices are supported, along with a range of mathematical operations that can be applied effectively to these arrays. For numerical calculations, NumPy is employed, and it serves as the foundation for many other scientific libraries.
- **SciPy:** SciPy expands on NumPy and provides more features for tasks requiring scientific computation. It has modules for signal processing, linear algebra, statistical operations, optimization, integration, interpolation, and more. SciPy provides specific methods for scientific applications, which is how it complements NumPy.
- **Matplotlib and Seaborn:** A potent plotting library for making static, interactive, and publishable-quality visuals is called Matplotlib. Seaborn offers a more advanced interface for the viewing of statistical data on top of Matplotlib. These libraries are essential for data visualization and outcome analysis in scientific research.
- **SymPy:** A Python library for symbolic mathematics is called SymPy. It enables for symbolic computation, making it possible to manipulate algebraic expressions and perform operations like calculus and equation-solving. For analytical calculations and the symbolic representation of mathematical expressions, SymPy is helpful.
- **Pandas:** Pandas is a tool for analyzing and manipulating data. It offers data structures for working with structured data, such as DataFrame and Series. Pandas is a popular tool for data exploration, cleaning, and preprocessing in scientific research.

- **IPython and Jupyter Notebooks:** IPython is an enhanced interactive Python shell that provides a more powerful and user-friendly experience compared to the standard Python interpreter. Jupyter Notebooks are web-based interactive computing environments that allow combining code, text, and visualizations in a single document. IPython and Jupyter Notebooks facilitate exploratory data analysis and interactive experimentation in scientific computing.
- **Image Processing:** Libraries like OpenCV and scikit-image provide tools for image processing and computer vision tasks.
- **Machine Learning and Deep Learning:** Tools for machine learning and deep learning applications in scientific computing are made available through libraries like scikit-learn and TensorFlow.

Scientific computing with Python allows researchers and scientists to perform complex calculations, analyze experimental data, visualize results, and develop and implement algorithms with ease. The extensive collection of libraries and tools in the Python ecosystem makes it a versatile and powerful language for scientific research and engineering applications.

REVIEW QUESTIONS

Q.1. What are basic programming constructs used in most programming languages?

Ans. Basic programming constructs used in most programming languages include:

Variables: Named storage locations to store data values.

Data Types: Define the type of data a variable can hold, such as integers, floating-point numbers, strings, etc.

Operators: Symbols used to perform operations on variables and values, such as arithmetic operators (+, –, *, /), comparison operators (>, <, ==), logical operators (AND, OR, NOT), etc.

Control Structures: Constructs used to control the flow of program execution, including:

Conditional Statements: if, else, elif (or switch-case in some languages).

Loops: for, while, do-while, foreach, etc.

Functions/Methods: Modular blocks of code that perform specific tasks and can be reused.

Input/Output: Mechanisms for taking input from the user and displaying output to the user.

Q.2. What are some common data structures used in programming?

Ans. Common data structures used in programming include:

Arrays: A collection of elements stored in contiguous memory locations, accessed using an index.

Linked Lists: A data structure consisting of a sequence of elements where each element points to the next one in the sequence.

Stacks: A Last In, First Out (LIFO) data structure where elements are added and removed from the same end.

Queues: A First In, First Out (FIFO) data structure where elements are added at the rear and removed from the front.

Trees: Hierarchical data structures consisting of nodes connected by edges, with a root node at the top and child nodes branching out.

Graphs: A collection of nodes (vertices) and edges that connect them, representing relationships between entities.

Hash Tables: A data structure that stores key-value pairs and allows for efficient retrieval of values based on keys.

Sets: A collection of unique elements with no particular order.

Multiple Choice Questions

Q.1. What is Python?

(*a*) A type of snake found in tropical regions. (*b*) A high-level programming language.

(*c*) A species of bird known for its colorful plumage.

(*d*) A database management system.

Q.2. Which symbol is used for single-line comments in Python?

(*a*) // (*b*) # (*c*) /* */ (*d*) --

Q.3. What is the result of 5 + 3 * 2 in Python?

(*a*) 16 (*b*) 11 (*c*) 10 (*d*) 13

Q.4. Which of the following data types is mutable in Python?

(*a*) Tuple (*b*) String (*c*) List (*d*) Set

Q.5. What does the len() function do in Python?

(*a*) Returns the length of a string.
(*b*) Returns the length of a list or sequence.
(*c*) Returns the length of a dictionary.
(*d*) All of the above.

Q.6. Which of the following is not a valid way to declare a variable in Python?

(*a*) variable_name = value
(*b*) 1_variable = value
(*c*) _variable = value
(*d*) variableName = value

Q.7. What is the output of the following code snippet?

```
my_list = [1, 2, 3, 4, 5]
print(my_list[1:4])
```

(*a*) [1, 2, 3, 4, 5] (*b*) [1, 2, 3] (*c*) [2, 3, 4] (*d*) [2, 3, 4, 5]

Q.8. Which statement is used to exit a loop prematurely in Python?

(*a*) break (*b*) exit (*c*) stop (*d*) halt

Q.9. What does the range() function return in Python?

(*a*) A list of numbers
(*b*) A tuple of numbers
(*c*) An iterator
(*d*) A dictionary

Q.10. Which of the following is used to define a function in Python?

(*a*) func (*b*) method (*c*) define (*d*) def

Answer to Multiple Choice Questions

1. (*b*) **2.** (*b*) **3.** (*d*) **4.** (*c*) **5.** (*d*) **6.** (*b*) **7.** (*c*) **8.** (*a*) **9.** (*c*) **10.** (*d*)

❑❑❑

3

NUMPY AND PANDAS LIBRARY

NUMPY

A strong Python package for numerical computation and array operations is called NumPy. The acronym is "Numerical Python." Large, multi-dimensional arrays and matrices are supported by NumPy, which also offers a selection of mathematical operations for effectively using huge arrays. Numerous other libraries used in data research and scientific computing, like Pandas and Matplotlib, are built upon it.

Here are some key features and functionalities of NumPy:

- **Ndarray:** The fundamental data structure in NumPy is the ndarray (n-dimensional array), which is a homogeneous, multi-dimensional array.

Arrays can have any number of dimensions and are similar to Python lists but provide more efficient storage and operations.

- **Array Creation:** Numpy.array() and Numpy.zeros() are two examples of functions that can be used to build new arrays from lists, tuples, or existing arrays in Python.

NumPy also provides functions to generate arrays with specific patterns, like numpy.arange(), numpy.linspace(), and numpy.random.rand().

- **Array Operations:** NumPy supports element-wise arithmetic operations (addition, subtraction, multiplication, division) and broadcasting to efficiently perform operations on arrays of different shapes.
- **Array Indexing and Slicing:** Arrays can be indexed and sliced to access specific elements or sub-arrays.

You can effectively extract particular areas of an array via slicing.

- **Universal Functions (ufuncs):** NumPy provides a wide range of built-in mathematical functions known as universal functions (ufuncs).

Ufuncs can be applied element-wise to arrays, making mathematical operations faster and more convenient.

- **Array Shape and Reshaping:** NumPy provides functions to get the shape of an array using .shape and to reshape arrays using .reshape(), .resize(), and others.
- **Aggregation and Statistical Functions:** NumPy includes functions to perform various aggregation operations on arrays, such as sum(), mean(), min(), max(), std(), and var(), among others.

- **Broadcasting:** NumPy allows arrays of different shapes to be combined and operated on, following certain broadcasting rules, which can simplify array operations.
- **Random Number Generation:** NumPy's random module provides functions to generate random numbers and arrays, such as numpy.random.rand(), numpy.random.randint(), and more.
- **Linear Algebra:** NumPy provides functions for linear algebra operations, such as matrix multiplication (numpy.dot()), matrix inversion (numpy.linalg.inv()), and eigenvalues (numpy.linalg.eig()).

To use NumPy, you need to import it into your Python script or Jupyter Notebook using the import numpy as np statement, where np is a common alias used for NumPy. Once imported, you can start using NumPy's array and mathematical functionalities to perform various numerical computations and data manipulations efficiently.

First, make sure you have NumPy installed. If you don't have it installed, you can install it using pip:

```
pip install numpy
```

Now, let's create a Python script and perform some array operations using NumPy:

```
import numpy as np

# Create a simple NumPy array
data = [1, 2, 3, 4, 5]
numpy_array = np.array(data)

print("Original array:")
print(numpy_array)
```

```
In [29]: # impart Librbary
         import numpy as np

         # Create a simple NumPy array
         data = [1, 2, 3, 4, 5]
         numpy_array = np.array(data)

         print("Original array:")
         print(numpy_array)

         Original array:
         [1 2 3 4 5]
```

```
# Perform some array operations
print("\nArray operations:")
print("Sum of elements:", numpy_array.sum())
print("Mean of elements:", numpy_array.mean())
print("Maximum element:", numpy_array.max())
print("Minimum element:", numpy_array.min())
```

```
In [29]: # impart Librbary
         import numpy as np

         # Create a simple NumPy array
         data = [1, 2, 3, 4, 5]
         numpy_array = np.array(data)

         print("Original array:")
         print(numpy_array)

         Original array:
         [1 2 3 4 5]

In [30]: # Perform some array operations
         print("\nArray operations:")
         print("Sum of elements:", numpy_array.sum())
         print("Mean of elements:", numpy_array.mean())
         print("Maximum element:", numpy_array.max())
         print("Minimum element:", numpy_array.min())

         Array operations:
         Sum of elements: 35
         Mean of elements: 3.0
         Maximum element: 5
         Minimum element: 1
```

```
# Broadcasting - adding a scalar to the array
print("\nBroadcasting:")
scalar = 10
result = numpy_array + scalar
print("Array after broadcasting:", result)
```

```
In [31]: # Broadcasting - adding a scalar to the array
         print("\nBroadcasting:")
         scalar = 10
         result = numpy_array + scalar
         print("Array after broadcasting:", result)

         Broadcasting:
         Array after broadcasting: (11 12 13 14 15]
```

```
# Element-wise operations
print("\nElement-wise operations:")
array1 = np.array([1, 2, 3])
array2 = np.array([4, 5, 6])
addition_result = array1 + array2
print("Addition:", addition_result)
multiplication_result = array1 * array2
print("Multiplication:", multiplication_result)
```

```
In [32]: # Element-wise operations
         print("\nElement-wise operations:")
         array1 = np.array(1[1, 2, 3])
         array2 = np.array([4, 5, 6])
         Element-wise operations:

In [33]: addition_result = array1 + array2
         print('Addition:", addition_result)
         Addition: [5 7 9]

In [34]: multiplication_result = array1 * array2
         print("Multiplication:", multiplication_result)
         Multiplication: [4 10 18]
```

```
# Matrix operations
print("\nMatrix operations:")
matrix1 = np.array([[1, 2], [3, 4]])
matrix2 = np.array([[5, 6], [7, 8]])

matrix_product = np.dot(matrix1, matrix2)
print("Matrix Product:")
print(matrix_product)
```

```
In [35]: # Matrix operations
         print("\nMatrix operations:")
         matrix1 = np.array([[1, 2], [3, 4]])
         matrix2 = np.array([[5, 6], [7, 8]])

         matrix_product = np.dot(matrix1, matrix2)
         print("Matrix Product:")
         print(matrix_product)
```

```
Matrix operations:
Matrix Product:
[[19 22]
 [43 50]]
```

PANDAS

A well-known Python package for data cleaning, analysis, and manipulation is called Pandas. It is constructed on top of NumPy and offers robust data structures and functions for working with tabular data, such as that found in spreadsheets and SQL tables, as well as structured data. Due to its flexibility and simplicity of use, Pandas is frequently used in data science, machine learning, and data analysis applications.

Key Features and Functionalities of Pandas:

1. **DataFrame:** The pandas library offers a two-dimensional labeled data structure called DataFrame. One of the most popular data structures for data analysis and manipulation. Similar to a spreadsheet or a SQL table, a DataFrame is a table having rows and columns. It enables effective storage and analysis of structured data.
   To work with pandas, make sure you have it installed. If not, you can install it using pip:
   pip install pandas
   Here is an illustration of how to construct and use a pandas DataFrame:

```
    import pandas as pd

# Create a DataFrame from a dictionary
data = {
    'Name': ['John', 'Alice', 'Bob', 'Emily'],
    'Age': [25, 28, 22, 30],
    'City': ['New York', 'Los Angeles', 'Chicago', 'San Francisco']
}

df = pd.DataFrame(data)
# Display the DataFrame
print(df)
```

```
In [38]: # import Library
         import pandas as pd
         # Create a DataFrame from a dictionary
         data = {
             'Name': ['John', 'Alice', 'Bob', 'Emily'],
             'Age': [25, 28, 22, 30],
             'City': ['New York', 'Los Angeles', 'Chicago', 'San Francisco']
         }
         df = pd.DataFrame(data)
```

```
In [39]: # Display the DataFrame
         print(df)
             Name   Age            City
         0   John    25        New York
         1   Alice   28     Los Angeles
         2   Bob     22         Chicago
         3   Emily   30   San Francisco
```

We import the Pandas library as pd in this example. Using a Python dictionary of data, we create a DataFrame df where the lists of values correspond to the data for each column and the keys of the dictionary correspond to the column names.

Pandas DataFrame has many useful methods and attributes to manipulate and analyze the data. Here are some common operations:

Accessing Columns: You can access a specific column by using the column name as an index:

print(df['Name'])

```
In [40]: print(df['Name'])
         0   John
         1   Alice
         2   Bob
         3   Emily
         Name: Name, dtype: object
```

Accessing Rows: You can access a specific row by using the iloc or loc attribute:

print(df.iloc[0]) # Access the first row

print(df.loc[1]) # Access the row with the label '1'

```
In [41]: print(df.iloc[0])  # Access the first row
         print(df.loc[1])  # Access the row with the Label '1'
         Name              John
         Age                 25
         City          New York
         Name: 0, dtype: object
         Name             Alice
         Age                 28
         City       Los Angeles
         Name: 1, dtype: object
```

Adding and Removing Columns: You can add a new column to the DataFrame or remove an existing column:

df['Gender'] = ['Male', 'Female', 'Male', 'Female'] # Add a new column

df.drop('City', axis=1, inplace=True) # Remove the 'City' column

Filtering Data: You can filter the DataFrame based on certain conditions:

young_people = df[df['Age'] < 30] # Get rows where Age < 30

Grouping and Aggregation: You can execute aggregation operations and aggregate data depending on one or more columns:

```
grouped_data = df.groupby('Gender')['Age'].mean() # Calculate the average age by gender
```

```
In [42]: df['Gender'] = ['Male', 'Female', 'Male', 'Female'] # Add a new column
         df.drop('City', axis=1, inplace=True) # Remove the 'City' column

In [43]: young_people = df[df['Age'] < 30] # Get rows where Age < 30

In [44]: grouped_data = df.groupby('Gender')['Age'].mean() # Calculate the average age by gender
```

2. **Series:** A Series is a named, one-dimensional array that can store several forms of data. A DataFrame is composed of multiple Series, where each Series represents a column in the DataFrame. It is similar to a NumPy array, but it also has an associated labeled index, allowing for more flexible and descriptive data representation. One way to conceptualize a series is as a single data column with labels for each piece.

```
# Create a Series from a list
data = [10, 20, 30, 40, 50]
series = pd.Series(data)

# Display the Series
print(series)
```

```
In [45]: # Create a Series from a list
         data = [10, 20, 30, 40, 50]
         series = pd.Series(data)

In [46]: # Display the Series
         print(series)
         0  10
         1  20
         2  30
         3  40
         4  50
         dtype: int64
```

In this example, we import the pandas library as pd. We create a Series series from a Python list data. The default index for the Series is automatically generated as integers starting from 0.

Pandas Series has many useful methods and attributes to manipulate and analyze the data. Here are some common operations:

Accessing Elements: You can access elements of the Series using the index:

```
print(series[2]) # Access the element at index 2
```

Custom Index: You can provide a custom index to the Series:

```
custom_index = ['A', 'B', 'C', 'D', 'E']
series_with_custom_index = pd.Series(data, index=custom_index)
print(series_with_custom_index)
```

```
In [47]: print(series[2]) # Access the element at index 2
         30
```

```
In [48]: custom_index = ['A', 'B', 'C', 'D', 'E']
         series_with_custom_index = pd.Series(data, index=custom_index)
         print(series_with_custom_index)
         A   10
         B   20
         C   30
         D   40
         E   50
         dtype: int64
```

Mathematical Operations: You can perform mathematical operations on Series:

```
# Add a scalar to all elements
result = series + 5
print(result)
```

```
In [49]: # Add a scalar to all elements
         result = series + 5
         print(result)
         0   15
         1   25
         2   35
         3   45
         4   55
         dtype: int64
```

```
# Element-wise multiplication
result = series * 2
print(result)
```

```
In [50]: # Element-wise multiplication
         result = series * 2
         print(result)
         0   20
         1   40
         2   60
```

```
3   80
4   100
dtype: int64
```

Filtering Data: You can filter the Series based on certain conditions:

```
filtered_series = series[series > 30]  # Get elements greater than 30
print(filtered_series)
```

```
In [51]: filtered_series = series[series > 30] # Get elements greater than 30
         3   40
         4   50
         dtype: int64
```

Series with Labels: You can also create a Series with labels directly:

```
data = {'A': 10, 'B': 20, 'C': 30, 'D': 40, 'E': 50}
series = pd.Series(data)
print(series)
```

```
In [52]: data = {'A': 10, 'B': 20, 'C': 30, 'D': 40, 'E': 50}
         series = pd.Series(data)
         print(series)
         A   10
         B   20
         C   30
         D   40
         E   50
         dtype: int64
```

3. **Data Reading and Writing:** Pandas has routines for reading data from many different file types, including CSV, Excel, SQL databases, and others. Pandas may also export data to these formats. The read_* and to_* methods in pandas make it simple to read data from a variety of file formats and write data to files. Here are a few typical ways to read and write data with pandas:

   Reading Data:

   Reading from CSV file: First u save a file in your system drive like in D drive saved the file with name data.csv. One file created with following data and stored in D drive

	Pregnancies	Glucose	BloodPressure	SkinThickness	Insulin	BMI\
0	4	110	92	0	0	37.6
1	10	168	74	0	0	38.0
2	10	139	80	0	0	27.1
3	1	189	60	23	846	30.1
4	5	166	72	19	175	25.8

	DiabetesPedigreeFunction	Age	Outcome
0	0.191	30	0
1	0.537	34	1
2	1.441	57	0
3	0.398	59	1

```
import pandas as pd
# Read data from a CSV file
df = pd.read_csv(' D:\data.csv')

# Display the DataFrame
print(df)
```

```
In [54]: import pandas as pd
         # Read data from a CSV file
         df = pd.read_csv(' D:\data.csv')

In [55]: # Display the DataFrame
```

	Pregnancies	Glucose	BloodPressure	SkinThickness	Insulin	BMI\
0	4	110	92	0	0	37.6
1	10	168	74	0	0	38.0
2	10	139	80	0	0	27.1
3	1	189	60	23	846	30.1
4	5	166	72	19	175	25.8

	DiabetesPedigreeFunction	Age	Outcome
0	0.191	30	0
1	0.537	34	1
2	1.441	57	0
3	0.398	59	1
4	0.587	51	1

Reading from Excel file: First u save a file in your system drive like in D drive saved the file with name data2.xlsx. One file created with following data and stored in D drive

	Pregnancies	SkinThickness	Insulin	BMI	DiabetesPedigreeFunction	Age
0	4	0	0	37.6	0.191	30
1	10	0	0	38.0	0.537	34
2	10	0	0	27.1	1.441	57
3	1	23	846	30.1	0.398	59
4	5	19	175	25.8	0.587	51

```
   Outcome
0        0
1        1
2        0
3        1
4        1
```

```
import pandas as pd
# Read data from an Excel file (Sheet name can be specified)
df = pd.read_excel('data2.xls', sheet_name='data')

# Display the DataFrame
print(df)
```

```
In [58]: import pandas as pd
         # Read data from an Excel file (Sheet name can be specified)
         df = pd.read_excel('D:\data2.xls', sheet_name='data')

In [59]: # Display the DataFrame
         print(df)
            Pregnancies  SkinThickness  Insulin   BMI  DiabetesPedigreeFunction  Age
         0            4              0        0  37.6                     0.191   30
         1           10              0        0  38.0                     0.537   34
         2           10              0        0  27.1                     1.441   57
         3            1             23      846  30.1                     0.398   59
         4            5             19      175  25.8                     0.587   51
            Outcome
         0        0
         1        1
         2        0
         3        1
         4        1
```

Reading from JSON file: Save JavaScript Object Notation (JSON) file in your drive

```
{
        "fruit": "Apple",
        "size": "Large",
        "color": "Red"
}
```

```
import pandas as pd
# Read data from a JSON file
df = pd.read_json("D:\data3-json.json", typ='series')
```

```
# Display the DataFrame
print(df)
```

```
In [62]: import pandas as pd
         # Read data from a JSON file
         df = pd.read_json("D:\data3-json", typ='series')

In [63]: # Display the DataFrame
         print(df)
         fruit    Apple
         size     Large
         color    Red
         dtype: object
```

Writing Data:

Writing to CSV file:

```
import pandas as pd

# Assume 'df' is the DataFrame you want to save
df.to_csv('output.csv', index=False)  # Set index=False to exclude row numbers in the output
```

Writing to Excel file:

```
import pandas as pd

# Assume 'df' is the DataFrame you want to save
df.to_excel('output.xlsx', sheet_name='Sheet1', index=False)
```

Writing to JSON file:

```
import pandas as pd

# Assume 'df' is the DataFrame you want to save
df.to_json('output.json', orient='records')
```

4. **Data Selection and Manipulation:** Pandas supports powerful data indexing and selection methods, including label-based and position-based indexing, as well as boolean indexing. Data can be filtered, sorted, and manipulated using various methods and functions.
   Assume you have a CSV file named "grades.csv" with the following data:

	Name	Math	Science	History
0	John	85	90	78
1	Alice	76	88	92
2	Bob	90	82	79
3	Emily	88	78	86

Data Selection and Manipulation:

```
import pandas as pd

# Read the data from the CSV file
df = pd.read_csv('D:\grades.csv')

# Display the DataFrame
print("Original DataFrame:")
print(df)
```

```
In [64]: import pandas as pd

         # Read the data from the CSV file
         df = pd.read_csv(D':\grade.csv')

In [65]: # Display the DataFrame
         print("Original DataFrame:")
         print(df)

         Original DataFrame:
                Name   Math   Science   History
         0      John     85        90        78
         1     Alice     76        88        92
         2       Bob     90        82        79
         3     Emily     88        78        86
```

```
# Selecting specific columns
math_scores = df['Math']
print("\nMath Scores:")
print(math_scores)
```

```
In [66]: # Selecting specific columns
         math_scores = df['Math']
         print("\nMath Scores:")
         print(math_scores)

         Math Scores:
         0   85
         1   76
         2   90
         3   88
         Name: Math, dtype: int64
```

```
# Selecting specific rows
alice_row = df.loc[df['Name'] == 'Alice']
print("\nAlice's Row:")
print(alice_row)
```

```
In [67]: # Selecting specific rows
         alice_row = df.loc[df['Name'] == 'Alice']
         print('\nAlice's Row:")
         print(alice_row)

         Alice's Row:
              Name    Math    Science   History
         1    Alice   76      88        92
```

```
# Filtering based on conditions
passed_math = df[df['Math'] >= 80]
print("\nStudents who passed Math:")
print(passed_math)
```

```
In [68]: # Filtering based on conditions
         passed_math = df[df['Math'] >= 80]
         print("\nStudents who passed Math:")
         print(passed_math)

         Students who passed Math:
              Name    Math    Science   History
         0    John    85      90        78
         2    Bob     90      82        79
         3    Emily   88      78        86
```

```
# Adding a new column
df['Total'] = df['Math'] + df['Science'] + df['History']
print("\nDataFrame with Total column:")
print(df)
```

```
In [69]: # Adding a new column
         df['Total'] = df['Math'] + df['Science'} + df['History']
         print('\nDataFrame with Total column:")
         print(df)
```

```
DataFrame with Total column:
    Name  Math  Science  History  Total
0   John    85       90       78    253
1  Alice    76       88       92    256
2    Bob    90       82       79    251
3  Emily    88       78       86    252
```

```
# Calculating average grade
df['Average'] = df[['Math', 'Science', 'History']].mean(axis=1)
print("\nDataFrame with Average column:")
print(df)
```

```
In [70]: # Calculating average grade
         df['Average'] = df[['Math', 'Science', 'History']].mean(axis=1)
         print("\nDataFrame with Average column:")
         print(df)

         DataFrame with Average column:
             Name  Math  Science  History  Total    Average
         0   John    85       90       78    253  84.333333
         1  Alice    76       88       92    256  85.333333
         2    Bob    90       82       79    251  83.666667
         3  Emily    88       78       86    252  84.000000
```

```
# Sorting the DataFrame
sorted_df = df.sort_values(by='Average', ascending=False)
print("\nSorted DataFrame by Average:")
print(sorted_df)
```

```
In [71]: # Sorting the DataFrame
         sorted_df = df.sort_values(by='Average', ascending=False)
         print("\nSorted DataFrame by Average:")
         print(sorted_df)

         Sorted DataFrame by Average:
             Name  Math  Science  History  Total    Average
         1  Alice    76       88       92    256  85.333333
         0   John    85       90       78    253  84.333333
         3  Emily    88       78       86    252  84.000000
         2    Bob    90       82       79    251  83.666667
```

```
# Deleting a column
df.drop('History', axis=1, inplace=True)
print("\nDataFrame after removing History column:")
print(df)
```

```
In [72]: Deleting a column
         df.drop('History', axis=1, inplace=True)
         print("\nDataFrame after removing History column:")
         print(df)

         DataFrame after removing History column:
               Name   Math   Science   Total    Average
         0     John     85        90     253  84.333333
         1    Alice     76        88     256  85.333333
         2      Bob     90        82     251  83.666667
         3    Emily     88        78     252  84.000000
```

In this example, we first read the data from the CSV file into a pandas DataFrame df. Then, we perform various data selection and manipulation operations, such as selecting specific columns, filtering rows based on conditions, adding new columns, calculating average grades, sorting the DataFrame, and deleting a column.

5. **Missing Data Handling:** Pandas provides functions to handle missing data, such as dropna() to remove rows or columns with missing values and fillna() to fill missing values with specified values. Handling missing data is a crucial aspect of data analysis and manipulation. In pandas, missing data is represented by NaN (Not a Number) values. Pandas provides several methods to detect, remove, and fill missing data in DataFrames. Some common techniques for missing data handling in pandas:

Checking for Missing Data:

```
import pandas as pd

# Sample DataFrame with missing data
data = {
    'A': [1, 2, None, 4, 5],
    'B': [None, 10, 15, None, 25],
    'C': [100, 200, 300, 400, None]
}
df = pd.DataFrame(data)

# Check for missing data in the DataFrame
print(df.isnull())
```

```
In [73]: import pandas as pd

         # Sample DataFrame with missing data
         dat = {
             'A': [1, 2, None, 4, 5],
             'B': [None, 10, 15, None, 25],
             'C': [100, 200, 300, 400, None]
         }

         df = pd.DataFrame(data)

In [74]: # Check for missing data in the DataFrame
         print(df.isnull())

             A       B       C
         0   False   True    False
         1   False   False   False
         2   True    False   False
         3   False   True    False
         4   False   False   True
```

Dropping Missing Values:

```
# Drop rows with any missing values
df.dropna(inplace=True)

# Drop columns with any missing values
df.dropna(axis=1, inplace=True)

In [75]: # Drop rows with any missing values
         df.dropna(inplace=True)

In [76]: # Drop columns with any missing values
         df.dropna(axis=1, inplace=True)

In [77]: df
Out[77]:
             A       B       C
         1   2.0     10.0    200.0
```

Filling Missing Values:

```
# Fill missing values with a specific value (e.g., 0)
df.fillna(0, inplace=True)

# Fill missing values with the mean of the column
df.fillna(df.mean(), inplace=True)
```

```
# Forward fill missing values (propagate the previous value forward)
df.fillna(method='ffill', inplace=True)

# Backward fill missing values (propagate the next value backward)
df.fillna(method='bfill', inplace=True)
```

```
In [78]: # Full missing values with a specific value (e.g., 0)
         df.fillna(0, inplace=True)

In [79]: # Fill missing values with the mean of the column
         df.fillna(df.mean(), inplace=True)

In [80]: # Forward fill missing values (propagate the previous value forward)
         df.fillna(method='ffill', inplace=True)

In [81]: # Backward fill missing values (propagate the next value backward)
         df.fillna(method='bfill', inplace=True)
```

Interpolation:

```
# Use interpolation to fill missing values (linear method)
df.interpolate(method='linear', inplace=True)
```

Replacing Specific Values:

```
# Replace specific values with another value
df.replace(10, 100, inplace=True)
```

```
In [83]: # Use interpolation to fill missing values (linear method)
         df.interpolate(method= 'linear', inplace=True)

In [84]: # Replace specific values with another value
         df.replace(10, 100, inplace=True)
```

6. **Grouping and Aggregation:** Pandas allows data to be grouped based on specific criteria using groupby() and then perform aggregation operations on the grouped data, such as sum(), mean(), count(), etc. Grouping and aggregation in pandas are powerful techniques for summarizing and analyzing data based on some categorical variables. The groupby method is used to group data in a pandas DataFrame based on one or more columns, and aggregation functions are then applied to each group to compute summary statistics. Let's go through an example to illustrate this:
   Assume you have a CSV file named "sales.csv" with the following data:

```
Date,City,Product,Quantity,Revenue
2023-08-01,Delhi,Apple,10,100
2023-08-01,Delhi,Banana,5,50
2023-08-01,Mumbai,Apple,8,80
2023-08-01,Mumbai,Orange,12,60
```

2023-08-02,Delhi,Apple,15,150
2023-08-02,Delhi,Banana,6,60
2023-08-02,Mumbai,Orange,10,50
2023-08-02,Mumbai,Grapes,5,40

	Date	City	Product	Quantity	Revenue
0	01-08-2023	Delhi	Apple	10	100
1	01-08-2023	Delhi	Banana	5	50
2	01-08-2023	Mumbai	Apple	8	80
3	01-08-2023	Mumbai	Orange	12	60
4	02-08-2023	Delhi	Apple	15	150
5	02-08-2023	Delhi	Banana	6	60
6	02-08-2023	Mumbai	Orange	10	50
7	02-08-2023	Mumbai	Grapes	5	40

Grouping and Aggregation:

```
import pandas as pd

# Read the data from the CSV file
df = pd.read_csv(' D:\sales.csv')

# Display the DataFrame
print("Original DataFrame:")
print(df)
```

```
In [1]: import pandas as pd
        # Read the data from the CSV file
        df = pd.read_csv('D:\sales.csv')

In [2]: # Display the DataFrame
        print("Original DataFrame:")
        print(df)
```

Original DataFrame:

	Date	City	Product	Quantity	Revenue
0	01-08-2023	Delhi	Apple	10	100
1	01-08-2023	Delhi	Banana	5	50
2	01-08-2023	Mumbai	Apple	8	80
3	01-08-2023	Mumbai	Orange	12	60
4	02-08-2023	Delhi	Apple	15	150
5	02-08-2023	Delhi	Banana	6	60
6	02-08-2023	Mumbai	Orange	10	50
7	02-08-2023	Mumbai	Grapes	5	40

```
# Grouping by 'City' and 'Product'
grouped_df = df.groupby(['City', 'Product'])

# Calculating total quantity and revenue for each group
aggregated_df = grouped_df.agg({
    'Quantity': 'sum',
    'Revenue': 'sum'
}).reset_index()

# Display the aggregated DataFrame
print("\nAggregated DataFrame:")
print(aggregated_df)
```

```
In [3]: # Grouping by 'City' and 'Product'
        grouped_df = df.groupby(['City', 'Product'])

In [4]: # Calculating total quantity and revenue for each group
        aggregated_df = grouped_df.agg({
            'Quantity': 'sum',
            'Revenue': 'sum'
        }).reset_index()

In [6]: # Display the aggregated DataFrame
        print("\nAggregated DataFrame:")
        print(aggregated_df)
```

Aggregated DataFrame:

	City	Product	Quantity	Revenue
0	Delhi	Apple	25	250
1	Delhi	Banana	11	110
2	Mumbai	Apple	8	80
3	Mumbai	Grapes	5	40
4	Mumbai	Orange	22	110

In this example, the data is initially read into a pandas DataFrame df from the CSV file. The data is then grouped based on the "City" and "Product" columns using the groupby method. Then, for each group, we use the agg method to determine the sum of "Quantity" and "Revenue." For a clearer presentation, the index of the generated DataFrame is reset using the reset_index method.

The resulting aggregated_df makes it simpler to evaluate and comprehend the data by providing a summary of the total 'Quantity' and 'Revenue' for each product in each city.

7. **Merging and Joining:** Pandas provides functions to merge and join DataFrames based on common columns or indices. Pandas provides several methods to combine data from different DataFrames based on specific columns or indices.

Make sure Pandas is installed first. You can install it if you haven't already by using the following command:

```
pip install pandas
```

Now, let's create two example DataFrames and see how to merge and join them.

```
import pandas as pd

# Example DataFrame 1
data1 = {
    'ID': [1, 2, 3, 4],
    'Name': ['Munesh', 'Vedansh', 'Anil', 'Prasiddha'],
    'Age': [44, 10, 35, 4]
}
df1 = pd.DataFrame(data1)

# Example DataFrame 2
data2 = {
    'ID': [3, 4, 5, 6],
    'Department': ['HR', 'Finance', 'Marketing', 'IT']
}
df2 = pd.DataFrame(data2)
```

```
In [7]:  data1 = {
             'ID': [1, 2, 3, 4],
             'Name': ['Munesh', 'Vedansh', 'Anil', 'Prasiddha'],
             'Age': [44, 10, 35, 4]
         }
         df1 = pd.DataFrame(data1)

In [8]:  data2 = {
             'ID': [3, 4, 5, 6],
             'Department': ['HR', 'Finance', 'Marketing', 'IT']
         }
         df2 = pd.DataFrame(data2)
```

Merge

Inner Merge: Only the rows with matching values in both DataFrames on the given column(s) are returned by an inner merge.

```
inner_merged = pd.merge(df1, df2, on='ID', how='inner')
print(inner_merged)
```

```
In [7]:  data1 = {
             'ID': [1, 2, 3, 4],
             'Name': ['Munesh', 'Vedansh', 'Anil', 'Prasiddha'],
```

```
        'Age': [44, 10, 35, 4]
    }
    df1 = pd.DataFrame(data1)
```

```
In [8]:  data2 = {
              'ID': [3, 4, 5, 6],
              'Department': ['HR', 'Finance', 'Marketing', 'IT']
          }
          df2 = pd.DataFrame(data2)
```

```
In [9]:  inner_merged = pd.merge(df1, df2, on='ID', how='inner')
         print(inner_merged)
                 ID        Name      Age    Department
         0       3         Anil      35     HR
         1       4         Prasiddha 4      Finance
```

Left Merge: The rows from both the left and right DataFrames that match are both returned by a left merge. NaN values will be filled in for rows in the correct DataFrame that don't match.

left_merged = pd.merge(df1, df2, on='ID', how='left')
print(left_merged)

```
In [10]: left_merged = pd.merge(df1, df2, on='ID', how='left')
         print(left_merged)
                 ID        Name      Age    Department
         0       1         Munesh    44     NaN
         1       2         Vedansh   10     NaN
         2       3         Anil      35     HR
         3       4         Prasiddha 4      Finance
```

Right Merge: The rows from both the left and right data frames that match are both returned by a right merge. NaN values will be inserted in for rows in the left DataFrame that don't match.

right_merged = pd.merge(df1, df2, on='ID', how='right')
print(right_merged)

```
In [11]: right_merged = pd.merge(df1, df2, on='ID', how='right')
         print(inner_merged)
                 ID        Name      Age    Department
         0       3         Anil      35.0   HR
         1       4         Prasiddha 4.0    Finance
         2       5         NaN       NaN    Marketing
         3       6         NaN       NaN    IT
```

Outer Merge: When there is a match in either the left or right DataFrame, an outer merge returns all rows. Rows with no matches will have NaN values filled in.

```
outer_merged = pd.merge(df1, df2, on='ID', how='outer')
print(outer_merged)
```

```
In [12]: outer_merged = pd.merge(df1, df2, on='ID', how='outer')
         print(outer_merged)
```

	ID	Name	Age	Department
0	1	Munesh	44.0	NaN
1	2	Vedansh	10.0	NaN
2	3	Anil	35.0	HR
3	4	Prasiddha	4.0	Finance
4	5	NaN	NaN	Marketing
5	6	NaN	NaN	IT

Join: The join() method in Pandas is used to join two DataFrames based on their indices.

```
df1.set_index('ID', inplace=True)
df2.set_index('ID', inplace=True)

joined_df = df1.join(df2, lsuffix='_df1', rsuffix='_df2')
print(joined_df)
```

```
In [13]: df1.set_index('ID', inplace=True)
         df2.set_index('ID', inplace=True)

         joined_df = df1.join(df2, 1suffix='_df1', rsuffix='_df2')
         print(joined_df)
```

ID	Name	Age	Department
1	Munesh	44	NaN
2	Vedansh	10	NaN
3	Anil	35	HR
4	Prasiddha	4	Finance

8. **Reshaping Data:** In Pandas, reshaping data is changing the layout of a DataFrame to a different shape to make the data easier to work with and analyze. Pandas typically use stacking, unstacking, pivoting, and melting as reshaping methods. Let's look at some instances of each. Data reshaping techniques supported by Pandas include pivot(), melt(), and stack(). We'll make use of the following DataFrame for these instances:

```
import pandas as pd
data = {
    'Name': ['Sinddha', 'Charu', 'Prasiddha'],
    'Math': [85, 78, 92],
    'Science': [90, 85, 88],
    'History': [80, 75, 85]
}
```

```
df = pd.DataFrame(data)
print(df)
```

```
In [14]: import pandas as pd

         data = {
             'Name': ['Sinddha', 'Charu', 'Prasiddha'],
             'Math': [85, 78, 92],
             'Science': [90, 85, 88],
             'History': [80, 75, 85]
         }

         df = pd.DataFrame(data)

In [15]: print(df)
```

	Name	Math	Science	History
0	Sindddha	85	90	80
1	Charu	78	85	75
2	Prasiddha	92	88	85

Stacking: By "stacking" the columns on top of one another, stacking converts data from a wide format (columns) to a long format (rows).

```
stacked_df = df.set_index('Name').stack().reset_index()
stacked_df.columns = ['Name', 'Subject', 'Score']

print(stacked_df)
```

```
In [16]: stacked_df = df.set_index('Name').stack().reset_index()
         stacked_df.columns = ['Name', 'Subject', 'Score']

         print(stacked_df)
```

	Name	Subject	Score
0	Sinddha	Math	85
1	Sinddha	Science	90
2	Sinddha	History	80
3	Charu	Math	78
4	Charu	Science	85
5	Charu	History	75
6	Prasiddha	Math	92
7	Prasiddha	Science	88
8	Prasiddha	History	85

Unstacking: Unstacking converts data from a long format (rows) back to a wide format (columns) by "unstacking" a specified level of the index.

```
unstacked_df = stacked_df.set_index(['Name', 'Subject'])['Score'].unstack().reset_index()
print(unstacked_df)
```

```
In [17]: unstacked_df = stacked_df.set_index(['Name', 'Subject'])['Score'].unstack().reset_index()
         print(unstacked_df)
         Subject    Name        History    Math    Science
         0          Charu       75         78      85
         1          Prasiddha   85         92      88
         2          Sinddha     80         85      90
```

Pivoting: Pivoting allows you to transform data by specifying new row and column indices and the values to populate the new DataFrame.

```
pivoted_df = df.pivot(index='Name', columns='Subject', values='Score').reset_index()
print(pivoted_df)
```

Output:

```
Subject Name      History    Math    Science
0       Sinddha   80         85      90
1       Charu     75         78      85
2       Prasiddha 85         92      88
```

Melting: Melting is the reverse of pivoting, where we convert a wide DataFrame to a long format.

```
melted_df = pd.melt(df, id_vars='Name', var_name='Subject', value_name='Score')
print(melted_df)
```

```
In [19]: melted_df = pd.melt(df, id_vars='Name', var_name='Subject', value_name='Score')
         print(melted_df)
                 Name        Subject    Score
         0       Sinddha     Math       85
         1       Charu       Math       78
         2       Prasiddha   Math       92
         3       Sinddha     Science    90
         4       Charu       Science    85
         5       Prasiddha   Science    88
         6       Sinddha     History    80
         7       Charu       History    75
         8       Prasiddha   History    85
```

9. **Time Series Data:** A time-indexed set of data points is referred to as time series data. It is frequently applied to a variety of fields, including environmental sciences, finance, and economics. Pandas allows for the representation of time series data using either the DatetimeIndex or the PeriodIndex to provide time-based operations. Let's walk through an example of utilizing Pandas to manipulate time series data. Pandas offers a wealth of help when working with time series data, including resampling and date and time manipulation.

Make sure Pandas is installed first. You can install it if you haven't already by using the following command.:

```
pip install pandas
```

Now, let's create an example DataFrame representing time series data:

```
import pandas as pd

# Create a date range from January 1, 2023 to January 10, 2023
date_range = pd.date_range(start='2023-01-01', end='2023-01-10', freq='D')

# Create time series data with random values
data = {
    'Date': date_range,
    'Temperature': [25, 28, 22, 23, 20, 19, 24, 26, 28, 27],
    'Rainfall': [0.1, 0.0, 0.5, 0.3, 0.0, 0.0, 0.2, 0.0, 0.0, 0.1]
}
df = pd.DataFrame(data)
print(df)
```

```
In [20]: import pandas as pd
         # Create a date range from January 1, 2023 to January 10, 2023
         date_range = pd.date_range(start='2023-01-01', end='2023-01-10', freq='D')

In [21]: # Create time series data with random values
         data = {
             'Date': date_range,
             'Temperature': [25, 28, 22, 23, 20, 19, 24, 26, 28, 27],
             'Rainfall': [0.1, 0.0, 0.5, 0.3, 0.0, 0.0, 0.2, 0.0, 0.0, 0.1]
         }
         df = pd.DataFrame(data)

In [22]: print(df)
```

	Date	Temperature	Rainfall
0	2023-01-01	25	0.1
1	2023-01-02	28	0.0
2	2023-01-03	22	0.5
3	2023-01-04	23	0.3
4	2023-01-05	20	0.0
5	2023-01-06	19	0.0
6	2023-01-07	24	0.2
7	2023-01-08	26	0.0
8	2023-01-09	28	0.0
9	2023-01-10	27	0.1

Having the time series data in the DataFrame now allows us to conduct a number of time-based actions:

Indexing and Slicing

```
# Set the 'Date' column as the index
df.set_index('Date', inplace=True)
# Access data for a specific date
print(df.loc['2023-01-05'])
```

```
In [23]: # Set the 'Date' column as the index
         df.set_index('Date', inplace=True)
```

```
In [24]: # Access data for a specific date
         print(df.loc['2023-01-05'])
         Temperature    20.0
         Rainfall        0.0
         Name: 2023-01-05  00:00:00,   dtype: float64
```

```
# Slicing data for a specific time period
print(df.loc['2023-01-03':'2023-01-07'])
```

```
In [25]: # Slicing data for a specific time period
         print(df.loc['2023-01-03' : '2023-01-07'])
                      Temperature      Rainfall
         Date
         2023-01-03        22             0.5
         2023-01-04        23             0.3
         2023-01-05        20             0.0
         2023-01-06        19             0.0
         2023-01-07        24             0.2
```

Resampling

```
# Resample data to get the daily average
daily_avg = df.resample('D').mean()

# Resample data to get the weekly sum
weekly_sum = df.resample('W').sum()
```

```
In [26]: # Resample data to get the daily average
         daily_avg = df.resample('D').mean()
```

```
In [27]: # Resample data to get the weekly sum
         weekly_sum = df.resample('W').sum()
```

Rolling Window

```
# Compute a 3-day rolling mean of 'Temperature'
rolling_mean = df['Temperature'].rolling(window=3).mean()
```

Time Shifting

```
# Shift the 'Temperature' data one day backward
df['Temperature_shifted'] = df['Temperature'].shift(1)

# Shift the 'Rainfall' data two days forward
df['Rainfall_shifted'] = df['Rainfall'].shift(-2)
```

```
In [28]: # Compute a 3-day rolling mean of 'Temperature'
         rolling_mean = df['Temperature'].rolling(window=3).mean()

In [29]: # Shift the 'Temperature' data one day backward
         df['Temperature_shifted'] = df['Temperature'].shift(1)

In [30]: # shift the 'Rainfall' data two days forward
         df['Rainfall_shifted'] = df['Rainfall'].shift(–2)
```

10. **Data Visualization:** Pandas provides basic data visualization capabilities built on top of the popular Python data visualization library, Matplotlib. Using Pandas, you can easily create various types of charts to visualize your data. Let's look at some Pandas-based data visualization examples. To produce illuminating plots and charts, Pandas can easily integrate with Matplotlib and other visualization packages. Make sure you have Matplotlib installed if you want to use these examples. You can install it if you haven't already by using the following command:

    ```
    pip install matplotlib
    ```

    Let's create an example DataFrame for visualization:

    ```
    import pandas as pd
    data = {
        'Name': ['Siddha', 'Charu', 'Prasiddha', 'Harsh', 'Ishita'],
        'Math': [85, 78, 92, 70, 88],
        'Science': [90, 85, 88, 75, 95],
        'History': [80, 75, 85, 90, 80]
    }
    df = pd.DataFrame(data)
    ```

    The DataFrame df looks like this:

	Name	Math	Science	History
0	Siddha	85	90	80
1	Charu	78	85	75
2	Prasiddha	92	88	85
3	Harsh	70	75	90
4	Ishita	88	95	80

```
In [31]: import pandas as pd
         data = {
             'Name': ['Siddha', 'Charu', 'Prasiddha', 'Harsh', 'Ishita'],
             'Math': [85, 78, 92, 70, 88],
             'Science': [90, 85, 88, 75, 95],
             'History': [80, 75, 85, 90, 80]
         }
         df = pd.DataFrame(data)

In [32]: print(df)
              Name   Math  Science  History
         0    Siddha    85       90       80
         1    Charu     78       85       75
         2  Prasiddha   92       88       85
         3    Harsh     70       75       90
         4    Ishita    88       95       80
```

Line Plot

```
import matplotlib.pyplot as plt

# Plotting the Math scores for each student
df.plot(x='Name', y='Math', kind='line', marker='o')
plt.title('Math Scores')
plt.xlabel('Name')
plt.ylabel('Math Score')
plt.show()
```

```
In [33]: import matplotlib.pyplot as plt

         # Plotting the Math scores for each student
         df.plot(x='Name', y='Math', kind='line', marker='o')
         plt.title('Math Scores')
         plt.xlabel('Name')
         plt.ylabel('Math Score')
         plt.show()
```

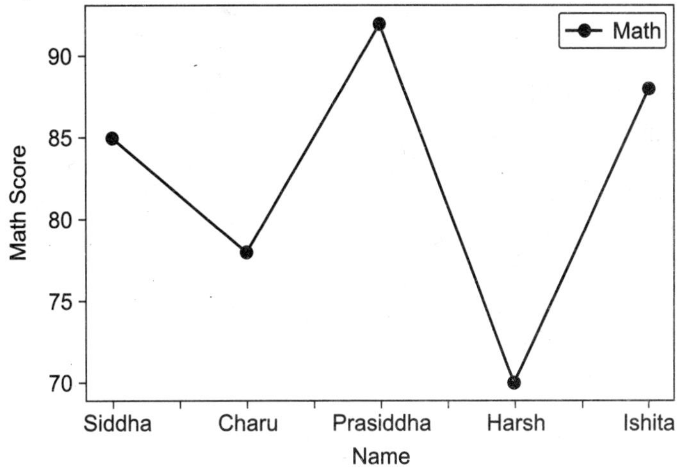

Bar Plot

```
# Plotting the average scores for each subject
df.mean().plot(kind='bar', color='skyblue')
plt.title('Average Scores')
plt.ylabel('Average Score')
plt.show()
```

In [35]:
```
# Plotting the average scores for each subject
df.mean().plot(king='bar', color='skyblue')
plt.title('Average Scores')
plt.ylabel('Average Scores')
plt.show()
```

```
C:\Users\Dr Anil Kumar Dubey\AppData\Local\Temp\ipykernel_11
DataFrame reductions (with 'numeric_only=None') is deprecated
columns before calling the reduction.
df.mean().plot(kind='bar', color='skyblue')
```

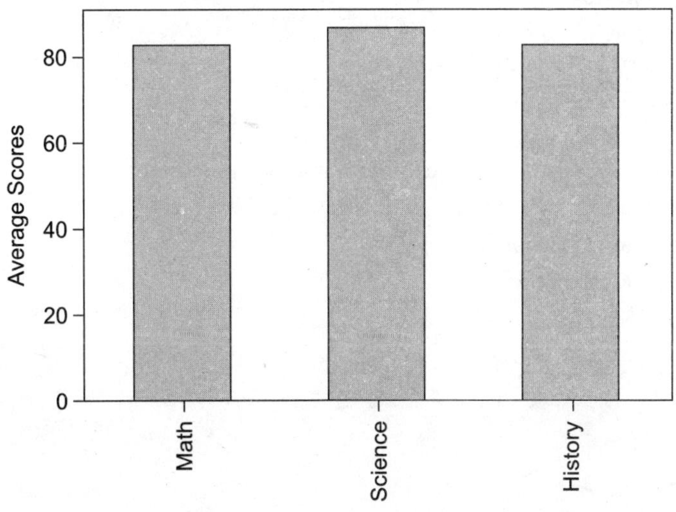

Histogram

```
# Plotting a histogram of Math scores
df['Math'].plot(kind='hist', bins=10, color='purple', alpha=0.6)
plt.title('Histogram of Math Scores')
plt.xlabel('Math Score')
plt.show()
```

```
In [36]: # Plotting a histogram of Math scores
         df['Math'].plot(kind='hist', bins=10, color='purple', alpha=0.6)
         plt.title('Histogram of Math Scores')
         plt.xlabel('Math Score')
         plt.show()
```

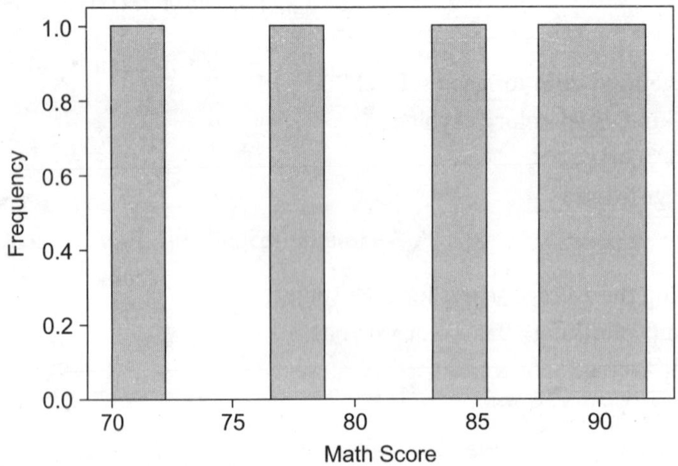

Scatter Plot

```
# Plotting a scatter plot between Math and Science scores
df.plot(x='Math', y='Science', kind='scatter', color='green', s=100)
plt.title('Math vs. Science Scores')
plt.xlabel('Math Score')
plt.ylabel('Science Score')
plt.show()
```

```
In [37]: # Plotting a scatter plot between Math and Science scores
         df.plot(x='Math', y='Science', kind='scatter', color='green', s=100)
         plt.title('Math vs. Science Scores')
         plt.xlabel('Math Score')
         plt.ylabel('Science Score')
         plt.show()
```

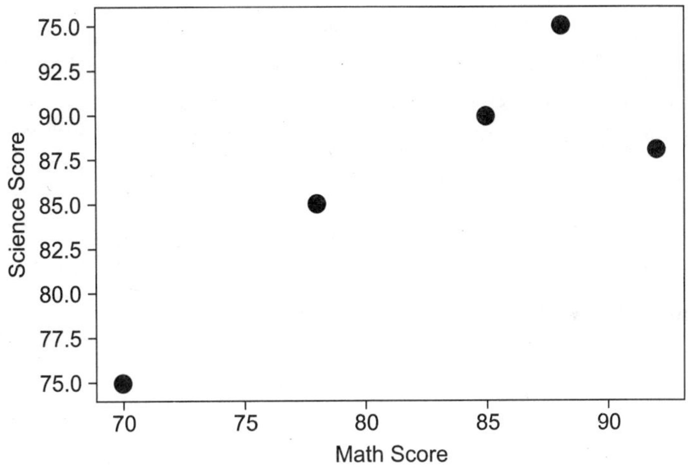

Box Plot

```
# Plotting a box plot for all subjects
df.plot(kind='box', color='orange')
plt.title('Box Plot of Scores')
plt.ylabel('Score')
plt.show()
```

```
In [38]: # Plotting a box plot for all subjects
         df.plot(kind='box', color='orange')
         plt.title('Box Plot of Scores')
         plt.ylabel('Score')
         plt.show()
```

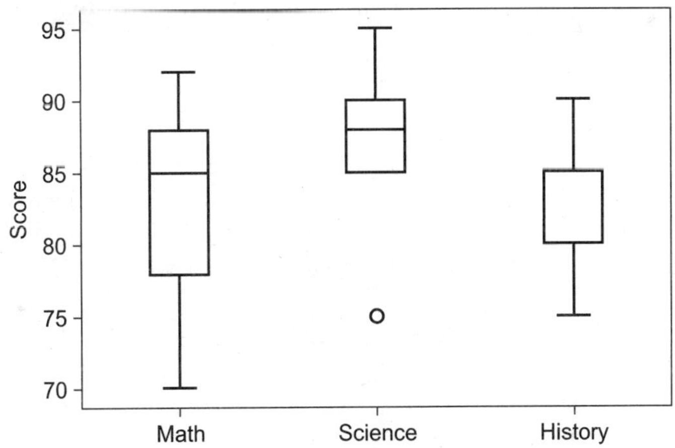

MATPLOTLIB

A well-liked Python library for producing static, interactive, and publication-quality graphics is called Matplotlib. It is frequently used to generate different kinds of charts and graphs as well as scientific charting and data visualization. Matplotlib is a crucial tool for data analysis and data sharing since it offers a flexible and simple interface for constructing a variety of graphs. Make sure Matplotlib is installed before using it:

```
pip install matplotlib
```

Here's an example:

```
import matplotlib.pyplot as plt

# Sample data
x = [1, 2, 3, 4, 5]
y = [10, 20, 15, 25, 30]

# Create a simple line plot
plt.plot(x, y, marker='o')
plt.title('Interactive Plot using Matplotlib')
plt.xlabel('X-axis')
plt.ylabel('Y-axis')

# Display the plot in the Jupyter Notebook
plt.show()
```

```
In [39]: import matplotlib.pyplot as plt
         # Sample data
         x = [1, 2, 3, 4, 5]
         y = [10, 20, 15, 25, 30]

In [42]: # Create a simple line plot
         plt.plot(x, y, marker='o')
         plt.title('Interactive Plot using Matplotlib')
         plt.xlabel('X-axis')
         plt.ylabel('Y-axis')
         # Display the plot in the Jupyter Notebook
         plt.show()
```

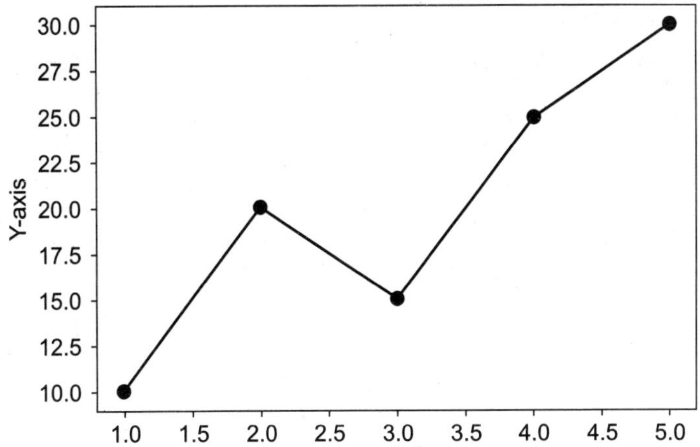

1. **Simple and Intuitive Interface:** An easy-to-use interface is provided by Matplotlib for building plots and charts. It enables altering the lines, markers, colors, labels, and titles of numerous story aspects.

```
import numpy as np
import pandas as pd
import matplotlib.pyplot as plt
from matplotlib.figure import Figure

# Sample data
x = [1, 2, 3, 4, 5]
y1 = [10, 15, 8, 12, 20]
y2 = [5, 10, 6, 8, 12]

# Create a figure and axes
fig=plt.figure()
fig, ax = plt.subplots()
ax.plot(x, y1)
ax.plot(x, y2)
print(fig, ax)
```

```
In [60]: import numpy as np
         import pandas as pd
         import matplotlib.pyplot as plt
         from matplotlib.figure import Figure
         # Sample data
         x = [1, 2, 3, 4, 5]
         y1 = [10, 15, 8, 12, 20]
         y2 = [5, 10, 6, 8, 12]
```

In [71]:
```
# Create a figure and axes
fig=plt.figure()
fig, ax = plt.subplots()
ax.plot(x, y1)
ax.plot(x, y2)
print(fig, ax)
Figure(432×288) AxesSubplot(0.125,0.125;0.775×0.755)
<Figure size 432×288 with 0 Axes>
```

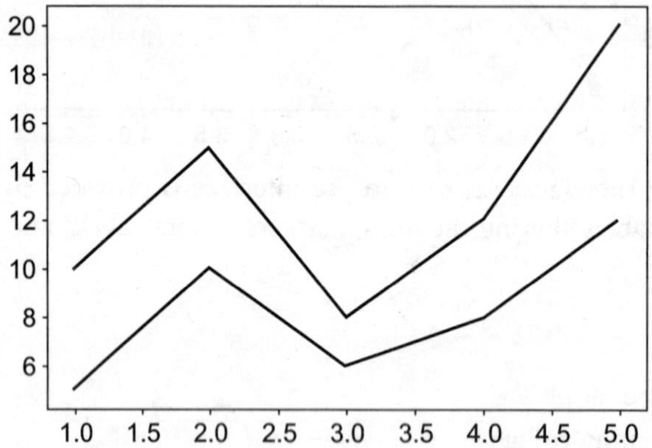


```
# Plot lines with markers and colors
ax.plot(x, y1, marker='o', color='blue', label='Line 1')
ax.plot(x, y2, marker='s', color='red', label='Line 2')

# Add labels to the axes
ax.set_xlabel('X-axis')
ax.set_ylabel('Y-axis')

# Add a title to the plot
ax.set_title('Example Plot with Lines, Markers, Colors, Labels, and Title')

# Add a legend to differentiate between lines
ax.legend()

# Display the plot
plt.show()
```

In [85]:
```
# Create a figure and axes
fig=plt.figure()
ax.plot(x, y1)
ax.plot(x, y2)
```

```
# Plot lines with markers and colors
ax.plot(x, y1, marker='o', color='blue', label='Line 1')
ax.plot(x, y2, marker='s', color='red', label='Line 2')

# Add Labels to the axes
ax.set_xlabel('X-axis')
ax.set_ylabel('Y-axis')

# Add a title to the plot
ax.set_title('Example Plot with Lines, markers, Colors, Labels, and Title')

# Add a Legend to differentiate between lines
ax.legend()
plt.show()
<Figure size 432x288 with 0 Axes>
```

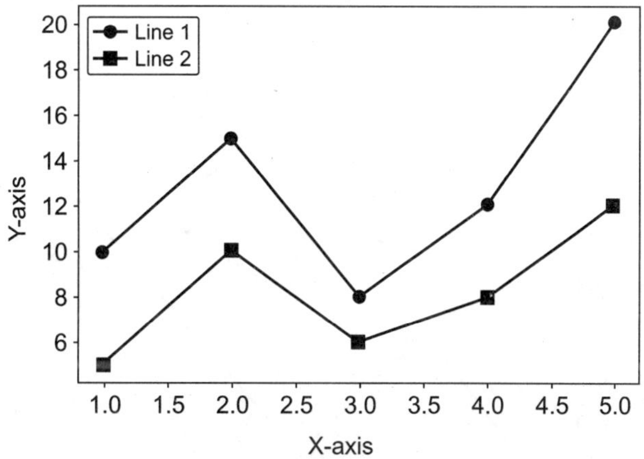

In this illustration, we made a figure and axes, plotted two lines using various markers and colors, labeled the axes, and gave the plot a title. To help you identify between the two lines, we have provided a legend. The resulting plot will show lines with markers in different hues (blue and red)—circles for line 1 and squares for line 2. The plot's title will be shown at the top and the X- and Y-axes will be labeled. The legend will also specify which line belongs to each label.

2. **Wide Variety of Plots:** Line plots, scatter plots, bar plots, histogram plots, pie charts, box plots, 3D graphs, and more are all supported by Matplotlib.

Line Plot

```
import matplotlib.pyplot as plt

# Sample data
x = [1, 2, 3, 4, 5]
y = [9, 16, 11, 17, 23]
```

```
# Create a line plot
plt.plot(x, y, marker='o', color='blue')
plt.title('Line Plot Example')
plt.xlabel('X-axis')
plt.ylabel('Y-axis')
plt.show()
```

```
In [86]: import matplotlib.pyplot as plt
         # Sample data
         x = [1, 2, 3, 4, 5]
         y = [9, 16, 11, 17, 23]
```

```
In [87]: # Create a line plot
         plt.plot(x, y, marker='o', color='blue')
         plt.title('Line Plot Example')
         plt.xlabel('X-axis')
         plt.ylabel('Y-axis')
         plt.show()
```

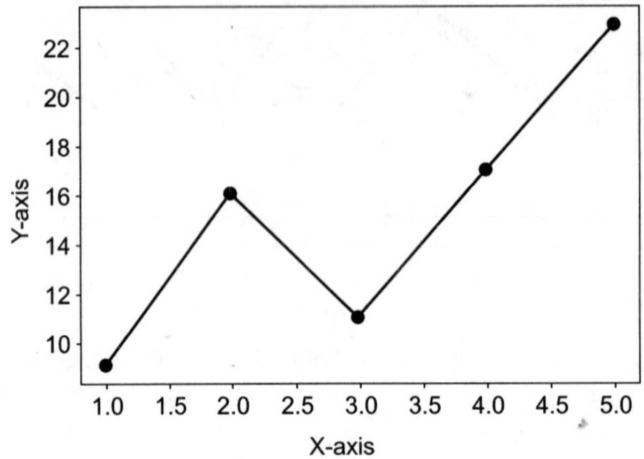

Scatter Plot

```
import matplotlib.pyplot as plt

# Sample data
x = [1, 2, 3, 4, 5]
y = [9, 16, 11, 17, 23]

# Create a scatter plot
plt.scatter(x, y, marker='o', color='red')
plt.title('Scatter Plot Example')
plt.xlabel('X-axis')
plt.ylabel('Y-axis')
```

```
plt.show()

In [88]: # Create a scatter plot
         plt.scatter(x, y, marker='o', color='red')
         plt.title('Scatter Plot Example')
         plt.xlabel('X-axis')
         plt.ylaberl('Y-axis')
         plt.show()
```

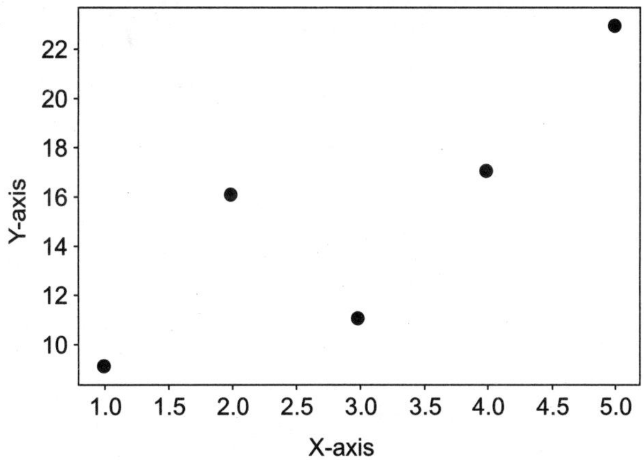

Bar Plot

```
import matplotlib.pyplot as plt

# Sample data
x = ['A', 'B', 'C', 'D', 'E']
y = [11, 16, 9, 14, 24]

# Create a bar plot
plt.bar(x, y, color='green')
plt.title('Bar Plot Example')
plt.xlabel('Categories')
plt.ylabel('Values')
plt.show()

In [89]: # Sample data
         x = ['A', 'B', 'C', 'D', 'E']
         y = [11, 16, 9, 14, 24]

In [90]: # Create a bar plot
         plt.bar(x, y, color='green')
         plt.title('Bar Plot Example')
         plt.xlabel('Categories')
```

```
plt.ylabel('Values')
plt.show()
```

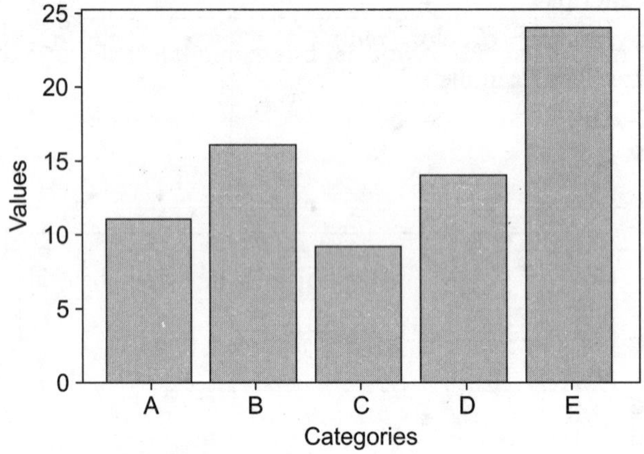

Histogram Plot

```
import matplotlib.pyplot as plt

# Sample data
data = [10, 15, 8, 12, 20, 25, 18, 16, 11, 9, 14]

# Create a histogram plot
plt.hist(data, bins=5, color='purple', alpha=0.6)
plt.title('Histogram Plot Example')
plt.xlabel('Bins')
plt.ylabel('Frequency')
plt.show()
```

```
In [91]: import matplotlib.pyplot as plt
         # Sample data
         data = [10, 15, 8, 12, 20, 25, 18, 16, 11, 9, 14]

In [92]: # Create a histogram plot
         plt.hist(dat, bins=5, color='purple', alpha=0.6)
         plt.title('Histogram Plot Example')
         plt.xlabel('Bins')
         plt.ylabel('Frequency')
         plt.show()
```

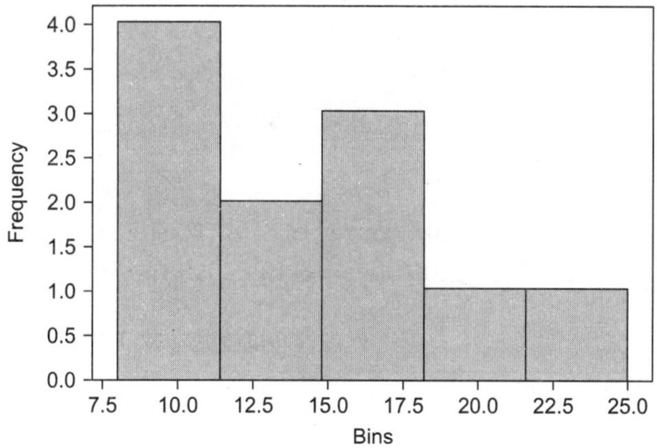

Pie Chart

```
import matplotlib.pyplot as plt

# Sample data
labels = ['A', 'B', 'C', 'D']
sizes = [15, 30, 25, 30]
colors = ['blue', 'green', 'red', 'orange']

# Create a pie chart
plt.pie(sizes, labels=labels, colors=colors, autopct='%1.1f%%')
plt.title('Pie Chart Example')
plt.show()
```

```
In [93]: import matplotlib.pyplot as plt
         # Sample data
         labels = ['A', 'B', 'C', 'D']
         sizes = [15, 30, 25, 30]
         colors = ['blue', 'green', 'red', 'orange']

In [94]: # Create a pie chart
         plt.pie(sizes, labels=labels, colors=colors, autopct='%1.1f%')
         plt.title('Pie Chart Example')
         plt.show()
```

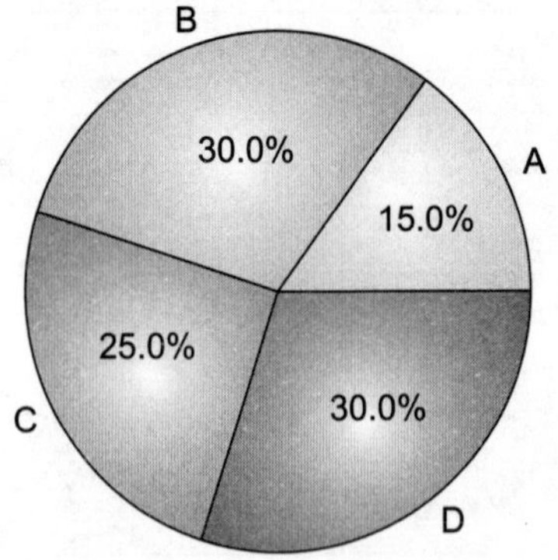

Box Plot

```
import matplotlib.pyplot as plt

# Sample data
data = [10, 15, 8, 12, 20, 25, 18, 16, 11, 9, 14]

# Create a box plot
plt.boxplot(data)
plt.title('Box Plot Example')
plt.ylabel('Values')
plt.show()
```

```
In [95]: import matplotlib.pyplot as plt
         # Sample data
         data = [10, 15, 8, 12, 20, 25, 18, 16, 11, 9, 14]

In [96]: # Create a box plot
         plt.boxplot(data)
         plt.title('Box Plot Example')
         plt.ylabel('Values')
         plt.show()
```

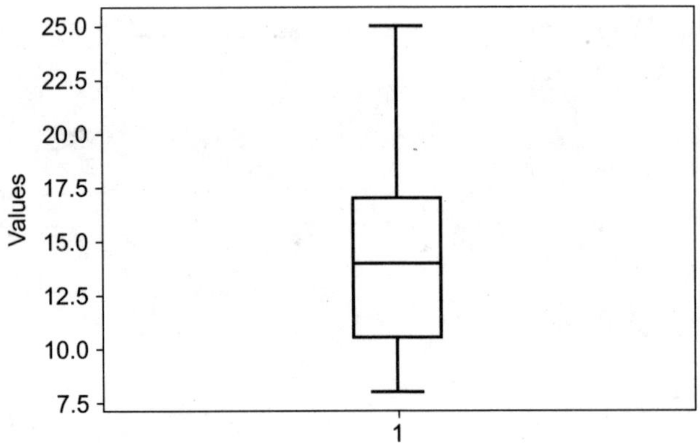

3D Plot

```
import matplotlib.pyplot as plt
import numpy as np

# Sample data for 3D plot
x = np.linspace(-5, 5, 100)
y = np.linspace(-5, 5, 100)
X, Y = np.meshgrid(x, y)
Z = np.sin(np.sqrt(X**2 + Y**2))

# Create a 3D surface plot
fig = plt.figure()
ax = fig.add_subplot(111, projection='3d')
ax.plot_surface(X, Y, Z, cmap='viridis')
ax.set_title('3D Plot Example')
ax.set_xlabel('X-axis')
ax.set_ylabel('Y-axis')
ax.set_zlabel('Z-axis')
plt.show()
```

```
In [97]: import matplotlib.pyplot as plt
         import numpy as np

         # Sample data for 3D plot
         x = np.linspace(-5, 5, 100)
         y = np.linspace(-5, 5, 100)
         X, Y = np.meshgrid(x, y)
         Z = np.sin(np.sqrt(X**2 + Y**2))

In [68]: # Create a 3D surface plot
         fig = plt.figure()
         ax = fig.add_subplot(111, projection='3d')
         ax.plot_surface(X, Y, Z, cmap='viridis')
         ax.set_title('3D Plot Example')
         ax.set_xlabel('X-axis')
         ax.set_ylabel('Y-axis')
         ax.set_zlabel('Z-axis')
         plt.show()
```

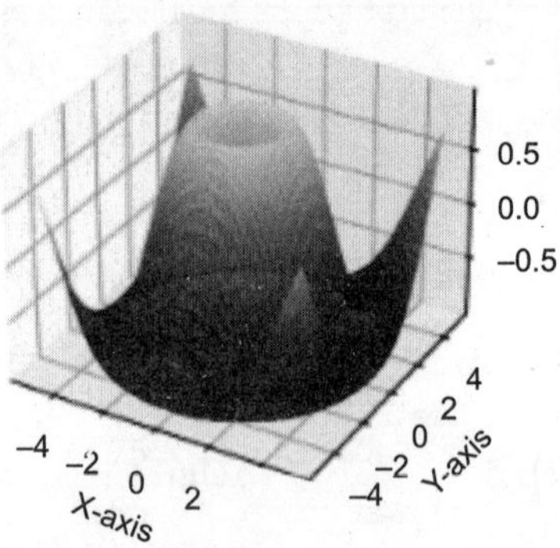

3. **Integration with NumPy and Pandas**: Matplotlib integrates seamlessly with NumPy arrays and Pandas DataFrames, allowing easy visualization of data structures. This integration makes it easier to see and analyze data by allowing you to immediately generate different types of charts from Pandas DataFrames and NumPy arrays. Here are some examples of how Pandas DataFrames and NumPy Arrays are used with Matplotlib:

Matplotlib with NumPy Arrays

```
import matplotlib.pyplot as plt
import numpy as np

# Sample NumPy array
x = np.linspace(0, 10, 100)
y = np.sin(x)

# Create a simple line plot
plt.plot(x, y)
plt.title('Line Plot with NumPy Array')
plt.xlabel('X-axis')
plt.ylabel('Y-axis')
plt.show()
```

```
In [99]: import matplotlib.pyplot as plt
         import numpy as np
         # Sample Numpy array
         x = np.linspace(0, 10, 100)
         y = np.sin(x)

In [100]: # Create a simple line plot
         plt.plot(x, y)
         plt.title('Line Plot with Numpy Array')
         plt.xlabel('X-axis')
         plt.ylabel('Y-axis')
         plt.show()
```

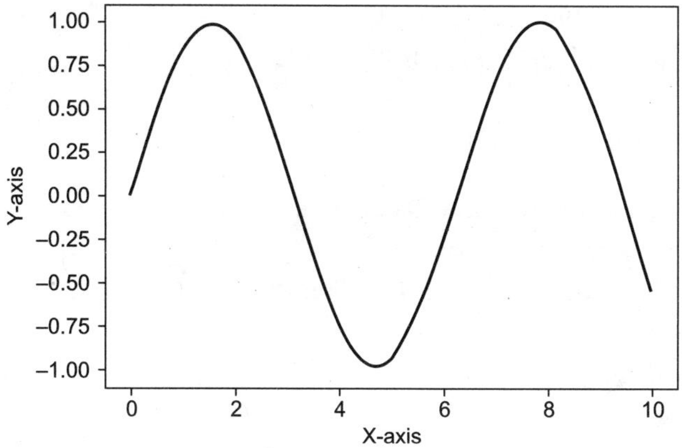

In this example, we created a line plot using a NumPy array x for the X-axis and another NumPy array y for the Y-axis.

Matplotlib with Pandas DataFrames

```
import matplotlib.pyplot as plt
import pandas as pd

# Sample data in a Pandas DataFrame
data = {
    'Name': ['Siddha', 'Charu', 'Prasiddha', 'Harsh', 'Ishita'],
    'Math': [85, 78, 92, 70, 88],
    'Science': [90, 85, 88, 75, 95],
    'History': [80, 75, 85, 90, 80]
}
df = pd.DataFrame(data)

# Create a bar plot from the DataFrame
df.plot(x–'Name', kind–'bar')
plt.title('Bar Plot with Pandas DataFrame')
plt.xlabel('Name')
plt.ylabel('Scores')
plt.show()
```

```
In [101]: import matplotlib.pyplot as plt
          import pandas as pd
          # Sample data in a Pandas DataFrame
          data = {
              'Name': ['Siddha', 'Charu', 'Prasiddha', 'Harsh', 'Ishita'],
              'Math': [85, 78, 92, 70, 88],
```

```
        'Science': [90, 85, 88, 75, 95],
        'History': [80, 75, 85, 90, 80]
    }
    df = pd.DataFrame(data)

In [102]: # Create a bar plot from the DataFrame
    df.plot(x='Name', kind='bar')
    plt.title('Bar Plot with Pandas DataFrame')
    plt.xlabel('Name')
    plt.ylabel('Scores)
    plt.show()
```

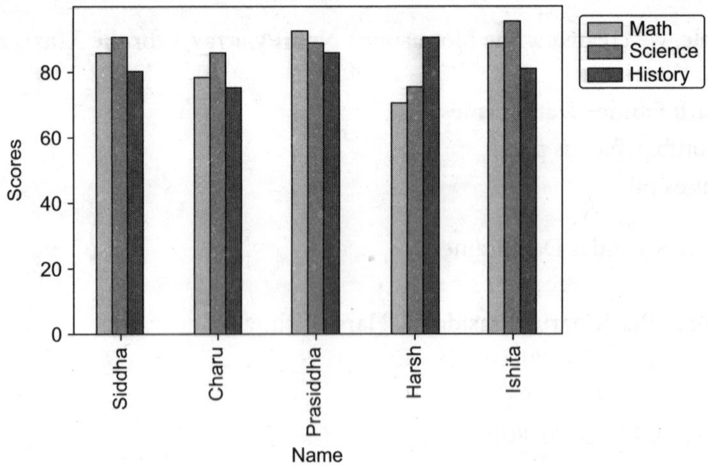

The 'Name' column serves as the X-axis in this example's bar plot, and the scores serve as the Y-axis.

4. **Publication-Quality Plots:** Matplotlib produces high-quality plots suitable for publication and presentation purposes. It provides options for exporting plots to various file formats, including PNG, PDF, SVG, and more. You can use the savefig() function to save your plots in the desired format. Let's see some examples:

   Exporting to PNG

```
import matplotlib.pyplot as plt
import numpy as np

# Sample data
x = np.linspace(0, 10, 100)
y = np.sin(x)

# Create a simple line plot
plt.plot(x, y)
plt.title('Line Plot Example')
plt.xlabel('X-axis')
plt.ylabel('Y-axis')
```

```
In [103]: import matplotlib.pyplot as plt
          import numpy as np

          # Sample data
          x = np.linspace(0, 10, 100)
          y = np.sin(x)

In [104]: # Create a simple Line plot
          plt.plot(x, y)
          plt.title('Line Plot Example')
          plt.xlabel('X-axis')
          plt.ylabel('Y-axis')
Out [104]: Text(0, 0.5, 'Y-axis')
```

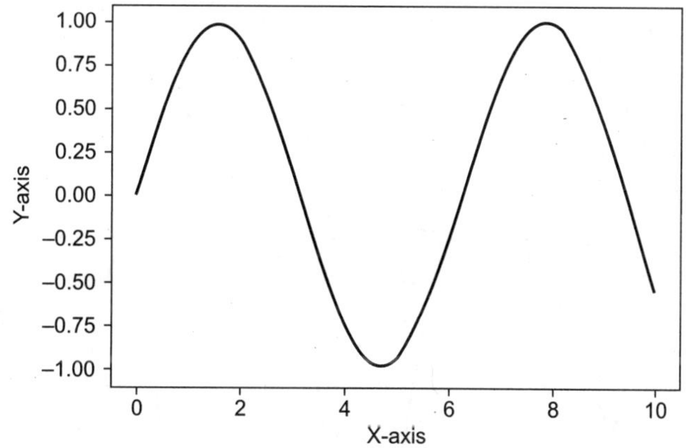


```
# Save the plot as a PNG file
plt.savefig('line_plot.png', dpi=300)

In [105]: # Save the plot as a PNG file
          plt.savefig('line_plot.png', dpi=300)
          <Figure size 432×288 with 0 Axes>
```

This will save the plot as a PNG file named "line_plot.png" with a resolution of 300 dpi (dots per inch).

Exporting to PDF

```
import matplotlib.pyplot as plt
import numpy as np

# Sample data
x – np.linspace(0, 20, 100)
y = np.sin(x)
```

```
# Create a simple line plot
plt.plot(x, y)
plt.title('Line Plot Example')
plt.xlabel('X-axis')
plt.ylabel('Y-axis')
```

```
In [108]: import matplotlib.pyplot as plt
          import numpy as np

          # Sample data
          x = np.linspace(0, 20, 100)
          y = np.sin(x)
```

```
In [109]: # Create a simple Line plot
          plt.plot(x, y)
          plt.title('Line Plot Example')
          plt.xlabel('X-axis')
          plt.ylabel('Y-axis')
Out [109]: Text(0, 0.5, 'Y-axis')
```

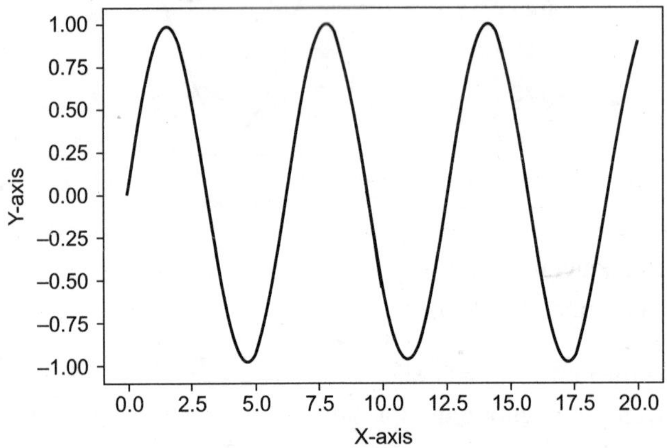


```
# Save the plot as a PDF file
plt.savefig('line_plot.pdf')
```

```
In [110]: # Save the plot as a PDF file
          plt.savefig('line_plot.pdf')
          <Figure size 432×288 with 0 Axes>
```

This will save the plot as a PDF file named "line_plot.pdf".

Exporting to SVG

```
import matplotlib.pyplot as plt
import numpy as np
```

```
# Sample data
x = np.linspace(0, 20, 100)
y = np.sin(x)

# Create a simple line plot
plt.plot(x, y)
plt.title('Line Plot Example')
plt.xlabel('X-axis')
plt.ylabel('Y-axis')

# Save the plot as an SVG file
plt.savefig('line_plot.svg')
```

```
In [111]: # Create a simple Line plot
          plt.plot(x, y)
          plt.title('Line Plot Example')
          plt.xlable('X-axis')
          plt.ylabel('Y-axis')
```

Out [111]: Text(0, 0.5, 'Y-axis')

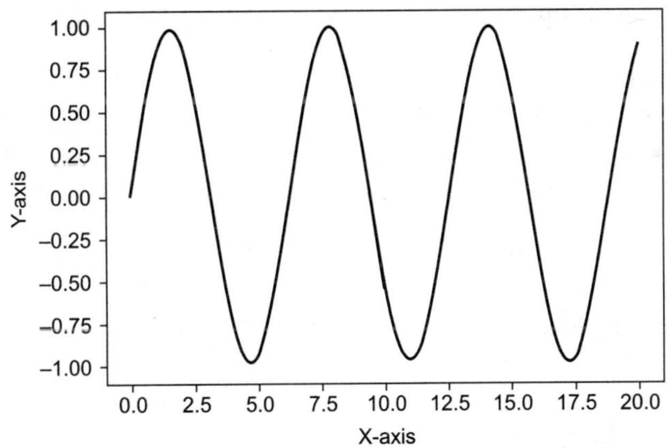


```
In [112]: # Save the plot as an SVG file
          plt.savefig('line_plot.svg')
```

This will save the plot as an SVG file named "line_plot.svg".

In each example, the savefig() function is used to save the plot in the desired format. You can specify the filename, and the file format will be determined based on the file extension provided (e.g., .png for PNG, .pdf for PDF, .svg for SVG). Remember to call savefig() before calling plt.show(). Also, you can customize the plot's appearance and settings before saving it to the file, just as you would do for displaying the plot on the screen using plt.plot(), plt.title(), plt.xlabel(), and other Matplotlib functions.

5. **Customization and Styling:** Matplotlib allows extensive customization and styling options for plots. You can control the appearance of plot elements such as axes, legends, grids, and annotations. Customization and styling in Matplotlib allow you to personalize the appearance of your plots, making them visually appealing and informative. You can customize various aspects of the plot, such as colors, markers, line styles, fonts, labels, titles, and more.

```
import matplotlib.pyplot as plt
import numpy as np

# Sample data
x = np.linspace(0, 20, 100)
y1 = np.sin(x)
y2 = np.cos(x)

# Create a figure and axes
fig=plt.figure()
fig, ax = plt.subplots()
ax.plot(x, y1)
ax.plot(x, y2)
```

```
In [116]: import matplotlib.pyplot as plt
          import numpy as np

          # Sample data
          x = np.linspace(0, 20, 100)
          y1 = np.sin(x)
          y2 = np.cos(x)

In [117]: # Create a figure and axes
          fig=plot.figure()
          fig, ax = plt.subplots()
          ax.plot(x, y1)
          ax.plot(x, y2)
Out [117]: [<matplotlib.lines.Line2D at 0×1dd8b0d92e0>
          <Figure size 432×288 with 0 Axes>
```

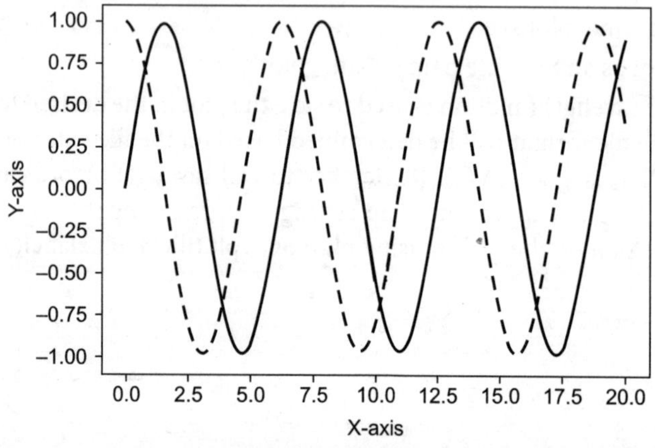

```
# Plot lines with customizations
ax.plot(x, y1, linestyle='-', color='blue', linewidth=2, label='Sin(x)')
ax.plot(x, y2, linestyle='--', color='red', linewidth=2, label='Cos(x)')

In [118]: # Create a figure and axes
          fig=plt.figure()
          fig, ax = plt.subplots()
          ax.plot(x, y1)
          ax.plot(x, y2)

          # Plot Lines with customizations
          ax.plot(x, y1, linestyle='-', color='blue', linewidth=2, label='Sin(x)')
          ax.plot(x, y2, linestyle='--', color='red', linewidth=2, label='Cos(x)')
Out[118]: [<matplotlib.lines.Line2D at 0×1dd8b14c3a0>]
          <Figure size 432×288 with 0 Axes>
```

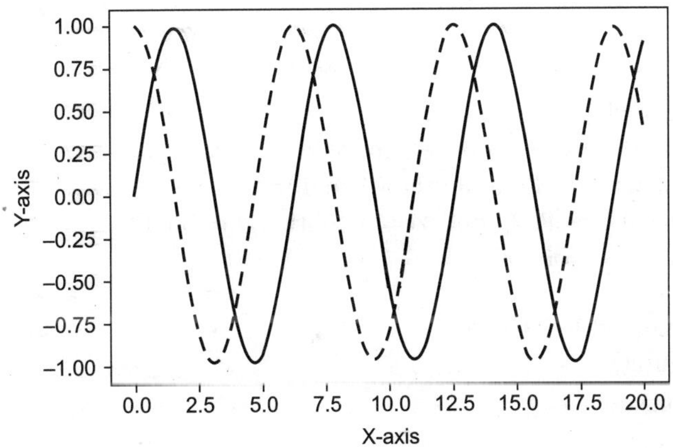


```
# Add markers
ax.scatter(x[::10], y1[::10], color='blue', marker='o', label='Sample Points Sin(x)')
ax.scatter(x[::10], y2[::10], color='red', marker='s', label='Sample Points Cos(x)')

In [119]: # Create a figure and axes
          fig=plt.figure()
          fig, ax = plt.subplots()
          ax.plot(x, y1)
          ax.plot(x, y2)

          # Plot Lines with customizations
          ax.plot(x, y1, linestyle='-', color='blue', linewidth=2, label='Sin(x)')
          ax.plot(x, y2, linestyle='--', color='red', linewidth=2, label='Cos(x)')
```

```
# Add markers
ax.scatter(x[::10], y1[::10], color='blue', marker='o', label='Sample Points Sin(x)')
ax.scatter(x[::10], y2[::10], color='red', marker='s', label='Sample Points Cos(x)')
```

Out [119]: <matplotlib.collections.PathCollection at 0×1dd8b1bff40>
<Figure size 432×288 with 0 Axes>

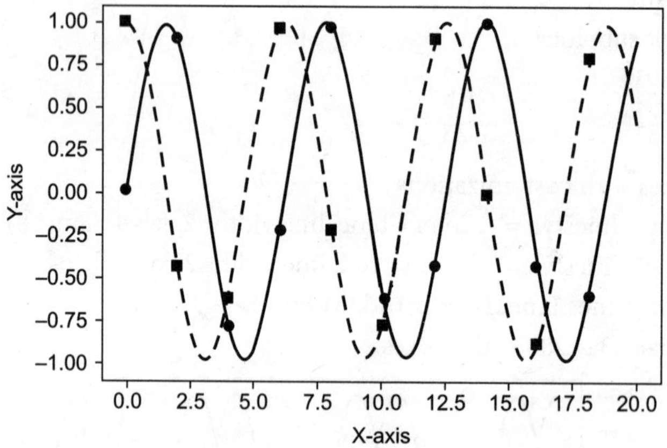


```
# Customize the axes and grid
ax.set_xlabel('X-axis', fontsize=12, fontweight='bold')
ax.set_ylabel('Y-axis', fontsize=12, fontweight='bold')
ax.set_title('Customized Line Plot', fontsize=14, fontweight='bold')
ax.grid(True, linestyle='--', alpha=0.6)
```

In [120]:
```
# Create a figure and axes
fig=plt.figure()
fig, ax = plt.subplots()
ax.plot(x, y1)
ax.plot(x, y2)

# Plot Lines with customizations
ax.plot(x, y1, linestyle='-', color='blue', linewidth=2, label='Sin(x)')
ax.plot(x, y2, linestyle='--', color='red', linewidth=2, label='Cos(x)')

# Add markers
ax.scatter(x[::10], y1[::10], color='blue', marker='o', label='Sample Points Sin(x)')
ax.scatter(x[::10], y2[::10], color='red', marker='s', label='Sample Points Cos(x)')

# Customize the axes and grid
ax.set_xlabel('X-axis', fontsize=12, fontweight='bold')
ax.set_ylabel('Y-axis', fontsize=12, fontweight='bold')
ax.set_title('Customized Line Plot', fontsize=14, fontweight='bold')
ax.grid(True, linestyle='--', alpha=0.6)
```

<Figure size 432×288 with 0 Axes>

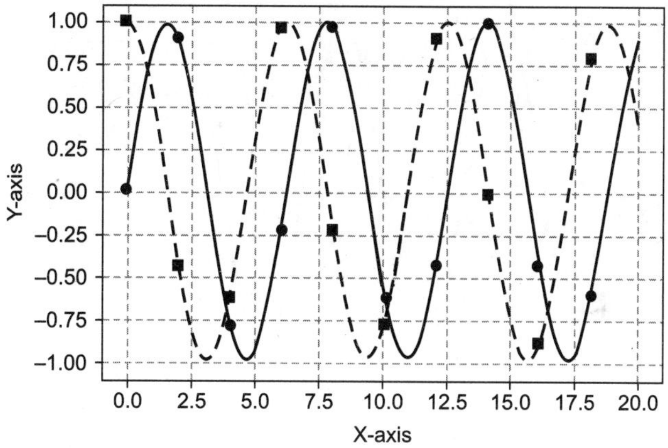


```
# Add a legend
ax.legend()
```

```
In [121]: # Create a figure and axes
          fig=plt.figure()
          fig, ax = plt.subplots()
          ax.plot(x, y1)
          ax.plot(x, y2)

          # Plot Lines with customizations
          ax.plot(x, y1, linestyle='-', color='blue', linewidth=2, label='Sin(x)')
          ax.plot(x, y2, linestyle='--', color='red', linewidth=2, label='Cos(x)')

          # Add markers
          ax.scatter(x[::10], y1[::10], color='blue', marker='o', label='Sample Points Sin(x)')
          ax.scatter(x[::10], y2[::10], color='red', marker='s', label='Sample Points Cos(x)')

          # Customize the axes and grid
          ax.set_xlabel('X-axis', fontsize=12, fontweight='bold')
          ax.set_ylabel('Y-axis', fontsize=12, fontweight='bold')
          ax.set_title('Customized Line Plot', fontsize=14, fontweight='bold')
          ax.grid(True, linestyle='--', alpha=0.6)

          # Add a Legend
          ax.legend()
Out[121]: <matplotlib.legend.Legend at 0x1dd8b2a8a90>
          <Figure size 432x288 with 0 Axes>
```

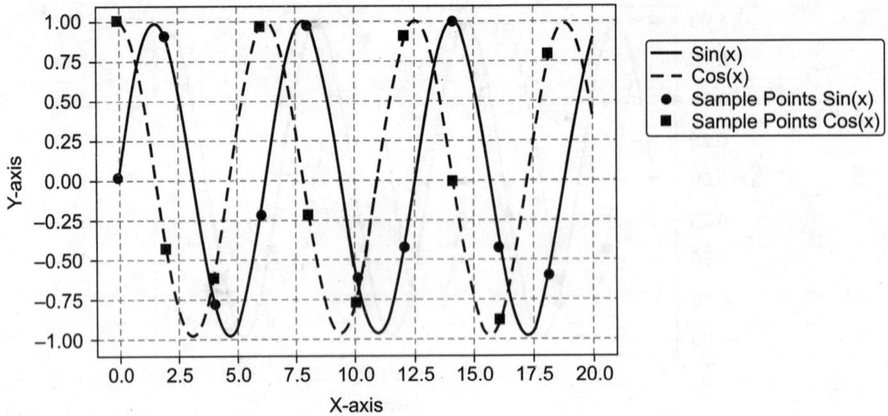


```
# Set the background color of the plot
ax.set_facecolor('lightgray')
```

```
In [123]: # Create a figure and axes
          fig=plt.figure()
          fig, ax = plt.subplots()
          ax.plot(x, y1)
          ax.plot(x, y2)

          # Plot Lines with customizations
          ax.plot(x, y1, linestyle='-', color='blue', linewidth=2, label='Sin(x)')
          ax.plot(x, y2, linestyle='--', color='red', linewidth=2, label='Cos(x)')

          # Add markers
          ax.scatter(x[::10], y1[::10], color='blue', marker='o', label='Sample Points Sin(x)')
          ax.scatter(x[::10], y2[::10], color='red', marker='s', label='Sample Points Cos(x)')

          # Customize the axes and grid
          ax.set_xlabel('X-axis', fontsize=12, fontweight='bold')
          ax.set_ylabel('Y-axis', fontsize=12, fontweight='bold')
          ax.set_title('Customized Line Plot', fontsize=14, fontweight='bold')
          ax.grid(True, linestyle='--', alpha=0.6)

          # Add a Legend
          ax.legend()

          # Set the background color of the plot
          ax.set_facecolor('lightgray')
          <Figure size 432x288 with 0 Axes>
```

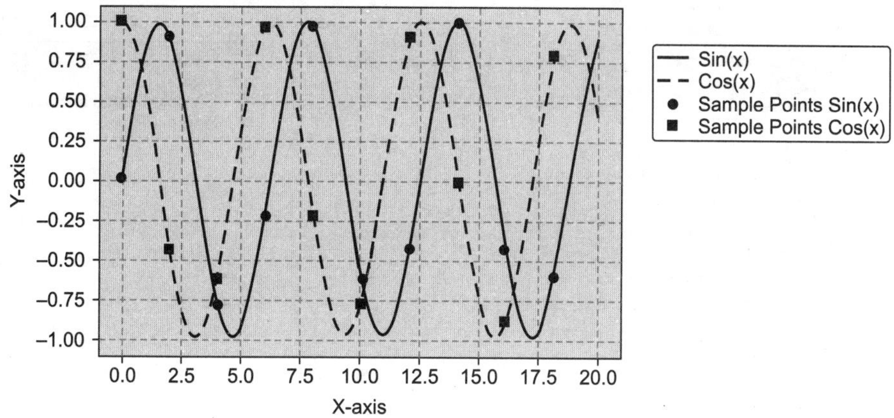


```
# Customize the tick labels
ax.tick_params(axis='both', which='major', labelsize=10, colors='black', length=6, width=1)
<Figure size 432x288 with 0 Axes>
```

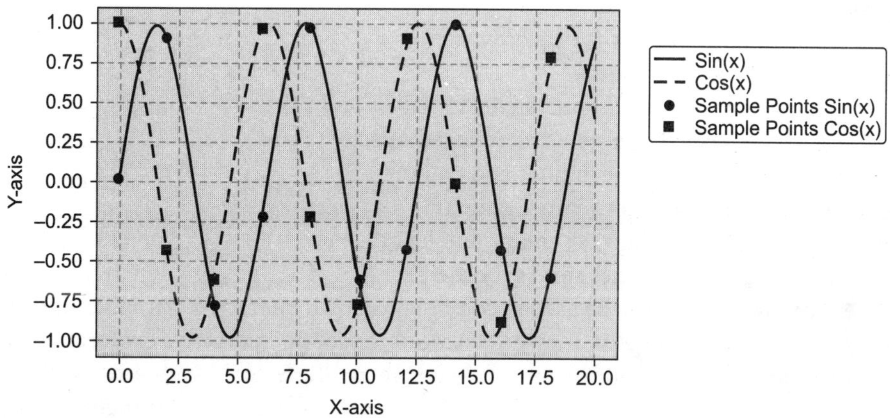


```
# Customize the spines (axes borders)
ax.spines['top'].set_visible(False)
ax.spines['right'].set_visible(False)
ax.spines['bottom'].set_linewidth(1)
ax.spines['left'].set_linewidth(1)

# Show the plot
plt.show()
<Figure size 432x288 with 0 Axes>
```

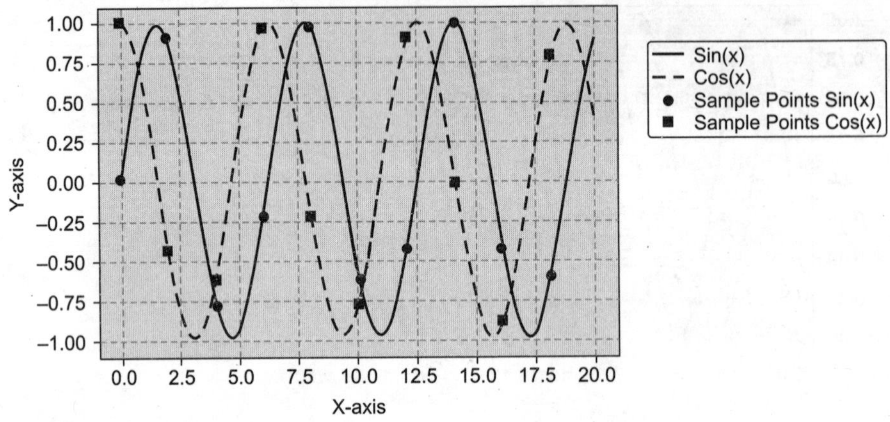

In this example, we used a combination of plot(), scatter(), and various customization functions to create a customized line plot. Here are some of the customizations used:

- Custom line styles: '-' for solid line and '--' for dashed line.
- Custom colors: 'blue' and 'red'.
- Markers: 'o' for circles and 's' for squares.
- Custom line and marker widths.
- Custom fonts, font sizes, and fontweights for labels and title.
- Gridlines with a dashed line style and reduced opacity (alpha).
- Legend to differentiate between lines and markers.
- Background color of the plot set to 'lightgray'.
- Custom tick labels with fontsize, colors, and length.
- Custom linewidth for the axes spines (borders).

6. **Interactive Plots:** Matplotlib can be used in combination with interactive backends like %matplotlib notebook or %matplotlib widget in Jupyter Notebook, enabling interactive exploration of plots.
7. **Subplots and Layouts:** Matplotlib supports creating multiple plots (subplots) within the same figure using the subplot() function or GridSpec. You can customize the arrangement and spacing of subplots using layout functions. Subplots in Matplotlib allow you to create multiple plots within a single figure, enabling you to display related visualizations side by side. You can control the arrangement and size of subplots to create complex layouts.

```
import matplotlib.pyplot as plt
import numpy as np

# Sample data
x = np.linspace(0, 20, 100)
y1 = np.sin(x)
y2 = np.cos(x)
y3 = np.sin(x) + np.cos(x)
```

```
In [130]: import matplotlib.pyplot as plt
          import numpy as np

          # Sample data
          x = np.linspace(0, 10, 100)
```

```
        y1 = np.sin(x)
        y2 = np.cos(x)
        y3 = np.sin(x) + np.cos(x)

# Create a figure and multiple axes (subplots)
fig, axes = plt.subplots(nrows=2, ncols=2, figsize=(10, 8))

# Plot 1: Line plot
axes[0, 0].plot(x, y1, color='blue', label='Sin(x)')
axes[0, 0].set_title('Line Plot of Sin(x)')
axes[0, 0].set_xlabel('X-axis')
axes[0, 0].set_ylabel('Y-axis')
axes[0, 0].legend()
```

```
In [4]:  # Create a figure and multiple axes (subplots)
         fig, axes = plt.subplots(nrows=2, ncols, figsize=(8, 6))

         # Plot 1: Line plot
         axes[0, 0].plot(x, y1, color='blue', label='Sin(x)')
         axes[0, 0].set_title('Line Plot of Sin(x)')
         axes[0, 0].set_xlabel('X-axis')
         axes[0, 0].set_ylabel('Y-axis')
         axes[0, 0].legend()
Out [4]: <matplotlib.legend.Legend at 0×264f638d100>
```

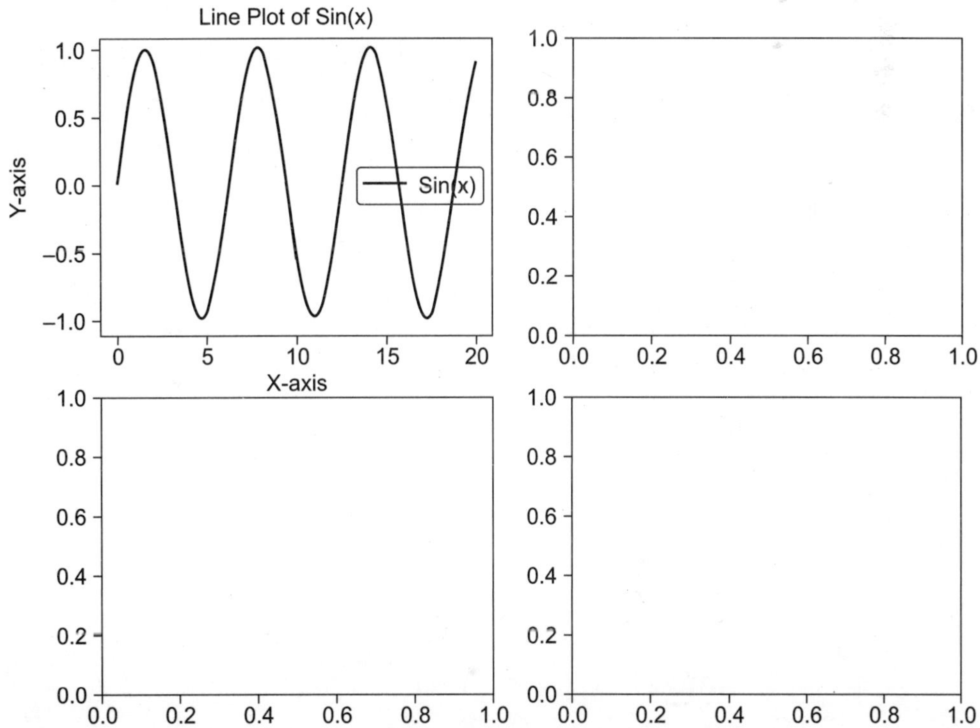

```
# Plot 2: Scatter plot
axes[0, 1].scatter(x[::10], y2[::10], color='red', marker='s', label='Cos(x) Sample Points')
axes[0, 1].set_title('Scatter Plot of Cos(x)')
axes[0, 1].set_xlabel('X-axis')
axes[0, 1].set_ylabel('Y-axis')
axes[0, 1].legend()
Out [5]: <matplotlib.legend.Legend at 0×264f6528b80>
```

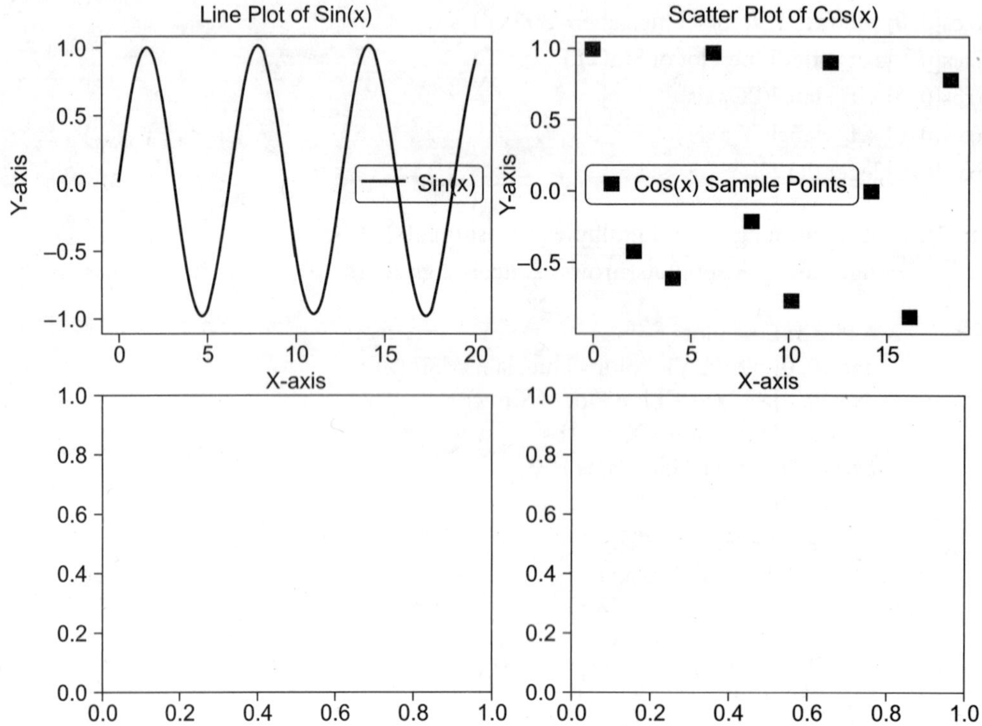


```
# Plot 3: Bar plot
categories = ['A', 'B', 'C', 'D', 'E']
values = [10, 15, 8, 12, 20]
axes[1, 0].bar(categories, values, color='green')
axes[1, 0].set_title('Bar Plot of Values')
axes[1, 0].set_xlabel('Categories')
axes[1, 0].set_ylabel('Values')
Out [6]: Text(0, 0.5, 'Values')
```

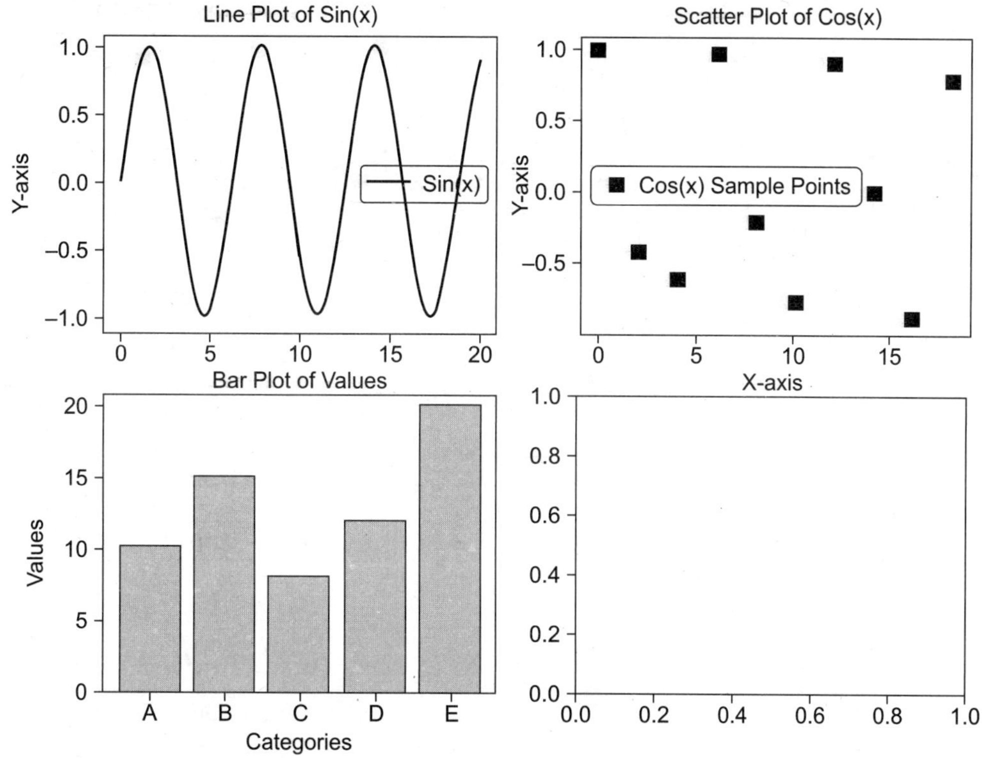


```
# Plot 4: Line plot with dashed line
axes[1, 1].plot(x, y3, color='purple', linestyle='--', label='Sin(x) + Cos(x)')
axes[1, 1].set_title('Line Plot of Sin(x) + Cos(x)')
axes[1, 1].set_xlabel('X-axis')
axes[1, 1].set_ylabel('Y-axis')
axes[1, 1].legend()
Out [7]:   <matplotlib.legend.Legend at 0x264f791a8c0>
```

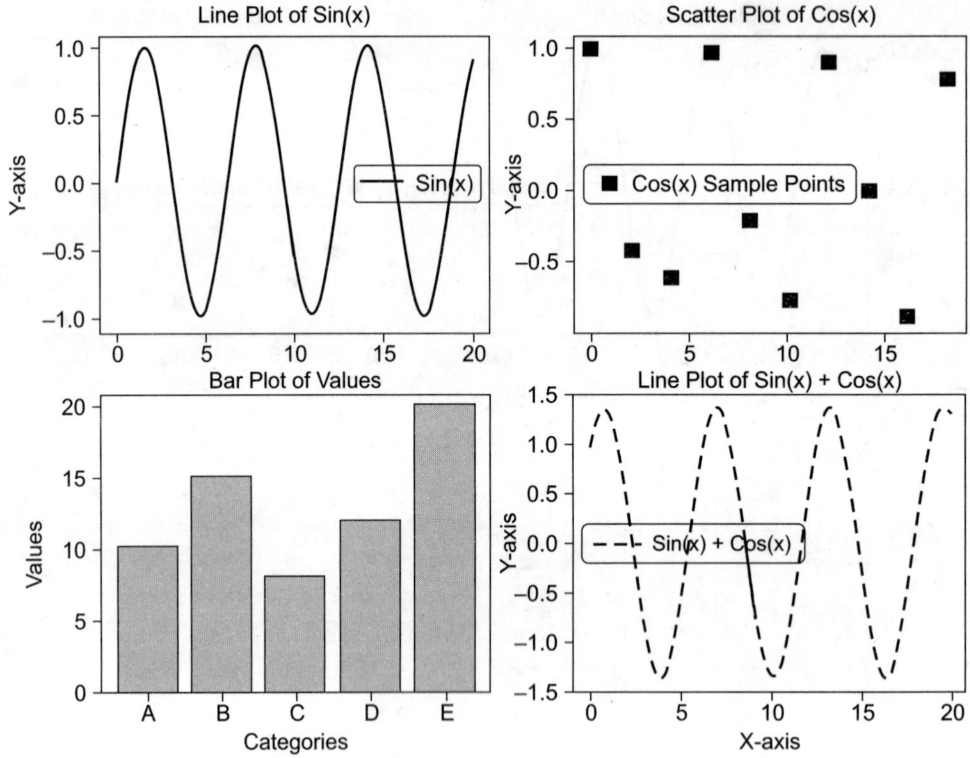


```
# Adjust the layout and spacing between subplots
plt.tight_layout()

# Show the plots
plt.show()
```

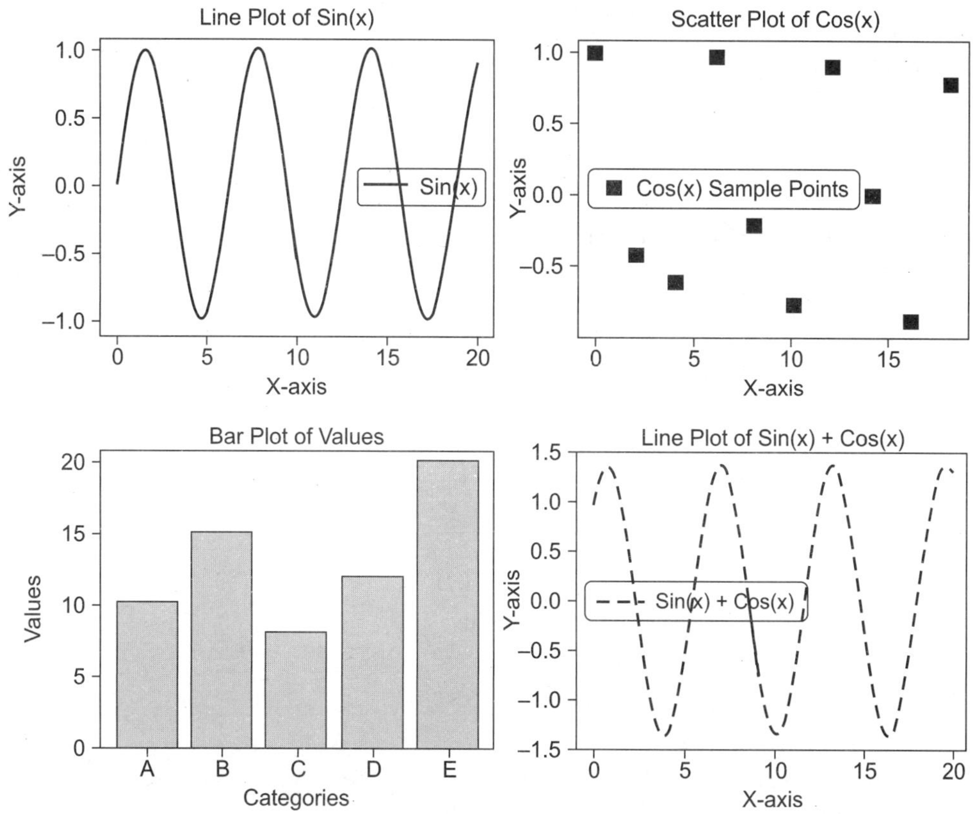

In this example, we used plt.subplots() to create a 2x2 grid of subplots (four plots in total) within a single figure. We then plotted different types of visualizations in each subplot. The figsize parameter in plt.subplots() controls the overall size of the figure. The axes variable is a 2D array that holds references to the individual axes (subplots). We used these axes to customize each subplot's appearance, including titles, labels, colors, markers, line styles, and legends. The plt.tight_layout() function is used to adjust the spacing between subplots automatically, ensuring that the plots do not overlap and the labels are visible.

This example demonstrates how to create a 2x2 grid of subplots, but you can modify the nrows and ncols parameters in plt.subplots() to create different arrangements, such as a 1x3 grid, 3x1 grid, or any other custom layout.

8. **Integration with GUI Toolkits:** Matplotlib can be used with various graphical user interface (GUI) toolkits such as Tkinter, PyQt, and wxPython, allowing integration with desktop applications.

Matplotlib Integration with Tkinter:

```
import tkinter as tk
import numpy as np
import matplotlib.pyplot as plt
from matplotlib.backends.backend_tkagg import FigureCanvasTkAgg

# Create the Tkinter application
root = tk.Tk()
root.title("Matplotlib with Tkinter")
```

```
# Create a figure and axis for Matplotlib
fig, ax = plt.subplots()
x = np.linspace(0, 2 * np.pi, 100)
y = np.sin(x)
ax.plot(x, y)
```

```
In [9]:    # Matplotlib Integration with Tkinter:
           import tkinter as tk
           import numpy as np
           import matplotlib.pyplot as plt
           from matplotlib.backends.backend_tkagg import FigureCanvasTkAgg
```

```
In [10]:   # Create the Tkinter application
           root = tk.Tk()
           root.title("Matplotlib with tkinter")
Out [10]:  ''
```

```
In [11]:   # Create a figure and axis for Matplotlib
           fig, ax = plt.subplots()
           x = np.linspace(0, 2 * np.pi, 100)
           y = np.sin(x)
           ax.plot(x, y)
Out [11]:  [<matplotlib.lines.Line2D at 0×264f7b49e80>]
```

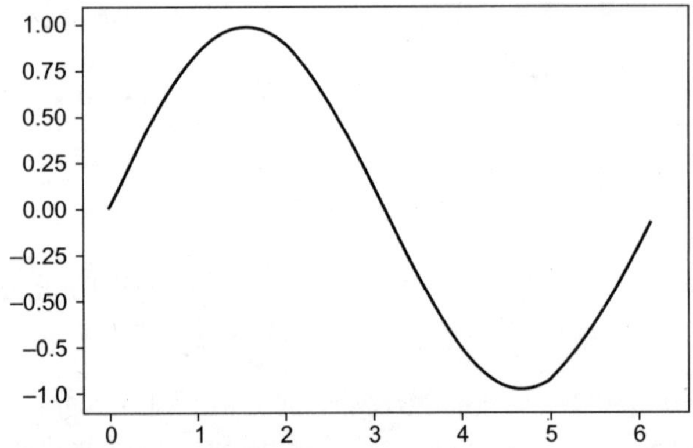


```
# Create a Tkinter canvas and display the Matplotlib figure on it
canvas = FigureCanvasTkAgg(fig, master=root)
canvas.draw()
canvas.get_tk_widget().pack()

# Run the Tkinter main loop
root.mainloop()
```

In [12]:
```
# Create a Tkinter canvas and display the Matplotlib figure on it
canvas = FigureCanvasTkAgg(fig, master=root)
canvas.draw()
canvas.get_tk_widget().pack()
```

In [ ]:

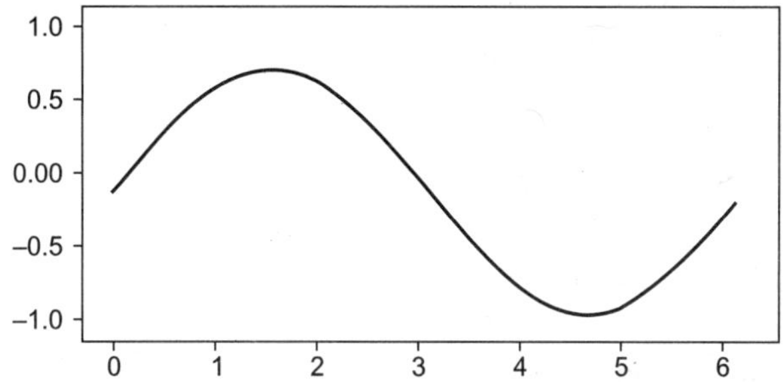

Matplotlib Integration with PyQt:

```
import sys
import numpy as np
import matplotlib.pyplot as plt
from matplotlib.backends.backend_qt5agg import FigureCanvasQTAgg as FigureCanvas
from PyQt5.QtWidgets import QApplication, QMainWindow, QVBoxLayout, QWidget

# Create the PyQt application
app = QApplication(sys.argv)
window = QMainWindow()
window.setWindowTitle("Matplotlib with PyQt")

# Create a QWidget for the Matplotlib figurc
central_widget = QWidget(window)
window.setCentralWidget(central_widget)

# Create a layout for the QWidget
layout = QVBoxLayout(central_widget)
```

In [14]:
```
Matplotlib Integration with PyQt:
import sys
import numpy as np
import matplotlib.pyplot as plt
from matplotlib.backends.backend_qt5agg import FigureCanvasQTAgg as FigureCanvas
from PyQt5.QtWidgets import QApplication, QMainWindow, QVBoxLayout, QWidget
```

```
In [15]:  # Create the PyQt application
          app = QApplication(sys.argv)
          window = QMainWindow()
          window.setWindowTitle("Matplotlib with PyQt")

In [16]:  # Create a QWidget for the Matplotlib figure
          central_widget = QWidget(window)
          window.setCentralWidget(central_widget)

In [17]:  # Create a layout for the QWidget
          layout = QVBoxLayout(central_widget)

# Create a figure and axis for Matplotlib
fig, ax = plt.subplots()
x = np.linspace(0, 2 * np.pi, 100)
y = np.sin(x)
ax.plot(x, y)

In [18]:  # Create a figure and axis for Matplotlib
          fig, ax = plt.subplots()
          x = np.linspace(0, 2 * np.pi, 100)
          y = np.sin(x)
          ax.plot(x, y)
Out [18]: [<matplotlib.lines.Line2D at 0x264f86e3490>]
```

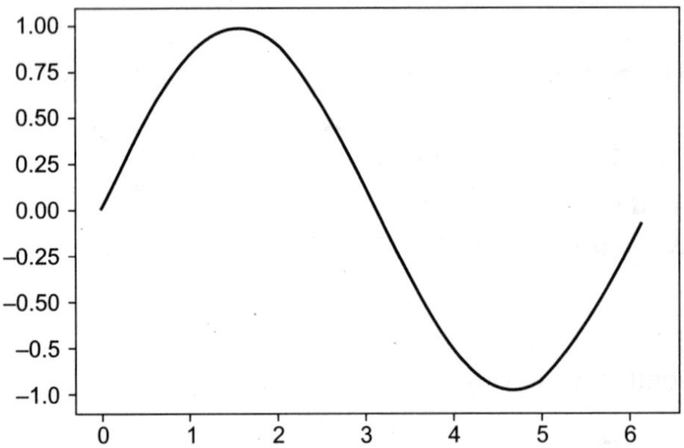


```
# Create a PyQt canvas and display the Matplotlib figure on it
canvas = FigureCanvas(fig)
layout.addWidget(canvas)

# Show the window
window.show()
sys.exit(app.exec_())
```

```
In [19]:  # Create a PyQt canvas and display the Matplotlib figure on it
           canvas = FigureCanvas(fig)
           layout.addWidget(canvas)

In [*]:   # Show the window
           window.show()
           sys.exit(app.exec_())

In [ ]:
```

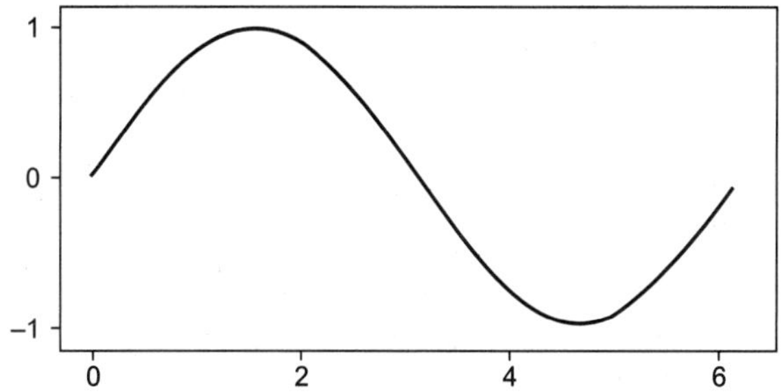

Matplotlib Integration with wxPython:

pip install wxPython

```
import wx
import numpy as np
import matplotlib.pyplot as plt
from matplotlib.backends.backend_wxagg import FigureCanvasWxAgg as FigureCanvas

# Create the wxPython application
app = wx.App(False)
frame = wx.Frame(None, wx.ID_ANY, "Matplotlib with wxPython", size=(600, 400))

# Create a panel for the Matplotlib figure
panel = wx.Panel(frame)

# Create a figure and axis for Matplotlib
fig, ax = plt.subplots()
x = np.linspace(0, 2 * np.pi, 100)
y = np.sin(x)
ax.plot(x, y)
```

```
In [23]:  Matplotlib Integration with wxPython:
           import wx
           import numpy as np
```

```
import matplotlib.pyplot as plt
from matplotlib.backends.backend_wxagg import FigureCanvasWxAgg as FigureCanvas
```

In [24]:
```
# Create the wxPython application
app = wx.App(False)
frame = wx.Frame(None, wx.ID_ANY, "Matplotlib with wxPython", size=(600, 400))
```

In [25]:
```
# Create a panel for the Matplotlib figure
panel = wx.Panel(frame)
```

In [26]:
```
# Create a figure and axis for Matplotlib
fig, ax = plt.subplots()
x = np.linspace(0, 2 * np.pi, 100)
y = np.sin(x)
ax.plot(x, y)
```

Out[26]:
```
[<matplotlib.lines.Line2D at 0×264fbed1f40>]
```

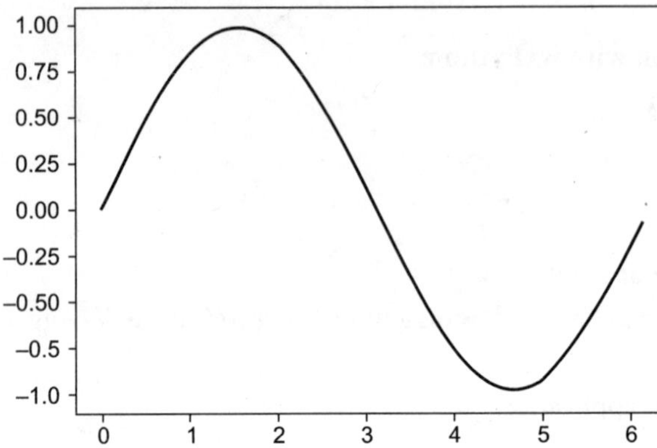


```
# Create a wxPython canvas and display the Matplotlib figure on it
canvas = FigureCanvas(panel, -1, fig)
sizer = wx.BoxSizer(wx.VERTICAL)
sizer.Add(canvas, 1, wx.EXPAND)
panel.SetSizer(sizer)

# Show the frame
frame.Show(True)
app.MainLoop()
```

In [5]:
```
# Create a wxPython canvas and display the Matplotlib figure on it
canvas = FigureCanvas(panel, -1, fig)
sizer = wx.BoxSizer(wx.VERTICAL)
sizer.Add(canvas, 1, wx.EXPAND)
panel.SetSizer(sizer)
```

```
In [*]:    # Show the frame
           frame.Show(True)
           app.MainLoop()
```

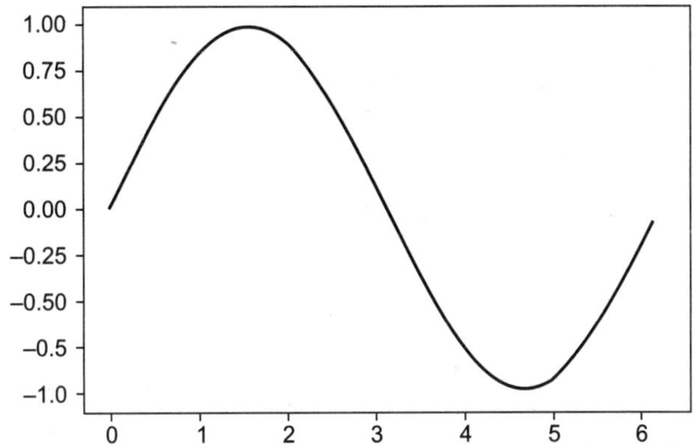

In all three examples, we create a simple Matplotlib plot and display it within the respective GUI framework. Each of these examples will open a window displaying the plotted sine wave.

9. **Seamless Integration with Pandas:** Matplotlib works well with Pandas for direct visualization of DataFrames and Series.

   To use Matplotlib, you need to import it into your Python script or Jupyter Notebook using the import matplotlib.pyplot as plt statement, where plt is a common alias used for Matplotlib. Once imported, you can use the various functions and methods provided by Matplotlib to create a wide range of visualizations, enabling effective data exploration and communication.

REVIEW QUESTIONS

Q.1. What is NumPy?

Ans. NumPy is a powerful Python library for numerical computing and array operations. It stands for "Numerical Python." NumPy provides support for large, multi-dimensional arrays and matrices, along with a collection of mathematical functions to operate on these arrays efficiently. It is the foundation for many other libraries used in data science and scientific computing, such as Pandas and Matplotlib.

Q.2. What is Pandas?

Ans. Pandas is a popular Python library for data manipulation, analysis, and cleaning. It is built on top of NumPy and provides powerful data structures and functions for working with structured data, including tabular data like spreadsheets and SQL tables. Pandas is widely used in data science, machine learning, and data analysis tasks due to its flexibility and ease of use.

Q.3. What is Matplotlib?

Ans. Matplotlib is a popular Python library for creating static, interactive, and publication-quality visualizations. It is widely used for data visualization, scientific plotting, and generating various types of charts and graphs. Matplotlib provides a flexible and straightforward interface for creating a wide range of plots, making it an essential tool for data analysis and data communication.

Multiple Choice Questions

Q.1. What does NumPy stand for?

(*a*) Numerical Python (*b*) Numeric Programming
(*c*) Numerical Processing (*d*) Numeric Pythagorean

Q.2. Which of the following data structures is provided by NumPy?

(*a*) Series (*b*) DataFrame (*c*) Array (*d*) Table

Q.3. What is the primary data structure used in Pandas for storing and manipulating data?

(*a*) Array (*b*) Series (*c*) List (*d*) Tuple

Q.4. Which Pandas function is used to read data from various file formats like CSV, Excel, and SQL databases?

(*a*) load_data() (*b*) read_file() (*c*) read_data() (*d*) read_csv()

Q.5. In Matplotlib, which function is used to create a scatter plot?

(*a*) scatter() (*b*) plot() (*c*) hist() (*d*) boxplot()

Q.6. What is the purpose of the np.zeros() function in NumPy?

(*a*) Create an array filled with zeros. (*b*) Create an array filled with ones.
(*c*) Create an empty array. (*d*) Create an array with random values.

Q.7. Which function is used to select specific rows and columns in a DataFrame in Pandas?

(*a*) slice() (*b*) select() (*c*) loc[] and iloc[] (*d*) subset()

Q.8. What is the purpose of the np.arange() function in NumPy?

(*a*) Create an array with evenly spaced values within a specified range.

(*b*) Create an array with random values. (*c*) Create an empty array.
(*d*) Create an array filled with zeros.

Q.9. Which Matplotlib function is used to add labels to the x and y axes of a plot?
(*a*) xlabel() and ylabel() (*b*) set_xlabel() and set_ylabel()
(*c*) add_xlabel() and add_ylabel() (*d*) label()

Q.10. What is the purpose of the np.random.rand() function in NumPy?
(*a*) Generate random integers.
(*b*) Generate random samples from a normal distribution.
(*c*) Generate random samples from a uniform distribution.
(*d*) Generate random permutation of sequence.

Q.11. Which Pandas function is used to drop rows with missing values from a DataFrame?
(*a*) dropna() (*b*) remove_missing() (*c*) drop_missing() (*d*) remove_na()

Q.12. Which Matplotlib function is used to add a title to a plot?
(*a*) set_title() (*b*) add_title() (*c*) title() (*d*) plot_title()

Q.13. What is the purpose of the np.mean() function in NumPy?
(*a*) Calculate the median of an array. (*b*) Calculate the mode of an array.
(*c*) Calculate the standard deviation of an array. (*d*) Calculate the mean (average) of an array.

Q.14. Which Pandas function is used to concatenate DataFrame objects along a particular axis?
(*a*) merge() (*b*) join() (*c*) concat() (*d*) append()

Q.15. In Matplotlib, which function is used to save a plot to a file?
(*a*) save() (*b*) export() (*c*) savefig() (*d*) to_file()

Q.16. What does the np.eye() function in NumPy do?
(*a*) Generate an identity matrix. (*b*) Generate a diagonal matrix.
(*c*) Generate an array filled with ones. (*d*) Generate an array filled with zeros.

Q.17. Which Pandas function is used to apply a function along an axis of a DataFrame?
(*a*) apply() (*b*) map() (*c*) transform() (*d*) applymap()

Q.18. In Matplotlib, what is the purpose of the plt.subplot() function?
(*a*) Add a subplot to the current figure. (*b*) Create a new figure.
(*c*) Set the properties of the current subplot. (*d*) Remove a subplot from the current figure.

Q.19. What is the purpose of the np.concatenate() function in NumPy?
(*a*) Calculate the dot product of two arrays. (*b*) Concatenate arrays along a specified axis.
(*c*) Multiply arrays element-wise. (*d*) Divide arrays element-wise.

Q.20. Which Pandas function is used to apply a rolling computation to a DataFrame?
(*a*) rolling() (*b*) window() (*c*) apply_rolling() (*d*) rolling_apply()

Answer to Multiple Choice Questions

1. (*a*) **2.** (*c*) **3.** (*b*) **4.** (*d*) **5.** (*a*) **6.** (*a*) **7.** (*c*) **8.** (*a*) **9.** (*a*)
10. (*c*) **11.** (*a*) **12.** (*c*) **13.** (*d*) **14.** (*c*) **15.** (*c*) **16.** (*a*) **17.** (*a*) **18.** (*a*)
19. (*b*) **20.** (*a*)

4

SCIKIT LEARN AND SCIPY LIBRARY

SCIKIT LEARN

A well-known open-source machine learning library for Python is called Scikit-learn, or sklearn. For machine learning tasks including classification, regression, clustering, dimensionality reduction, model selection, and preprocessing, it offers a large range of techniques and tools. On top of NumPy and SciPy, Scikit-learn is constructed, and it works well with other data manipulation tools like Pandas. Using the command below, install Scikit-learn using pip

```
pip install scikit-learn
```

1. **User-Friendly API:** Scikit-learn provides a dependable and approachable API that makes it simple to use and test out various machine learning methods.
2. **Wide Range of Algorithms:** A wide range of supervised and unsupervised learning methods, such as support vector machines (SVM), decision trees, random forests, k-nearest neighbors (KNN), clustering algorithms, and more, are included in the library. We will test four different methods using the well-known Iris dataset: Decision Tree, K-Nearest Neighbors, Support Vector Machine (SVM), and Random Forest.

```
import numpy as np
import pandas as pd
from sklearn.datasets import load_iris
from sklearn.model_selection import train_test_split
from sklearn.tree import DecisionTreeClassifier
from sklearn.neighbors import KNeighborsClassifier
from sklearn.svm import SVC
from sklearn.ensemble import RandomForestClassifier
from sklearn.metrics import accuracy_score, classification_report

# Load the Iris dataset
iris = load_iris()
X, y = iris.data, iris.target
```

```
# Split the data into training and testing sets
X_train, X_test, y_train, y_test = train_test_split(X, y, test_size=0.3, random_state=42)
```

In [1]:
```
import Library
import numpy as np
import pandas as pd
from sklearn.datasets import load_iris
from sklearn.model_selection import train_test_split
from sklearn.tree import DecisionTreeClassifier
from sklearn.neighbors import KNeighborsClassifier
from sklearn.svm import SVC
from sklearn.ensemble import RandomForestClassifier
from sklearn.metrics import accuracy_score, classification_report
C:\ProgramData\Anaconda3\lib\site-packages\scipy\_init_.py:146:        UserWarming:
A NumPy version >=1.16.5 and <1.23.0 is required for this version of SciPy (detected
version 1.25.0
    warning.warn(f" A NumPy version >=(np_minversion) and <{np_maxversion}"
```

In [2]:
```
# Load the Iris dataset
iris = load_iris()
X, y = iris.data, iris.target
```

In [3]:
```
# Split the data into training and testing sets
X_train, X_test, y_train, y_test = train_test_split(X, y, test_size=0.3, random_state=42)
```

```
# 1. Decision Tree Classifier
dt_classifier = DecisionTreeClassifier()
dt_classifier.fit(X_train, y_train)
y_pred_dt = dt_classifier.predict(X_test)
acc_dt = accuracy_score(y_test, y_pred_dt)
print("Decision Tree Classifier Accuracy:", acc_dt)
print(classification_report(y_test, y_pred_dt))
```

In [4]:
```
# 1. Decision Tree Classifier
dt_classifier = DecisionTreeClassifier()
dt_classifier.fit(X_train, y_train)
y_pred_dt = dt_classifier.predict(X_test)
acc_dt = accuracy_score(y_test, y_pred_dt)
print("Decision Tree Classifier Accuracy:", acc_dt)
print(classification_report(y_test, y_pred_dt))
```

```
Decision Tree Classifier Accuracy: 1.0
              precision    recall  f1-score   support
0                  1.00      1.00      1.00        19
1                  1.00      1.00      1.00        13
2                  1.00      1.00      1.00        13

accuracy                               1.00        45
macro avg          1.00      1.00      1.00        45
weighted avg       1.00      1.00      1.00        45
```

```
# 2. K-Nearest Neighbors Classifier
knn_classifier = KNeighborsClassifier()
knn_classifier.fit(X_train, y_train)
y_pred_knn = knn_classifier.predict(X_test)
acc_knn = accuracy_score(y_test, y_pred_knn)
print("K-Nearest Neighbors Classifier Accuracy:", acc_knn)
print(classification_report(y_test, y_pred_knn))
```

```
In [5]:  # 2. K-Nearest Neighbors Classifier
         knn_classifier = KNeighborsClassifier()
         knn_classifier.fit(X_train, y_train)
         y_pred_knn = knn_classifier.predict(X_test)
         acc_knn = accuracy_score(y_test, y_pred_knn)
         print("K-Nearest Neighbors Classifier Accuracy:", acc_knn)
         print(classification_report(y_test, y_pred_knn))
```

```
K-Nearest Neighbors Classifier Accuracy: 1.0
              precision    recall  f1-score   support
0                  1.00      1.00      1.00        19
1                  1.00      1.00      1.00        13
2                  1.00      1.00      1.00        13
accuracy                               1.00        45
macro avg          1.00      1.00      1.00        45
weighted avg       1.00      1.00      1.00        45
```

```
# 3. Support Vector Machine (SVM) Classifier
svm_classifier = SVC()
svm_classifier.fit(X_train, y_train)
y_pred_svm = svm_classifier.predict(X_test)
acc_svm = accuracy_score(y_test, y_pred_svm)
print("Support Vector Machine Classifier Accuracy:", acc_svm)
print(classification_report(y_test, y_pred_svm))
```

In [6]:
```
# 3. Support Vector Machine (SVM) Classifier
svm_classifier = SVC()
svm_classifier.fit(X_train, y_train)
y_pred_svm = svm_classifier.predict(X_test)
acc_svm = accuracy_score(y_test, y_pred_svm)
print("Support Vector Machine Classifier Accuracy:", acc_svm)
print(classification_report(y_test, y_pred_svm))
```

Support Vector Machine Classifier Accuracy: 1.0

	precision	recall	f1-score	support
0	1.00	1.00	1.00	19
1	1.00	1.00	1.00	13
2	1.00	1.00	1.00	13
accuracy			1.00	45
macro avg	1.00	1.00	1.00	45
weighted avg	1.00	1.00	1.00	45

```
# 4. Random Forest Classifier
rf_classifier = RandomForestClassifier()
rf_classifier.fit(X_train, y_train)
y_pred_rf = rf_classifier.predict(X_test)
acc_rf = accuracy_score(y_test, y_pred_rf)
print("Random Forest Classifier Accuracy:", acc_rf)
print(classification_report(y_test, y_pred_rf))
```

In [7]:
```
# 4. Random Forest Classifier
rf_classifier = RandomForestClassifier()
rf_classifier.fit(X_train, y_train)
y_pred_rf = rf_classifier.predict(X_test)
acc_rf = accuracy_score(y_test, y_pred_rf)
print("Random Forest Classifier Accuracy:", acc_rf)
print(classification_report(y_test, y_pred_rf))
```

Random Forest Classifier Accuracy: 1.0

	precision	recall	f1-score	support
0	1.00	1.00	1.00	19
1	1.00	1.00	1.00	13
2	1.00	1.00	1.00	13
accuracy			1.00	45
macro avg	1.00	1.00	1.00	45
weighted avg	1.00	1.00	1.00	45

This example demonstrates how to use scikit-learn to train and assess several classifiers. We divide the dataset into training and testing sets, train each classifier using the training data, and then use the test data to test our predictions. To assess how well each algorithm performs, we calculate the accuracy and print a categorization report.

3. **Model Selection and Evaluation:** Scikit-learn offers tools for hyperparameter tuning, cross-validation, and model selection to evaluate the effectiveness of machine learning models and prevent overfitting. An illustration of using these tools with the well-known Iris dataset is given below.

```
import numpy as np
import pandas as pd
from sklearn.datasets import load_iris
from sklearn.model_selection import train_test_split, cross_val_score, GridSearchCV
from sklearn.tree import DecisionTreeClassifier
from sklearn.ensemble import RandomForestClassifier

# Load the Iris dataset
iris = load_iris()
X, y = iris.data, iris.target

# Split the data into training and testing sets
X_train, X_test, y_train, y_test = train_test_split(X, y, test_size=0.3, random_state=42)
```

```
In [8]:    import numpy as np
           import pandas as pd
           from sklearn.datasets import load_iris
           from sklearn.model_selection import train_test_split, cross_val_score, GridSearchCV
           from sklearn.tree import DecisionTreeClassifier
           from sklearn.ensemble import RandomForestClassifier

In [9]:    # Load the Iris dataset
           iris = load_iris()
           X, y = iris.data, iris.target

In [10]:   # Split the data into training and testing sets
           X_train, X_test, y_train, y_test = train_test_split(X, y, test_size=0.3, random_state=42)
```

```
# 1. Model Selection and Cross-validation with Decision Tree Classifier
dt_classifier = DecisionTreeClassifier()

# Cross-validation with 5 folds
cross_val_scores_dt = cross_val_score(dt_classifier, X_train, y_train, cv=5)
print("Cross-validation scores for Decision Tree Classifier:", cross_val_scores_dt)
print("Mean cross-validation score for Decision Tree Classifier:", np.mean(cross_val_scores_dt))
```

In [11]:
```
# 1. Model Selection and Cross-validation with Decision Tree Classifier
dt_classifier = DecisionTreeClassifier()
```

In [12]:
```
# Cross-validation with 5 folds
cross_val_scores_dt = cross_val_score(dt_classifier, X_train, y_train, cv=5)
print("Cross-validation scores for Decision Tree Classifier:", cross_val_scores_dt)
print("Mean cross-validation score for Decision Tree Classifier:", np.mean(cross_val_
scores_dt))
Cross-validation scores for Decision Tree Classifier: [0.95238095 0.9047619 0.9047619
0.95238095 0.95238095]
Mean cross-validation score for Decision Tree Classifier: 0.9333333333333333
```

```
# 2. Hyperparameter Tuning with GridSearchCV and Random Forest Classifier
rf_classifier = RandomForestClassifier()

# Define hyperparameter grid for Random Forest
param_grid = {
    'n_estimators': [50, 100, 150],
    'max_depth': [None, 10, 20],
    'min_samples_split': [2, 5, 10]
}

# GridSearchCV for hyperparameter tuning
grid_search = GridSearchCV(rf_classifier, param_grid, cv=5)
grid_search.fit(X_train, y_train)

print("Best hyperparameters for Random Forest Classifier:", grid_search.best_params_)
print("Best cross-validation score for Random Forest Classifier:", grid_search.best_score_)
```

In [13]:
```
# 2. Hyperparameter Tuning with GridSearchCV and Random Forest Classifier
rf_classifier = RandomForestClassifier()

# Define hyperparameter grid for Random Forest
param_grid = {
    'n_estimators': [50, 100, 150],
    'max_depth': [None, 10, 20],
    'min_samples_split': [2, 5, 10]
}
```

In [14]:
```
# GridSearchCV for hyperparameter tuning
grid_search = GridSearchCV(rf_classifier, param_grid, cv=5)
grid_search.fit(X_train, y_train)
```

```
print("Best hyperparameters for Random Forest Classifier:", grid_search.best_params_)
print("Best cross-validation score for Random Forest Classifier:", grid_search.best_
score_)

Best hyperparameters for Random Forest Classifier: {'max_depth': None, 'min_samples_
split': 2, 'n_estimator': 100}
Best cross-validation score for Random Forest Classifier: 0.9428571428571428
```

```
# Evaluate the best model on the test set
best_rf_classifier = grid_search.best_estimator_
y_pred_rf = best_rf_classifier.predict(X_test)
acc_rf = np.mean(y_pred_rf == y_test)
print("Accuracy of the best Random Forest Classifier on the test set:", acc_rf)
```

```
In [15]:  # Evaluate the best model on the test set
          best_rf_classifier = grid_search.best_estimator_
          y_pred_rf = best_rf_classifier.predict(X_test)
          acc_rf = np.mean(y_pred_rf == y_test)
          print("Accuracy of the best Random Forest Classifier on the test set:", acc_rf)

          Accuracy of the best Random Forest Classifier on the test set: 1.0
```

In this illustration, we choose a model and cross-validate it using five folds using the Decision Tree Classifier. To evaluate the effectiveness of the model, the cross-validation scores are computed, and the mean score is determined.

For hyperparameter tuning, we use the Random Forest Classifier and define a hyperparameter grid containing different values for 'n_estimators', 'max_depth', and 'min_samples_split'. GridSearchCV is employed to search through this parameter grid and find the best combination of hyperparameters that maximize the cross-validation score.

Finally, we evaluate the best Random Forest model obtained from hyperparameter tuning on the test set to get an estimate of its performance on unseen data. This process helps us choose the best model and avoid overfitting by optimizing the hyperparameters based on cross-validation performance.

4. **Preprocessing and Feature Engineering:** Scikit-learn includes various preprocessing techniques such as scaling, normalization, one-hot encoding, and feature extraction. Below is an example that demonstrates various preprocessing techniques using scikit-learn on the famous Iris dataset:

```
import numpy as np
import pandas as pd
from sklearn.datasets import load_iris
from sklearn.model_selection import train_test_split
from sklearn.preprocessing import StandardScaler, MinMaxScaler, OneHotEncoder
from sklearn.decomposition import PCA
```

```
# Load the Iris dataset
iris = load_iris()
X, y = iris.data, iris.target

# Split the data into training and testing sets
X_train, X_test, y_train, y_test = train_test_split(X, y, test_size=0.3, random_state=42)

# 1. Feature Scaling with StandardScaler
scaler = StandardScaler()
X_train_scaled = scaler.fit_transform(X_train)
X_test_scaled = scaler.transform(X_test)
```

```
In [16]:  import numpy as np
          import pandas as pd
          from sklearn.datasets import load_iris
          from sklearn.model_selection import train_test_split
          from sklearn.preprocessing import StandardScaler, MinMaxScaler, OneHotEncoder
          from sklearn.decomposition import PCA

In [17]:  # Load the Iris dataset
          iris = load_iris()
          X, y = iris.data, iris.target

In [18]:  # Split the data into training and testing sets
          X_train, X_test, y_train, y_test = train_test_split(X, y, test_size=0.3, random_state=42)

In [19]:  # 1. Feature Scaling with StandardScaler
          scaler = StandardScaler()
          X_train_scaled = scaler.fit_transform(X_train)
          X_test_scaled = scaler.transform(X_test)
```

```
# 2. Feature Scaling with MinMaxScaler
min_max_scaler = MinMaxScaler()
X_train_minmax_scaled = min_max_scaler.fit_transform(X_train)
X_test_minmax_scaled = min_max_scaler.transform(X_test)

# 3. One-Hot Encoding for Categorical Variables
# In this example, there are no categorical variables in the Iris dataset,
# so we'll create an artificial example with some dummy categorical data.
colors = ['red', 'blue', 'green']
```

```
categorical_data = np.random.choice(colors, size=(X.shape[0], 1))
encoder = OneHotEncoder()
categorical_data_encoded = encoder.fit_transform(categorical_data).toarray()

# 4. Feature Extraction with Principal Component Analysis (PCA)
pca = PCA(n_components=2)
X_train_pca = pca.fit_transform(X_train)
X_test_pca = pca.transform(X_test)
```

```
In [20]: # 2. Feature Scaling with MinMaxScaler
         min_max_scaler = MinMaxScaler()
         X_train_minmax_scaled = min_max_scaler.fit_transform(X_train)
         X_test_minmax_scaled = min_max_scaler.transform(X_test)
```

```
In [21]: # 3. One-Hot Encoding for Categorical Variables
         # In this example, there are no categorical variables in the Iris dataset,
         # so we'll create an artificial example with some dummy categorical data.
         colors = ['red', 'blue', 'green']
         categorical_data = np.random.choice(colors, size=(X.shape[0], 1))
         encoder = OneHotEncoder()
         categorical_data_encoded = encoder.fit_transform(categorical_data).toarray()
```

```
In [22]: # 4. Feature Extraction with Principal Component Analysis (PCA)
         pca = PCA(n_components=2)
         X_train_pca = pca.fit_transform(X_train)
         X_test_pca = pca.transform(X_test)
```

```
# Display the results
print("Original Data Shape:", X.shape)
print("Scaled Data Shape (StandardScaler):", X_train_scaled.shape)
print("Scaled Data Shape (MinMaxScaler):", X_train_minmax_scaled.shape)
print("Encoded Categorical Data Shape:", categorical_data_encoded.shape)
print("PCA Transformed Data Shape:", X_train_pca.shape)
```

```
In [23]: # Display the results
         print("Original Data Shape:", X.shape)
         print("Scaled Data Shape (StandardScaler):", X_train_scaled.shape)
         print("Scaled Data Shape (MinMaxScaler):", X_train_minmax_scaled.shape)
         print("Encoded Categorical Data Shape:", categorical_data_encoded.shape)
         print("PCA Transformed Data Shape:", X_train_pca.shape)
```

```
Original Data Shape: (150, 4)
Scaled Data Shape (StandardScaler): (105, 4)
Scaled Data Shape (MinMaxScaler): (105, 4)
Encoded Categorical Data Shape: (150, 3)
PCA Transformed Data Shape: (105, 2)
```

- StandardScaler and MinMaxScaler are two separate scalers that were employed in this instance for feature scaling. While MinMaxScaler scales the features to a particular range (often [0, 1]), StandardScaler scales the features to have zero mean and unit variance.
- We generate a fake example using dummy categorical data represented by colors as there are no categorical variables in the Iris dataset. The categorical data is transformed into binary vectors using one-hot encoding, where each category is represented by a binary feature.
- Used Principal Component Analysis (PCA) to extract features from the data while reducing the data's dimensionality. To facilitate visualization, we condense the feature space in this case to two dimensions.

Not all datasets will necessitate using each of these preprocessing methods, so keep that in mind. The type of data being processed and the machine learning method being utilized determine which pretreatment procedures should be employed. These preparation methods can be crucial for enhancing model performance and ensuring that the data are in a format that the selected algorithm can use.

5. **Pipelines:** Scikit-learn supports the creation of complex machine learning workflows using pipelines, enabling easy chaining of data preprocessing steps and model training.
6. **Integration with NumPy and Pandas:** Scikit-learn works seamlessly with NumPy arrays and Pandas DataFrames, allowing easy integration with data manipulation libraries.
7. **Consistent Documentation:** Scikit-learn provides extensive and well-documented APIs along with examples and tutorials, making it easy for users to learn and understand the library.
8. **Active Development and Community Support:** Scikit-learn is actively developed and maintained by a large community of contributors, ensuring regular updates and improvements.
9. **Interoperability with Other Libraries:** Scikit-learn can be combined with other popular libraries like Matplotlib, Pandas, and NumPy to create end-to-end data science workflows.

   For many machine learning activities, academia, business, and research all frequently use Scikit-learn. It provides a strong basis for more complicated machine learning projects and is a great place for novices to learn machine learning. Scikit-learn must first be installed using the pip install scikit-learn command before being imported into a Python script or Jupyter notebook using the import sklearn command. You may then explore and use its numerous functions to create, train, and assess machine learning models from there.

SCIPY

Scipy is an open-source Python library built on top of NumPy that offers extra capabilities for a variety of technical and scientific computing tasks. It is widely used for tasks related to mathematics, statistics, optimization, signal processing, integration, interpolation, and much more. Scipy is a powerful tool for researchers, engineers, and data scientists who require advanced computational capabilities.

1. **scipy.linalg**: Linear algebra functions like matrix decomposition, eigenvalue problems, solving linear systems of equations, etc.

Matrix Decomposition - LU Decomposition: A matrix is factorized into a lower triangular matrix (L) and an upper triangular matrix (U) by the LU decomposition method. It is frequently employed to effectively solve linear systems.

```
import numpy as np
from scipy.linalg import lu

# Create a square matrix
A = np.array([[4, 2, 1], [3, 5, 2], [1, 1, 3]])

# Perform LU decomposition
P, L, U = lu(A)

print("Matrix A:")
print(A)
print("Lower triangular matrix L:")
print(L)
print("Upper triangular matrix U:")
print(U)
print("Permutation matrix P:")
print(P)
```

```
In [31]:  import numpy as np
          from scipy.linalg import lu
          # Create a square matrix
          A = np.array([[4, 2, 1], [3, 5, 2], [1, 1, 3]])

In [32]:  # Perform LU decomposition
          P, L, U = lu(A)
          print("Matrix A:")
          print(A)
          print("Lower triangular matrix L:")
          print(L)
          print("Upper triangular matrix U:")
          print(U)
          print("Permutation matrix P:")
          print(P)
          Matrix A:
          [[4  2  1]
           [3  5  2]
           [1  1  3]]
```

```
Lower triangular matrix L:
[[1.          0.          0.          ]
 [0.75        1.          0.          ]
 [0.25        0.14285714  1.          ]]
Upper triangular matrix U:
[[4.          2.          1.          ]
 [0.          3.5         1.25        ]
 [0.          0.          0.57142857  ]]
Permutation matrix P:
[[1.  0.  0.]
 [0.  1.  0.]
 [0.  0.  1.]]
```

Eigenvalue Problems: Finding the eigenvalues and eigenvectors of a square matrix is done using eigenvalue problems.

```
from scipy.linalg import eig

# Create a square matrix
A = np.array([[3, -1], [1, 1]])

# Find eigenvalues and eigenvectors
eigenvalues, eigenvectors = eig(A)

print("Matrix A:")
print(A)
print("Eigenvalues:")
print(eigenvalues)
print("Eigenvectors:")
print(eigenvectors)
```

```
In [33]:  from scipy.linalg import eig
          # Create a square matrix
          A = np.array([[3, -1], [1, 1]])

In [34]:  # Find eigenvalues and eigenvectors
          eigenvalues, eigenvectors = eig(A)
          print("Matrix A:")
          print(A)
          print("Eigenvalues:")
          print(eigenvalues)
          print("Eigenvectors:")
          print(eigenvectors)
```

```
Matrix A:
[[3  -1]
 [1   1]]
Eigenvalues:
[2.00000002+0.j  j 1.99999998+0.j]
Eigenvectors:
[[0.70710679  0.70710677]
 [0.70710677  0.70710679]]
```

Solving Linear Systems of Equations: Scipy.linalg.solve can be used to resolve linear systems of equations with the formula Ax = b.

```
from scipy.linalg import solve

# Create the coefficient matrix A and the right-hand side vector b
A = np.array([[3, 1], [1, 2]])
b = np.array([9, 8])

# Solve the linear system Ax = b
x = solve(A, b)
print("Matrix A:")
print(A)
print("Vector b:")
print(b)
print("Solution x:")
print(x)
```

```
In [35]:  from scipy.linalg import solve
          # Create the coefficient matrix A and the right-hand side vector b
          A = np.array([[3, 1], [1, 2]])
          b = np.array([9, 8])

In [36]:  # Solve the linear system Ax = b
          x = solve(A, b)
          print("Matrix A:")
          print(A)
          print("Vector b:")
          print(b)
          print("Solution x:")
          print(x)
          Matrix A:
          [[3  1]
           [1  2]]
```

```
Vector b:
[9  8]
Solution x:
[2.  3.]
```

The library offers many more functions for solving various linear algebra problems, including singular value decomposition, matrix inversion, matrix exponentiation, and more.

2. **scipy.integrate**: Integration and ODE (Ordinary Differential Equation) solvers.

Integration - Single and Multiple Integrals:

```
import numpy as np
from scipy.integrate import quad, dblquad

# Single integration of a function
result, error = quad(np.sin, 0, np.pi)
print("Integration of sin(x) from 0 to pi:", result)

# Double integration of a function
def f(x, y):
    return x * y

result, error = dblquad(f, 0, 1, lambda x: 0, lambda x: 2)
print("Double integration of xy over [0, 1] and [0, 2]:", result)
```

```
In [37]:  import numpy as np
          from scipy.integrate import quad, dblquad
          # Single integration of a function
          result, error = quad(np.sin, 0, np.pi)
          print("Integration of sin(x) from 0 to pi:", result)

In [38]:  # Double integration of a function
          def f(x, y):
              return x * y
          result, error = dblquad(f, 0, 1, lambda x: 0, lambda x: 2)
          print("Double integration of xy over [0, 1] and [0, 2]:", result)
          Double integration of xy over [0, 1] and [0, 2]: 0.9999999999999999999
```

Solving Ordinary Differential Equations (ODEs):

```
import numpy as np
from scipy.integrate import solve_ivp
import matplotlib.pyplot as plt
```

```
# Define the ODE function
def dydt(t, y):
    return -2 * y

# Initial condition
y0 = 1.0

# Time span for integration
t_span = (0, 5)
```

```
In [39]:  import numpy as np
          from scipy.integrate import solve_ivp
          import matplotlib.pyplot as plt
          # Define the ODE function
          def dydt(t, y):
              return -2 * y
          # Initial condition
          y0 = 1.0

In [40]:  # Time span for integration
          t_span = (0, 5)
```

```
# Integrate the ODE
sol = solve_ivp(dydt, t_span, [y0], t_eval=np.linspace(0, 5, 100))

# Plot the solution
plt.plot(sol.t, sol.y[0])
plt.xlabel('Time')
plt.ylabel('y(t)')
plt.title('Solution of dy/dt = -2y')
plt.grid(True)
plt.show()
```

```
In [41]:  # Integrate the ODE
          sol = solve_ivp(dydt, t_span, [y0], t_eval=np.linspace(0, 5, 100))
          # Plot the solution
          plt.plot(sol.t, sol.y[0])
          plt.xlabel('Time')
          plt.ylabel('y(t)')
          plt.title('Solution of dy/dt = -2y')
          plt.grid(True)
          plt.show()
```

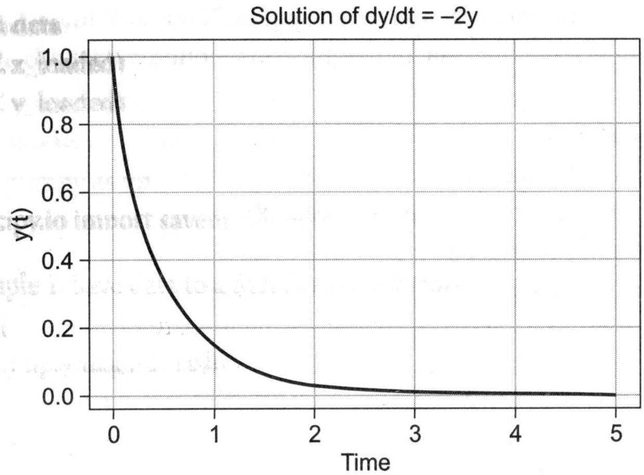

In the first example, we use quad to perform a single integration of the np.sin function over the interval [0, π]. In the second example, we use dblquad to perform a double integration of the f(x, y) = xy function over the intervals [0, 1] and [0, 2]. In the third example, we solve the simple first-order ODE dy/dt = -2y with an initial condition y(0) = 1.0. The solve_ivp function is used to solve the ODE over the time span [0, 5] and obtain the numerical solution. The solution is then plotted using Matplotlib.

These examples illustrate the capabilities of scipy.integrate for performing integration and solving ordinary differential equations in Python.

3. **scipy.optimize**: Optimization algorithms for finding the minimum or maximum of functions.

```
import numpy as np
from scipy.optimize import minimize_scalar

# Define the function to be minimized
def quadratic_function(x):
    return x**2 - 4*x + 4

# Find the minimum of the function using the 'bounded' method
result = minimize_scalar(quadratic_function, bounds=(-10, 10), method='bounded')

# Print the result
print("Minimum value found:", result.fun)
print("Value of x at the minimum:", result.x)
```

```
In [42]:  import numpy as np
          from scipy.optimize import minimize_scalar
          # Define the function to be minimized
          def quadratic_function(x):
              return x**2 - 4*x + 4
```

In [43]:
```
# Find the minimum of the function using the 'bounded' method
result = minimize_scalar(quadratic_function, bounds=(-10, 10), method='bounded')
```

In [44]:
```
# Print the result
print("Minimum value found:", result.fun)
print("Value of x at the minimum:", result.x)
Minimum value found: 0.0
Value of x at the minimum: 2.0
```

In this instance, f(x) = x2 - 4x + 4 is a straightforward quadratic function. To determine the minimum value of this function inside the bounds (-10, 10), we utilize scipy.optimize.minimize_scalar. This optimization uses the bounded technique.

Other optimization techniques that are included in Scipy can also be used.Find the least or maximum of more complex functions through optimizing. Popular techniques include "BFGS," "L-BFGS-B," "TNC," "COBYLA," etc. It's critical to select the best approach based on the function and problem at hand because each method has unique benefits and drawbacks.

Here is an illustration of how to get the minimum of the same function using a different approach (L-BFGS-B):

```
from scipy.optimize import minimize
result = minimize(quadratic_function, x0=0, method='L-BFGS-B', bounds=[(-10, 10)])

print("Minimum value found:", result.fun)
print("Value of x at the minimum:", result.x)
```

In [45]:
```
from scipy.optimize import minimize
result = minimize(quadratic_function, x0=0, method='L-BFGS-B', bounds=[(-10, 10)])
print("Minimum value found:", result.fun)
print("Value of x at the minimum:", result.x)
Minimum value found: [0.]
Value of x at the minimum: [2.]
```

Both examples will give you the same minimum value, but the paths taken to find the minimum might differ depending on the chosen optimization method.

4. **scipy.signal:** Signal processing functions like filtering, windowing, convolution, etc.

Filtering - Low-pass Filter:

```
import numpy as np
import matplotlib.pyplot as plt
from scipy.signal import butter, filtfilt

# Generate a noisy signal
t = np.linspace(0, 1, 1000)
signal = np.sin(2 * np.pi * 5 * t) + 0.5 * np.random.randn(len(t))
```

```
# Define the cutoff frequency for the low-pass filter
cutoff_freq = 8 # Hz

# Design a low-pass Butterworth filter
b, a = butter(N=6, Wn=cutoff_freq, btype='low', fs=1000)

# Apply the filter to the signal using filtfilt (zero-phase filtering)
filtered_signal = filtfilt(b, a, signal)
```

```
In [46]:  Filtering - Low-pass Filter:
          import numpy as np
          import matplotlib.pyplot as plt
          from scipy.signal import butter, filtfilt
          # Generate a noisy signal
          t = np.linspace(0, 1, 1000)
          signal = np.sin(2 * np.pi * 5 * t) + 0.5 * np.random.randn(len(t))
```

```
In [47]:  # Define the cutoff frequency for the low-pass filter
          cutoff_freq = 8  # Hz
```

```
In [48]:  # Design a low-pass Butterworth filter
          b, a = butter(N=6, Wn=cutoff_freq, btype='low', fs=1000)
          # Apply the filter to the signal using filtfilt (zero-phase filtering)
          filtered_signal = filtfilt(b, a, signal)
```

```
# Plot the original and filtered signals
plt.figure()
plt.plot(t, signal, label='Original Signal')
plt.plot(t, filtered_signal, label='Filtered Signal')
plt.xlabel('Time (s)')
plt.ylabel('Amplitude')
plt.title('Low-pass Filtering')
plt.legend()
plt.grid(True)
plt.show()
```

```
In [49]:  # Plot the original and filtered signals
          plt.figure()
          plt.plot(t, signal, label='Original Signal')
          plt.plot(t, filtered_signal, label='Filtered Signal')
```

```
plt.xlabel('Time (s)')
plt.ylabel('Amplitude')
plt.title('Low-pass Filtering')
plt.legend()
plt.grid(True)
plt.show()
```

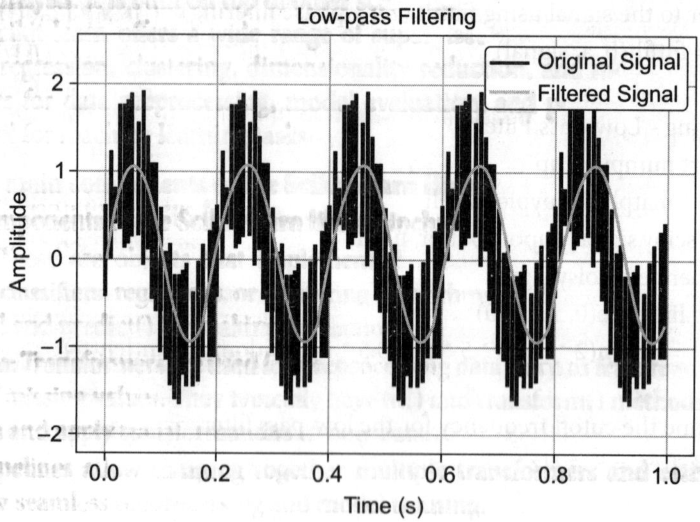

Windowing:

```
import numpy as np
import matplotlib.pyplot as plt
from scipy.signal import windows

# Generate a 100-sample Hann window
window = windows.hann(100)

# Plot the window
plt.figure()
plt.plot(window)
plt.xlabel('Sample')
plt.ylabel('Amplitude')
plt.title('Hann Window')
plt.grid(True)
plt.show()
```

```
In [50]: Windowing
         import numpy as np
         import matplotlib.pyplot as plt
```

```
from scipy.signal import windows
# Generate a 100-sample Hann window
window = windows.hann(100)
```

```
In [51]:  # Plot the window
          plt.figure()
          plt.plot(window)
          plt.xlabel('Sample')
          plt.ylabel('Amplitude')
          plt.title('Hann Window')
          plt.grid(True)
          plt.show()
```

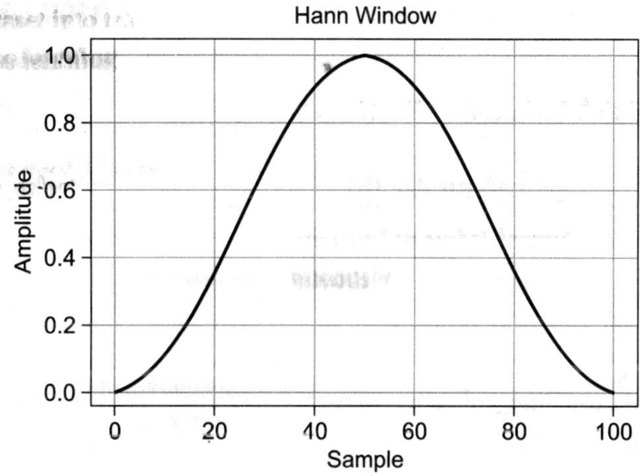

Convolution:

```
import numpy as np
import matplotlib.pyplot as plt
from scipy.signal import convolve

# Define two 1D signals
signal1 = np.array([1, 2, 3, 4, 5])
signal2 = np.array([1, 1, 1])

# Perform convolution between the two signals
conv_result = convolve(signal1, signal2, mode='full')
```

```
In [52]:  Convolution
          import numpy as np
```

```
          import matplotlib.pyplot as plt
          from scipy.signal import convolve

          # Define two 1D signals
          signal1 = np.array([1, 2, 3, 4, 5])
          signal2 = np.array([1, 1, 1])

In [53]:  # Perform convolution between the two signals
          conv_result = convolve(signal1, signal2, mode='full')

# Plot the original signals and the convolution result
plt.figure()
plt.subplot(311)
plt.stem(signal1, use_line_collection=True)
plt.title('Signal 1')
plt.grid(True)

plt.subplot(312)
plt.stem(signal2, use_line_collection=True)
plt.title('Signal 2')
plt.grid(True)

plt.subplot(313)
plt.stem(conv_result, use_line_collection=True)
plt.title('Convolution Result')
plt.grid(True)

plt.tight_layout()
plt.show()

In [54]:  # Plot the original signals and the convolution result
          plt.figure()
          plt.subplot(311)
          plt.stem(signal1, use_line_collection=True)
          plt.title('Signal 1')
          plt.grid(True)
          plt.subplot(312)
          plt.stem(signal2, use_line_collection=True)
          plt.title('Signal 2')
          plt.grid(True)
          plt.subplot(313)
```

```
plt.stem(conv_result, use_line_collection=True)
plt.title('Convolution Result')
plt.grid(True)
plt.tight_layout()
plt.show()
```

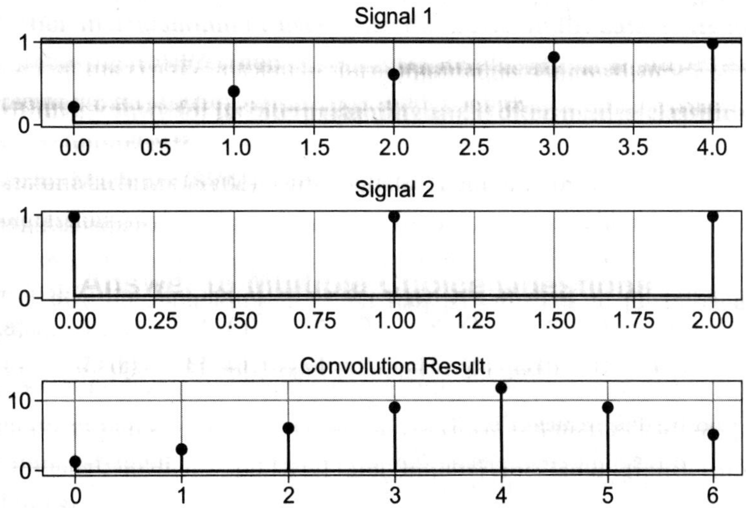

Here, apply a low-pass Butterworth filter to a noisy sine wave signal to remove high-frequency noise and preserve the low-frequency component.

Create a Hann window of size 100 and visualize the window's shape. Windowing is commonly used in signal processing to reduce spectral leakage when applying the Fourier Transform.

Convolute two signals (signal1 and signal2) using a 1D convolution algorithm, then plot the original signals and the convolutional output. Fundamental signal processing operations like filtering and feature extraction use convolution.

These illustrations demonstrate a few of the signal processing options offered by scipy.signal. The library provides a large range of tools and functions to efficiently carry out various signal processing operations.

5. **scipy.interpolate**: Interpolation and smoothing of data.

```
import numpy as np
import matplotlib.pyplot as plt
from scipy.interpolate import interp1d

# Generate some data points (sin function)
x = np.linspace(0, 2*np.pi, 10)
y = np.sin(x)

# Create a higher-resolution grid for interpolation
x_interp = np.linspace(0, 2*np.pi, 100)
```

```
# Perform interpolations using different methods
linear_interp = interp1d(x, y, kind='linear')
cubic_interp = interp1d(x, y, kind='cubic')
quadratic_interp = interp1d(x, y, kind='quadratic')
```

```
In [55]:  import numpy as np
          import matplotlib.pyplot as plt
          from scipy.interpolate import interp1d
          # Generate some data points (sin function)
          x = np.linspace(0, 2*np.pi, 10)
          y = np.sin(x)
```

```
In [56]:  # Create a higher-resolution grid for interpolation
          x_interp = np.linspace(0, 2*np.pi, 100)
```

```
In [57]:  # Perform interpolations using different methods
          linear_interp = interp1d(x, y, kind='linear')
          cubic_interp = interp1d(x, y, kind='cubic')
          quadratic_interp = interp1d(x, y, kind='quadratic')
```

```
# Calculate interpolated values on the higher-resolution grid
y_linear_interp = linear_interp(x_interp)
y_cubic_interp = cubic_interp(x_interp)
y_quadratic_interp = quadratic_interp(x_interp)

# Plot the original data and the interpolated results
plt.figure()
plt.plot(x, y, 'bo', label='Original Data')
plt.plot(x_interp, y_linear_interp, 'r-', label='Linear Interpolation')
plt.plot(x_interp, y_cubic_interp, 'g-', label='Cubic Interpolation')
plt.plot(x_interp, y_quadratic_interp, 'purple', label='Quadratic Interpolation')
plt.xlabel('X')
plt.ylabel('Y')
plt.title('Data Interpolation using interp1d')
plt.legend()
plt.grid(True)
plt.show()
In [58]:  # Calculate interpolated values on the higher-resolution grid
          y_linear_interp = linear_interp(x_interp)
          y_cubic_interp = cubic_interp(x_interp)
          y_quadratic_interp = quadratic_interp(x_interp)
```

In [59]:
```
# Plot the original data and the interpolated results
plt.figure()
plt.plot(x, y, 'bo', label='Original Data')
plt.plot(x_interp, y_linear_interp, 'r-', label='Linear Interpolation')
plt.plot(x_interp, y_cubic_interp, 'g-', label='Cubic Interpolation')
plt.plot(x_interp, y_quadratic_interp, 'purple', label='Quadratic Interpolation')
plt.xlabel('X')
plt.ylabel('Y')
plt.title('Data Interpolation using interp1d')
plt.legend()
plt.grid(True)
plt.show()
```

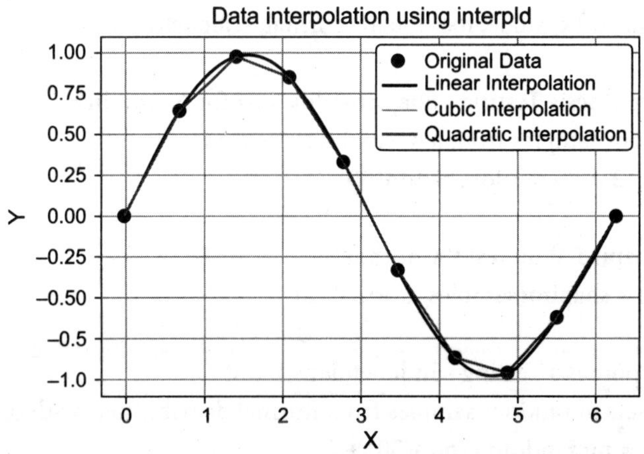

In this example, we generate some data points from a sine function (np.sin(x)) with 10 data points evenly spaced in the range [0, 2*pi]. We then create a higher-resolution grid (x_interp) for interpolation with 100 data points within the same range.

We use scipy.interpolate.interp1d to perform data interpolation using three different methods:

Linear Interpolation (kind='linear'): This method provides a straight line interpolation between data points.

Cubic Interpolation (kind='cubic'): This method provides a smooth cubic spline interpolation between data points.

Quadratic Interpolation (kind='quadratic'): This method provides a parabolic interpolation between data points.

After performing the interpolations, we plot the original data along with the interpolated results to visualize how each method approximates the function between the given data points.

The choice of interpolation method depends on the properties of the data and the required smoothness of the interpolated curve, and it is beneficial for estimating values at places that fall between the available data points.

6. **scipy.stats**: Probability distributions, statistical functions, and hypothesis testing.
   import numpy as np

```
import matplotlib.pyplot as plt
from scipy.stats import norm, t, chi2, f, shapiro, ttest_ind

# Example 1: Probability Distributions
# Generate random samples from a normal distribution with mean 0 and standard deviation 1
samples_normal = np.random.randn(1000)

# Fit a normal distribution to the data
mean_normal, std_normal = norm.fit(samples_normal)

# Example 2: Statistical Functions
# Calculate the cumulative distribution function (CDF) of the normal distribution at a specific point
x_value = 1.5
cdf_value = norm.cdf(x_value, loc=mean_normal, scale=std_normal)

# Example 3: Hypothesis Testing - Shapiro-Wilk Test for Normality
# Generate random samples from a normal distribution
samples_normal_2 = np.random.randn(50)

# Perform the Shapiro-Wilk test for normality
statistic, p_value = shapiro(samples_normal_2)

# Example 4: Hypothesis Testing - Independent T-test
# Generate two sets of random samples from normal distributions with different means
samples_group1 = np.random.randn(50) + 2
samples_group2 = np.random.randn(50)

# Perform an independent t-test to compare the means of the two groups
t_statistic, p_value_ttest = ttest_ind(samples_group1, samples_group2)

# Example 5: Hypothesis Testing - Chi-Square Test
# Create a contingency table for a chi-square test
observed_values = np.array([[30, 20], [15, 35]])

# Perform the chi-square test
chi2_statistic, p_value_chi2, _, _ = chi2.contingency.expected_freq(observed_values)

# Example 6: Hypothesis Testing - F-test
# Generate two sets of random samples from normal distributions with different variances
samples_group1_var1 = np.random.randn(50)
samples_group1_var2 = 2 * np.random.randn(50)
```

```
# Perform an F-test to compare the variances of the two groups
f_statistic, p_value_ftest = f.variat(samples_group1_var1, samples_group1_var2)

# Print the results
print("Mean and Standard Deviation of Normal Distribution:", mean_normal, std_normal)
print("CDF of Normal Distribution at x =", x_value, ":", cdf_value)
print("Shapiro-Wilk Test for Normality - Statistic:", statistic, "p-value:", p_value)
print("Independent T-test - Statistic:", t_statistic, "p-value:", p_value_ttest)
print("Chi-Square Test - Statistic:", chi2_statistic, "p-value:", p_value_chi2)
print("F-test - Statistic:", f_statistic, "p-value:", p_value_ftest)
```

Here,

Probability Distributions: In order to estimate the parameters (mean and standard deviation) of a normal distribution, we create random samples from the distribution and fit the distribution to the data.

Statistical Functions: We determine the normal distribution's cumulative distribution function (CDF) at a certain location.

Hypothesis Testing - Shapiro-Wilk Test for Normality: To determine if the data is distributed normally, we create random samples from a normal distribution.

Hypothesis Testing - Independent T-test: To compare the means of the two groups, we create two sets of random samples from normal distributions, each with a distinct mean.

Hypothesis Testing - Chi-Square Test: To determine if the two categorical variables are independent, we construct a contingency table and run the chi-square test.

Hypothesis Testing - F-test: We generate two sets of random samples from normal distributions with different variances and perform an F-test to compare the variances of the two groups.

These are just a few examples of the statistical functionalities provided by scipy.stats. The library offers a wide range of probability distributions, statistical functions, and hypothesis testing methods to help analyze and interpret data in various scientific and engineering applications.

7. **scipy.spatial**: Spatial algorithms and data structures for points and distances.

```
import numpy as np
from scipy.spatial import distance, KDTree

# Example 1: Distance Calculation
# Create two points in 2D space
point1 = np.array([1, 2])
point2 = np.array([4, 6])

# Calculate Euclidean distance between the two points
euclidean_distance = distance.euclidean(point1, point2)
print("Euclidean Distance between point1 and point2:", euclidean_distance)
```

```
# Calculate Manhattan distance between the two points
manhattan_distance = distance.cityblock(point1, point2)
print("Manhattan Distance between point1 and point2:", manhattan_distance)

# Calculate Chebyshev distance between the two points
chebyshev_distance = distance.chebyshev(point1, point2)
print("Chebyshev Distance between point1 and point2:", chebyshev_distance)

# Example 2: KDTree
# Create a set of points in 2D space
points = np.array([[1, 2], [4, 6], [2, 5], [7, 3], [3, 1]])

# Build a KDTree data structure
kdtree = KDTree(points)

# Query the KDTree to find the nearest neighbor for a given point
query_point = np.array([6, 2])
distances, indices = kdtree.query(query_point, k=2)
```

```
In [70]:  import numpy as np
          from scipy.spatial import distance, KDTree
          # Example 1: Distance Calculation

          # Create two points in 2D space
          point1 = np.array([1, 2])
          point2 = np.array([4, 6])

          # Calculate Euclidean distance between the two points
          euclidean_distance = distance.euclidean(point1, point2)
          print("Euclidean Distance between point1 and point2:", euclidean_distance)

          # Calculate Manhattan distance between the two points
          manhattan_distance = distance.cityblock(point1, point2)
          print("Manhattan Distance between point1 and point2:", manhattan_distance)

          # Calculate Chebyshev distance between the two points
          chebyshev_distance = distance.chebyshev(point1, point2)
          print("Chebyshev Distance between point1 and point2:", chebyshev_distance)

          # Example 2: KDTree
          # Create a set of points in 2D space
          points = np.array([[1, 2], [4, 6], [2, 5], [7, 3], [3, 1]])
```

```
    # Build a KDTree data structure
    kdtree = KDTree(points)

    # Query the KDTree to find the nearest neighbor for a given point
    query_point = np.array([6, 2])
    distances, indices = kdtree.query(query_point, k=2)

print("Query Point:", query_point)
print("Nearest Neighbor Points:", points[indices])
print("Distances to Nearest Neighbors:", distances)
```

```
Euclidean Distance between point1 and point2: 5.0
Manhattan Distance between point1 and point2: 7
Chebyshev Distance between point1 and point2: 4
Query Point: [6  2]
Nearest Neighbor Points: [[7  3]
[3  1]
Distances to Nearest Neighbors: [1.41421356  3.16227766]
```

Here,

Calculation of Distance: Using two points (point1 and point2) that we have created in 2D space, we may determine their distances using a variety of metrics, such as the Euclidean, Manhattan, and Chebyshev distances.

KDTree: Using scipy.spatial, we construct a KDTree data structure from a set of points (points) in 2D space.KDTree. A geographic data structure called KDTree enables quick nearest neighbor searches for a given point. The KDTree is then used to determine the distances between two of a query point's closest neighbors.

These examples show a few of the spatial data structures and algorithms that are offered by scipy.spatial. It is helpful for applications like clustering, search, and closest neighbor problems in that the library offers a variety of spatial features.

8. **scipy.special**: Special mathematical functions like Bessel functions, Gamma functions, etc.

```
import numpy as np
import matplotlib.pyplot as plt
from scipy.special import jn, gamma

# Example 1: Bessel Functions
# Calculate the first-order Bessel function of the first kind (J0) for various values of x
x = np.linspace(0, 10, 100)
bessel_J0 = jn(0, x)

# Calculate the first-order Bessel function of the second kind (Y0) for the same values of x
bessel_Y0 = jn(0, x, True)
```

```
# Plot the Bessel functions
plt.figure()
plt.plot(x, bessel_J0, label='J0(x)')
plt.plot(x, bessel_Y0, label='Y0(x)')
plt.xlabel('x')
plt.ylabel('Value')
plt.title('Bessel Functions (J0 and Y0)')
plt.legend()
plt.grid(True)
plt.show()
```

```
In [72]:  import numpy as np
          import matplotlib.pyplot as plt
          from scipy.special import jn, gamma

          # Example 1: Bessel Functions
          # Calculate the first-order Bessel function of the first kind (J0) for various values of x
          x = np.linspace(0, 10, 100)
          bessel_J0 = jn(0, x)
          # Calculate the first-order Bessel function of the second kind (Y0) for the same values of x
          bessel_Y0 = jn(0, x, True)

          # Plot the Bessel functions
          plt.figure()
          plt.plot(x, bessel_J0, label='J0(x)')
          plt.plot(x, bessel_Y0, label='Y0(x)')
          plt.xlabel('x')
          plt.ylabel('Value')
          plt.title('Bessel Functions (J0 and Y0)')
          plt.legend()
          plt.grid(True)
          plt.show()
```

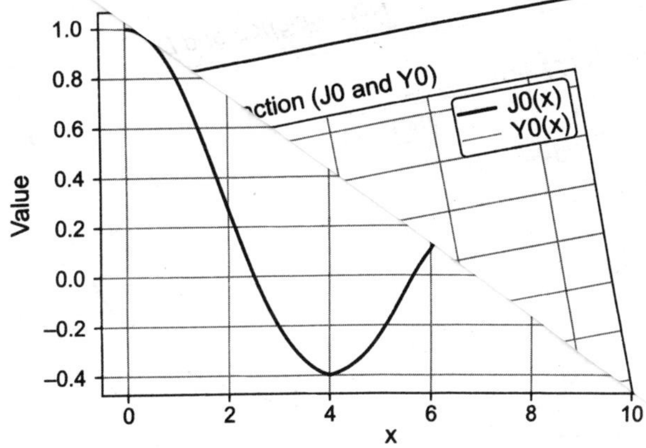


```
# Example 2: Gamma Function
# Calculate the Gamma function for a range of positive values
x_gamma = np.linspace(0.1, 5, 100)
gamma_values = gamma(x_gamma)

# Plot the Gamma function
plt.figure()
plt.plot(x_gamma, gamma_values, label='Gamma(x)')
plt.xlabel('x')
plt.ylabel('Value')
plt.title('Gamma Function')
plt.legend()
plt.grid(True)
plt.show()
```

```
In [73]:  # Example 2: Gamma Function

          # Calculate the Gamma function for a range of positive values
          x_gamma = np.linspace(0.1, 5, 100)
          gamma_values = gamma(x_gamma)

          # Plot the Gamma function
          plt.figure()
          plt.plot(x_gamma, gamma_values, label='Gamma(x)')
          plt.xlabel('x')
          plt.ylabel('Value')
          plt.title('Gamma Function')
          plt.legend()
          plt.grid(True)
          plt.show()
```

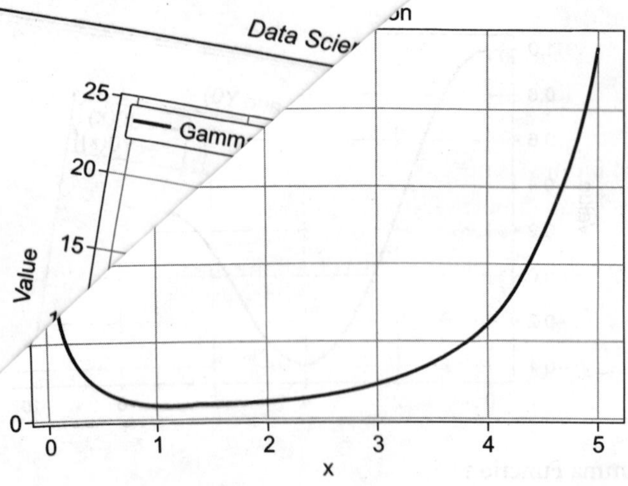

Here,

Bessel Functions: We calculate the first-order Bessel function of the first kind (J0) and the first-order Bessel function of the second kind (Y0) for a range of values of x. Bessel functions are special functions that arise in various physical and engineering problems, especially in the context of wave phenomena.

Gamma Function: We calculate the Gamma function for a range of positive values of x. The Gamma function is a generalization of the factorial function to real and complex numbers. It has applications in statistics, probability theory, and many areas of mathematics.

9. **scipy.io**: Input and output functions for various file formats. Example to demonstrate how to save and load data in the NumPy array format using scipy.io.

```
import numpy as np
from scipy.io import savemat, loadmat

# Example 1: Save data to a MATLAB file (.mat)
data = {
    'x': np.arange(0, 10),
    'y': np.sin(np.arange(0, 10))
}

# Save the data to a MATLAB file
savemat('data.mat', data)

# Example 2: Load data from a MATLAB file (.mat)
loaded_data = loadmat('data.mat')

# Access the loaded data
x_loaded = loaded_data['x']
y_loaded = loaded_data['y']
```

```
# Print the loaded data
print("Loaded x:", x_loaded)
print("Loaded y:", y_loaded)
```

```
In [74]:  import numpy as np
          from scipy.io import savemat, loadmat

          # Example 1: Save data to a MATLAB file (.mat)
          data = {
                'x': np.arange(0, 10),
                'y': np.sin(np.arange(0, 10))
          }

          # Save the data to a MATLAB file
          savemat('data.mat', data)

          # Example 2: Load data from a MATLAB file (.mat)
          loaded_data = loadmat('data.mat')

          # Access the loaded data
          x_loaded = loaded_data['x']
          y_loaded = loaded_data['y']

          # Print the loaded data
          print("Loaded x:", x_loaded)
          print("Loaded y:", y_loaded)
          Loaded x: [[ 0 1, 2, 3, 4, 5, 6, 7, 8, 9]]
          Loaded y: [[0.   0.84147098   0.90929743   0.14112001   -0.7568025   -0.95892427
                   -0.2794155   0.6569866   0.98935825   -0.41211849]]
```

Here,

- We create a dictionary data containing two NumPy arrays x and y.
- We use scipy.io.savemat to save this data to a MATLAB file named data.mat.
- We then use scipy.io.loadmat to load the data from the data.mat file into a new variable loaded_data, which is returned as a dictionary.
- We access the loaded data by indexing the dictionary with the appropriate keys ('x' and 'y') and store them in variables x_loaded and y_loaded.
- Finally, we print the loaded data to verify that it matches the original data.

Scipy complements NumPy by providing more advanced and specialized numerical algorithms. It is a powerful library for scientific computing and research in various domains like physics, engineering, economics, data analysis, and machine learning.

To use Scipy, you need to install it first. You can install it using pip:

pip install scipy

Once installed, you can import and use the desired submodules and functions in your Python code. For example:

```
import numpy as np
import scipy.linalg as la

# Example of matrix inversion
A = np.array([[1, 2], [3, 4]])
inv_A = la.inv(A)
print("Inverse of A:")
print(inv_A)
```

```
In [24]:  import numpy as np
          import scipy.linalg as la

In [25]:  # Example of matrix inversion
          A = np.array([[1, 2], [3, 4]])
          inv_A = la.inv(A)
          print("Inverse of A:")
          print(inv_A)
          Inverse of A:
          [[-2.   1. ]
           [1.5  -0.5]]
```

```
# Example of integration
from scipy.integrate import quad

result, _ = quad(np.sin, 0, np.pi/2)
print("Integration of sin(x) from 0 to pi/2:", result)
```

```
In [26]:  # Example of integration
          from scipy.integrate import quad
          result, _ = quad(np.sin, 0, np.pi/2)
          print("Integration of sin(x) from 0 to pi/2:", result)
          Integration of sin(x) from 0 to pi/2: 0.9999999999999999
```

```
# Example of optimization
from scipy.optimize import minimize

# Define a function to minimize
def func(x):
    return (x[0] - 2) ** 2 + (x[1] - 3) ** 2
```

```
# Minimize the function
res = minimize(func, [0, 0])
print("Minimum value:", res.fun)
print("Optimal parameters:", res.x)
```

```
In [27]:  # Example of optimization
          from scipy.optimize import minimize
          # Define a function to minimize
          def func(x):
          return (x[0] - 2) ** 2 + (x[1] - 3) ** 2
```

```
In [28]:  # Minimize the function
          res = minimize(func, [0, 0])
          print("Minimum value:", res.fun)
          print("Optimal parameters:", res.x)
```

Scipy library has extensive documentation, so be sure to check the official Scipy documentation for more detailed information and examples: https://docs.scipy.org/doc/scipy/reference/

REVIEW QUESTIONS

Q.1. What is the Scikit-learn library and what are its main functionalities?

Ans. Scikit-learn is a machine learning library in Python that provides simple and efficient tools for data mining and data analysis. It is built on top of other scientific computing libraries such as NumPy, SciPy, and Matplotlib. Scikit-learn offers a wide range of supervised and unsupervised learning algorithms for classification, regression, clustering, dimensionality reduction, and model selection. Additionally, it provides utilities for data preprocessing, model evaluation, and performance metrics, making it a comprehensive tool for machine learning tasks.

Q.2. Describe the main components of the Scikit-learn library.

Ans. The main components of the Scikit-learn library include:

Estimators: These are objects that implement the main API for building and fitting models. Estimators can be classifiers, regressors, or clustering algorithms, and they have methods such as fit() for training the model and predict() for making predictions.

Transformers: Transformers are used for preprocessing data, such as feature scaling, normalization, and imputation of missing values. They typically have fit() and transform() methods to learn parameters from training data and apply transformations to new data.

Pipelines: Pipelines allow chaining together multiple transformers and estimators into a single workflow, enabling seamless preprocessing and model training.

Model Selection: Scikit-learn provides utilities for model selection and hyperparameter tuning, such as cross-validation, grid search, and randomized search.

Metrics: The library offers a wide range of metrics for evaluating model performance, including accuracy, precision, recall, F1-score, mean squared error, and many others.

Q.3. What is the SciPy library and how does it relate to Scikit-learn?

Ans. SciPy is an open-source library in Python for scientific and technical computing. It builds on top of NumPy and provides additional functionality for optimization, integration, interpolation, linear algebra, signal processing, and more. While Scikit-learn focuses specifically on machine learning algorithms and tools, SciPy provides a broader set of scientific computing tools that can be used in conjunction with Scikit-learn. For example, SciPy's optimization algorithms can be useful for tuning hyperparameters in machine learning models, and its linear algebra routines can be used for tasks such as solving systems of equations or performing matrix decompositions. Overall, SciPy complements Scikit-learn by providing additional capabilities for scientific computing tasks beyond machine learning.

Multiple Choice Questions

Q.1. What is the primary purpose of scikit-learn?

(*a*) Data manipulation and analysis
(*b*) Deep learning
(*c*) Machine learning
(*d*) Natural language processing

Q.2. Which of the following algorithms is NOT included in scikit-learn?

(*a*) Linear Regression
(*b*) Decision Trees
(*c*) Convolutional Neural Networks
(*d*) Support Vector Machines

Q.3. What is the primary function of the fit() method in scikit-learn?

(*a*) To make predictions
(*b*) To transform data
(*c*) To train a model
(*d*) To evaluate a model

Q.4. Which scikit-learn module is used for data preprocessing, such as scaling features?

(*a*) sklearn.preprocessing
(*b*) sklearn.model_selection
(*c*) sklearn.metrics
(*d*) sklearn.feature_extraction

Q.5. Which of the following is NOT a metric for evaluating classification models in scikit-learn?

(*a*) Mean Absolute Error
(*b*) Accuracy
(*c*) Precision
(*d*) F1 Score

Q.6. What is the purpose of the GridSearchCV class in scikit-learn?

(*a*) To perform grid search for hyperparameter tuning
(*b*) To perform cross-validation
(*c*) To split the dataset into training and testing sets
(*d*) To fit a machine learning model

Q.7. Which scikit-learn module is used for feature extraction from text data?

(*a*) sklearn.preprocessing
(*b*) sklearn.feature_extraction
(*c*) sklearn.feature_selection
(*d*) sklearn.decomposition

Q.8. What is the purpose of the fit_transform() method in scikit-learn?

(*a*) To fit a model and transform data simultaneously
(*b*) To fit a model
(*c*) To transform data
(*d*) To evaluate a model

Q.9. Which scikit-learn module is used for unsupervised learning algorithms?

(*a*) sklearn.linear_model
(*b*) sklearn.ensemble
(*c*) sklearn.cluster
(*d*) sklearn.neighbors

Q.10. What is the purpose of the predict() method in scikit-learn?

(*a*) To train a model
(*b*) To transform data
(*c*) To make predictions
(*d*) To evaluate a model

Q.11. Which of the following is NOT a clustering algorithm available in scikit-learn?

(*a*) K-means
(*b*) Hierarchical Clustering
(*c*) DBSCAN
(*d*) Random Forest

Q.12. What is the purpose of the train_test_split() function in scikit-learn?

(*a*) To split the dataset into training and testing sets
(*b*) To fit a model
(*c*) To perform hyperparameter tuning
(*d*) To perform cross-validation

Q.13. Which scikit-learn module is used for ensemble learning algorithms?

(*a*) sklearn.linear_model
(*b*) sklearn.ensemble
(*c*) sklearn.cluster
(*d*) sklearn.neighbors

Q.14. What is the purpose of the cross_val_score() function in scikit-learn?

(*a*) To perform feature selection
(*b*) To perform hyperparameter tuning
(*c*) To perform cross-validation
(*d*) To make predictions

Q.15. Which scikit-learn module is used for model evaluation metrics?

(*a*) sklearn.preprocessing
(*b*) sklearn.model_selection
(*c*) sklearn.metrics
(*d*) sklearn.feature_extraction

Q.16. What is the primary purpose of the fit() method in a scikit-learn transformer?

(*a*) To make predictions (*b*) To transform data (*c*) To train a model (*d*) To evaluate a model

Q.17. Which scikit-learn module is used for linear models?

(*a*) sklearn.linear_model
(*b*) sklearn.ensemble
(*c*) sklearn.cluster
(*d*) sklearn.neighbors

Q.18. What is the purpose of the score() method in scikit-learn?

(*a*) To fit a model
(*b*) To transform data
(*c*) To make predictions
(*d*) To evaluate a model

Q.19. Which scikit-learn module is used for support vector machines?

(*a*) sklearn.linear_model
(*b*) sklearn.ensemble
(*c*) sklearn.svm
(*d*) sklearn.neighbors

Q.20. What is the purpose of the transform() method in a scikit-learn transformer?

(*a*) To make predictions
(*b*) To transform data
(*c*) To train a model
(*d*) To evaluate a model

Answer to Multiple Choice Questions

1. (*c*) **2.** (*c*) **3.** (*c*) **4.** (*a*) **5.** (*a*) **6.** (*a*) **7.** (*b*) **8.** (*a*) **9.** (*c*)
10. (*c*) **11.** (*d*) **12.** (*a*) **13.** (*b*) **14.** (*c*) **15.** (*c*) **16.** (*c*) **17.** (*a*) **18.** (*d*)
19. (*c*) **20.** (*b*)

□□□

5

DATA MANIPULATION

DATA MANIPULATION

Data transformation and modification to improve its suitability for analysis, visualization, and other data-related tasks is referred to as data manipulation. Data is filtered, sorted, aggregated, merged, reshaped, and cleaned, among other activities. Data manipulation is a crucial step in the data analysis workflow, as it helps to prepare the data for further processing and gain meaningful insights.

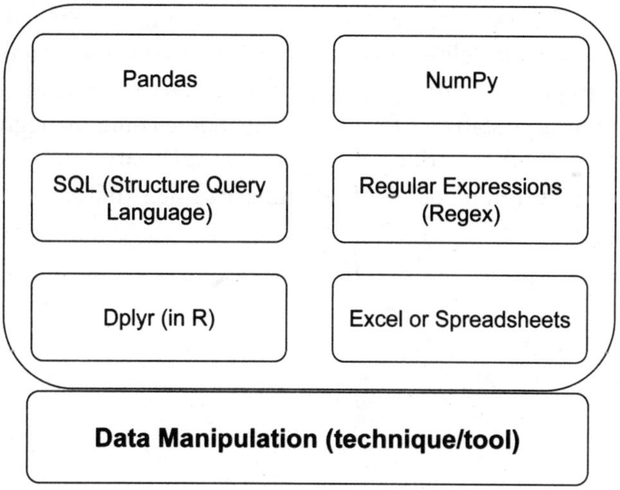

Fig. 5.1: Common Techniques and tools for Data Manipulation

Here are some common techniques and tools for data manipulation:

(a) Pandas: Pandas is a potent Python package for handling and analyzing data. It offers two main data structures for processing structured data, DataFrame and Series.

(b) NumPy: NumPy is another essential library for data manipulation, especially when working with numerical data in arrays.

(c) SQL (Structured Query Language): For data stored in databases, SQL is a powerful language for data manipulation. You can use SQL queries to filter, sort, and aggregate data directly within databases.

(d) **Regular Expressions (Regex):** Regular expressions are helpful for pattern matching and string manipulation, making them valuable when dealing with unstructured text data.

(e) **Dplyr (in R):** If you are working in R, the dplyr package provides an efficient and user-friendly set of tools for data manipulation tasks similar to Pandas in Python.

(f) **Excel or Spreadsheets:** For simple data manipulation tasks, spreadsheets like Microsoft Excel or Google Sheets can be useful tools.

Data manipulation is often an iterative process, and data analysts and data scientists frequently perform multiple operations to clean, reshape, and transform data until it's ready for analysis. Understanding data manipulation techniques and using the appropriate tools can significantly streamline the data analysis workflow and lead to more accurate and insightful results.

GROUP SUMMARIES

Group summaries, also known as aggregations, involve calculating summary statistics or metrics for subsets of data grouped based on one or more categorical variables. It is a common data manipulation technique used in data analysis to gain insights into specific groups within a dataset. Python's Pandas library provides powerful tools for performing group summaries efficiently. Here's how you can perform group summaries using Pandas:

(a) **Loading Data**: Fill a Pandas DataFrame with your data. The DataFrame needs columns for grouping by and columns for numeric data that you want to compute summary statistics for.

(b) **Grouping Data**: Use the groupby() function to group the data based on one or more columns. The groupby() function splits the DataFrame into groups based on the specified column(s).

(c) **Applying Aggregations:** After grouping the data, you can apply various aggregation functions to calculate summary statistics for each group. Some common aggregation functions include sum(), mean(), median(), count(), min(), max(), std(), var(), and describe().

Example: Here is an illustration of a group summary using Pandas:

```
import pandas as pd
# Sample data
data = {
    'Category': ['A', 'N', 'A', 'N', 'A', 'N'],
'Value': [10, 20, 30, 15, 25, 18]
}

# Create a DataFrame
df = pd.DataFrame(data)

# Group by 'Category' and calculate mean and sum for each group
grouped_df = df.groupby('Category').agg({
    'Value': ['mean', 'sum']
})

print(grouped_df)
```

```
In [1]:  import pandas as pd
         # Sample data
         data = {
               'Category': ['A', 'N', 'A', 'N', 'A', 'N'],
               'Value': [10, 20, 30, 15, 25, 18]
         }

In [2]:  # Create a DataFrame
         df = pd.DataFrame(data)

In [3]:  # Group by 'Category' and calculate mean and sum for each group
         grouped_df = df.groupby('Category').agg({
               'Value': ['mean', 'sum']
         })
         print(grouped_df)
                        value
                  mean          sum
         Category
         A        21.666667     65
         N        17.66667      53
```

In this example, we divided the data into groups based on the 'Category' column, and for each group, we computed the mean and total of the 'Value' column. The summary statistics for each category are contained in the resulting DataFrame, grouped_df.

Group summaries are valuable for comparing different groups, understanding the distribution of data within groups, and identifying patterns or trends in the data. By leveraging the groupby() function and various aggregation functions in Pandas, you can perform efficient and insightful group summaries for your data analysis tasks.

CROSSTAB, PIVOT AND RESHAPE DATA

Crosstab, pivot, and reshaping are data manipulation techniques used to restructure data for better analysis and presentation. These methods are frequently used in Python utilizing Pandas, a potent data manipulation and analysis tool.

5.1 CROSSTAB

A crosstab, short for cross-tabulation, is used to compute a frequency table of two or more variables. It shows how data is distributed across several categories, making it simpler to compare and understand how different variables relate to one another.

```
import pandas as pd
# Sample data
data = {
    'Category': ['A', 'N', 'A', 'N', 'A', 'N'],
```

```
    'Value': [10, 20, 30, 15, 25, 18]
}

# Create a DataFrame
df = pd.DataFrame(data)

# Perform crosstab
cross_tab = pd.crosstab(df['Category'], df['Value'])

print(cross_tab)
```

```
In [6]:   import pandas as pd

          # Sample data
          data = {
                'Category': ['A', 'N', 'A', 'N', 'A', 'N'],
                'Value': [10, 20, 30, 15, 25, 18]
          }

          # Create a DataFrame
          df = pd.DataFrame(data)

          # Perform crosstab
          cross_tab = pd.crosstab(df['Category'], df['Value'])

          print(cross_tab)

          Value     10   15   18   20   25   30
          Category
          A          1    0    0    0    1    1
          N          0    1    1    1    0    0
```

In this example, we created a crosstab to show the frequency of each 'Value' in each 'Category.'

5.2 PIVOT

Pivoting is a technique to reshape data by converting rows into columns and vice versa. It is helpful when you want to transform long-format data into wide-format or vice versa, making it easier to analyze and visualize data.

```
import pandas as pd

# Create a DataFrame
df = pd.DataFrame({'team': ['A', 'A', 'B', 'B'],
    'position': ['G', 'F', 'G', 'F'],
```

```
    'points': [11, 13, 11, 8]})
print(df)

# Perform pivot
pivot_df = df.pivot_table(index='team', columns='position', values='points', aggfunc='sum')
print(pivot_df)
```

```
In [17]:  import pandas as pd

          # Create a DataFrame
          df = pd.DataFrame({'team': ['A', 'A', 'B', 'B'],
                'position': ['G', 'F', 'G', 'F'],
                'points': [11, 13, 11, 8]})

In [18]:  print(df)
             team    position    points
          0    A        G          11
          1    A        F          13
          2    B        G          11
          3    B        F           8

In [19]:  # Perform pivot
          pivot_df = df.pivot_table(index='team', columns='position', values='points',
          aggfunc='sum')
          print(pivot_df)
          position    F    G
          team
          A          13   11
          B           8   11
```

In this example, we pivoted the data to display 'position' as columns, and 'team' as the index, with corresponding 'points' for each combination.

5.3 RESHAPE DATA

Pandas provides various functions for reshaping data, such as melt(), stack(), unstack(), and transpose(). These functions allow you to convert data between different formats to suit your analysis requirements.

```
import pandas as pd
# Sample data
data = {
    'team': ['A', 'B'],
    'points_A': [11, 13],
    'points_B': [11, 8]
}
```

```
# Create a DataFrame
df = pd.DataFrame(data)

# Reshape data using melt
melted_df = pd.melt(df, id_vars='team', var_name='Variable', value_name='Value')

print(melted_df)
```

```
In [21]:  import pandas as pd

          # Sample data
          data = {
                'team': ['A', 'B'],
                'points_A': [11, 13],
                'points_B': [11, 8]
          }

          # Create a DataFrame
          df = pd.DataFrame(data)
          # Reshape data using melt
          melted_df = pd.melt(df, id_vars='team', var_name='Variable', value_name='Value')
          print(melted_df)
                team    variable    value
          0      A      points_A     11
          1      B      points_A     13
          2      A      points_B     11
          3      B      points_B      8
```

In this example, we used melt() to transform the data from wide-format to long-format.

MANAGING MISSING VALUES

Data preprocessing and analysis need careful management of missing values. Missing values are frequent in datasets from the real world and can occur for a variety of reasons, including incorrect data entry by the user, incorrect data collection, or corrupted data. The Pandas package for Python offers a number of strategies for handling missing values correctly. Several methods for utilizing Pandas to manage missing values:

(a) **Detecting Missing Values:** The isnull() and notnull() methods in Pandas can be used to find missing data in a DataFrame.
    Use df.isnull().sum() to count the number of missing values in each column.

```
import pandas as pd
```

```
# Sample DataFrame with some missing values
data = {
    'Name': ['Siddha', 'Charu', 'Prasiddha', None, 'Pihu'],
    'Age': [11, 14, None, 22, None],
    'City': ['Delhi', None, 'Panjab', 'Uttar Pradesh', 'Rajasthan']
}

df = pd.DataFrame(data)

# Using isnull() to detect missing values
print("DataFrame:")
print(df)
```

```
In [22]:  import pandas as pd

          # Sample DataFrame with some missing values
          data = {
              'Name': ['Siddha', 'Charu', 'Prasiddha', None, 'Pihu'],
              'Age': [11, 14, None, 22, None],
              'City': ['Delhi', None, 'Panjab', 'Uttar Pradesh', 'Rajasthan']
          }
          df = pd.DataFrame(data)

          # Using isnull() to detect missing values
          print("DataFrame:")
          print(df)

          DataFrame:
                  Name   Age           City
          0     Siddha  11.0          Delhi
          1      Charu  14.0           None
          2  Prasiddha   NaN         Punjab
          3       None  22.0  Uttar Pradesh
          4       Pihu   NaN      Rajasthan
```

```
# Check for missing values
print("\nUsing isnull():")
print(df.isnull())
```

```
In [23]:  # Check for missing values
          print("\nUsing isnull():")
          print(df.isnull())
```

```
Using isnull():
        Name    Age     City
0       False   False   False
1       False   False   True
2       False   True    False
3       True    False   False
4       False   True    False
```

```
# Using notnull() to detect non-missing values
print("\nUsing notnull():")
print(df.notnull())
```

```
In [24]: # Using notnull() to detect non-missing values
         print("\nUsing notnull():")
         print(df.notnull())

         Using notnull():
                 Name    Age     City
         0       True    True    True
         1       True    True    False
         2       True    False   True
         3       False   True    True
         4       True    False   True
```

Output:

```
DataFrame:
        Name        Age     City
0       Siddha      11.0    Delhi
1       Charu       14.0    None
2       Prasiddha   NaN     Punjab
3       None        22.0    Uttar Pradesh
4       Pihu        NaN     Rajasthan

Using isnull():
        Name    Age     City
0       False   False   False
1       False   False   True
2       False   True    False
3       True    False   False
4       False   True    False
```

Using notnull():

	Name	Age	City
0	True	True	True
1	True	True	False
2	True	False	True
3	False	True	True
4	True	False	True

(b) **Removing Missing Values:** Use dropna() to remove rows or columns containing missing values. Be cautious when using this method, as it can result in significant data loss. Example: df.dropna(axis=0) removes rows with any missing value, while df.dropna(axis=1) removes columns with any missing value.

```
import pandas as pd

# Sample DataFrame with some missing values
data = {
    'Name': ['Siddha', 'Charu', 'Prasiddha', None, 'Pihu'],
    'Age': [11, 14, None, 22, None],
    'City': ['Delhi', None, 'Panjab', 'Uttar Pradesh', 'Rajasthan']
}

df = pd.DataFrame(data)

# Using isnull() to detect missing values
print("DataFrame:")
print(df)
```

```
In [25]:  import pandas as pd

          # Sample DataFrame with some missing values
          data = {
              'Name': ['Siddha', 'Charu', 'Prasiddha', None, 'Pihu'],
              'Age': [11, 14, None, 22, None],
              'City': ['Delhi', None, 'Panjab', 'Uttar Pradesh', 'Rajasthan']
          }

          df = pd.DataFrame(data)

          # Using isnull() to detect missing values
          print("DataFrame:")
          print(df)
```

```
DataFrame:
        Name   Age           City
0     Siddha  11.0          Delhi
1      Charu  14.0           None
2  Prasiddha   NaN         Punjab
3       None  22.0  Uttar Pradesh
4       Pihu   NaN      Rajasthan
```

```
# Remove rows containing any missing value (default behavior)
df_dropna_rows = df.dropna()

print("\nDataFrame after dropping rows with missing values:")
print(df_dropna_rows)
```

```
In [26]: # Remove rows containing any missing value (default behavior)
         df_dropna_rows = df.dropna()
         print("\nDataFrame after dropping rows with missing values:")
         print(df_dropna_rows)

         DataFrame after dropping rows with missing values:
              Name   Age   City
         0  Siddha  11.0  Delhi
```

Output:

```
DataFrame:
        Name   Age           City
0     Siddha  11.0          Delhi
1      Charu  14.0           None
2  Prasiddha   NaN         Punjab
3       None  22.0  Uttar Pradesh
4       Pihu   NaN      Rajasthan

DataFrame after dropping rows with missing values:
     Name   Age   City
0  Siddha  11.0  Delhi
```

As you can see, the rows with index 1, 2, 3 and 4, which contain missing values, have been removed from the DataFrame.

If you want to remove columns containing any missing values, you can use the axis parameter:

```
# Remove columns containing any missing value
df_dropna_columns = df.dropna(axis=1)

print("\nDataFrame after dropping columns with missing values:")
print(df_dropna_columns)
```

In [27]:
```
# Remove columns containing any missing value
df_dropna_columns = df.dropna(axis=1)
print("\nDataFrame after dropping columns with missing values:")
print(df_dropna_columns)
```

```
DataFrame after dropping columns with missing values:
Empty DataFrame
Columns: [ ]
Index: [0, 1, 2, 3, 4]
```

Output:

```
DataFrame after dropping columns with missing values:
Empty DataFrame
Columns: []
Index: [0, 1, 2, 3, 4]
```

In this case, all column 'Name', 'Age' and 'City' contain missing values, so have been removed from the DataFrame.

Keep in mind that the dropna() method by default creates a new DataFrame and does not alter the existing DataFrame. The inplace=True argument can be used to change the DataFrame in place:

```
# Remove rows containing any missing value and modify the DataFrame in place
df.dropna(inplace=True)

print("\nDataFrame after dropping rows in place:")
print(df)
```

In [28]:
```
# Remove rows containing any missing value and modify the DataFrame in place
df.dropna(inplace=True)
print("\nDataFrame after dropping rows in place:")
print(df)
```

```
DataFrame after dropping rows in place:
     Name     Age    City
0    Siddha   11.0   Delhi
```

Output:

```
DataFrame after dropping rows in place:
     Name     Age    City
0    Siddha   11.0   Delhi
```

(c) **Filling Missing Values (Imputation):** To replace missing data with a given value or a statistical measure (mean, median, or mode), use the fillna() function. For instance, df.fillna(0) and df['column'] both fill in missing values with 0.The function fillna(df['column'].mean()) replaces missing values in a column with that column's mean.

```
# Fill missing values in 'Age' column with a specific value (e.g., 0)
df_filled_age = df['Age'].fillna(0)

print("\nDataFrame after filling missing values in 'Age' column:")
print(df_filled_age)
```

```
In [29]:  # Fill missing values in 'Age' column with a specific value (e.g., 0)
          df_filled_age = df['Age'].fillna(0)

          print("\nDataFrame after filling missing values in 'Age' column:")
          print(df_filled_age)

          DataFrame after filling missing values in 'Age' column:
          0  11.0
          Name: Age, dtype: float64
```

Output:

DataFrame after filling missing values in 'Age' column:
0 11.0
Name: Age, dtype: float64

You can see in the result that the value 0 was used to fill in the missing entries in the 'Age' column. Additionally, you can substitute the mean, median, or any other value for any missing variables. As an illustration, let's substitute the mean of the non-missing values for the missing values in the 'Age' column:

```
# Fill missing values in 'Age' column with the mean of non-missing values
mean_age = df['Age'].mean()
df_filled_age_mean = df['Age'].fillna(mean_age)

print("\nDataFrame after filling missing values in 'Age' column with mean:")
print(df_filled_age_mean)
```

```
In [30]:  # Fill missing values in 'Age' column with the mean of non-missing values
          mean_age = df['Age'].mean()
          df_filled_age_mean = df['Age'].fillna(mean_age)

          print("\nDataFrame after filling missing values in 'Age' column with mean:")
          print(df_filled_age_mean)

          DataFrame after filling missing values in 'Age' column:
          0  11.0
          Name: Age, dtype: float64
```

Output:

DataFrame after filling missing values in 'Age' column with mean:

```
0    11.0
Name: Age, dtype: float64
```

The mean of the non-missing values (11.0) has been used to fill in the gaps in the 'Age' column in this instance.

(d) **Interpolation:** In a time series or ordered dataset, Pandas offers interpolation methods like interpolate() to approximate missing values based on nearby values.

```
import pandas as pd
import numpy as np

# Sample DataFrame with some missing values
data = {
    'Date': pd.date_range('2023-07-01', periods=6, freq='D'),
    'Temperature': [15, None, 20, None, None, 40],
}

df = pd.DataFrame(data)

print("Original DataFrame:")
print(df)
```

```
In [31]:  import pandas as pd
          import numpy as np

          # Sample DataFrame with some missing values
          data = {
              'Date': pd.date_range('2023-07-01', periods=6, freq='D'),
              'Temperature': [15, None, 20, None, None, 40],
          }

          df = pd.DataFrame(data)

          print("Original DataFrame:")
          print(df)

          Original DataFrame:
                   Date   Temperature
          0  2023-07-01          15.0
          1  2023-07-02           NaN
          2  2023-07-03          20.0
          3  2023-07-04           NaN
          4  2023-07-04           NaN
          5  2023-07-06          40.0
```

```
# Interpolate missing values in the 'Temperature' column using linear interpolation
df_interpolated = df.interpolate(method='linear')

print("\nDataFrame after interpolating missing values:")
print(df_interpolated)
```

```
In [32]:  # Interpolate missing values in the 'Temperature' column using linear interpolation
          df_interpolated = df.interpolate(method='linear')

          print("\nDataFrame after interpolating missing values:")
          print(df_interpolated)

          DataFrame after interpolating missing values:
                   Date   Temperature
          0  2023-07-01     15.000000
          1  2023-07-02     17.500000
          2  2023-07-03     20.000000
          3  2023-07-04     26.666667
          4  2023-07-04     33.333333
          5  2023-07-06     40.000000
```

Output:

```
Original DataFrame:
        Date   Temperature
0  2023-07-01      15.0
1  2023-07-02      NaN
2  2023-07-03      20.0
3  2023-07-04      NaN
4  2023-07-05      NaN
5  2023-07-06      40.0

DataFrame after interpolating missing values:
        Date   Temperature
0  2023-07-01  15.000000
1  2023-07-02  17.500000
2  2023-07-03  20.000000
3  2023-07-04  26.666667
4  2023-07-05  33.333333
5  2023-07-06  40.000000
```

By applying linear interpolation between the current values, the missing values in the 'Temperature' column have been filled in this example. Based on the index and the column values, the interpolate() method determines the intermediate values.

(e) **Imputation using Scikit-learn:** Scikit-learn's SimpleImputer class allows for more advanced imputation strategies, such as using the mean / median / most frequent value, or a constant to replace missing values.

```
import pandas as pd
from sklearn.impute import SimpleImputer

# Sample DataFrame with some missing values
data = {
    'Age': [22, None, 31, 18, None, 34],
    'Salary': [30000, 50000, None, 40000, None, 51000],
}

df = pd.DataFrame(data)

print("Original DataFrame:")
print(df)
```

```
In [45]:  import pandas as pd
          from sklearn.impute import SimpleImputer

          # Sample DataFrame with some missing values
          data = {
              'Age': [22, None, 31, 18, None, 34],
              'Salary': [30000, 50000, None, 40000, None, 51000],
          }

          df = pd.DataFrame(data)

          print("Original DataFrame:")
          print(df)

          Original DataFrame:
               Age     Salary
          0    22.0    30000.0
          1    NaN     50000.0
          2    31.0    NaN
          3    18.0    40000.0
          4    NaN     NaN
          5    34.0    51000.0
```

```
# Initialize the SimpleImputer with strategy='mean' to fill missing values with the mean
imputer = SimpleImputer(strategy='mean')
```

```
# Fit the imputer on the DataFrame and perform imputation
df_imputed = pd.DataFrame(imputer.fit_transform(df), columns=df.columns)

print("\nDataFrame after imputation:")
print(df_imputed)
```

In [46]:
```
# Initialize the SimpleImputer with strategy='mean' to fill missing values with the mean
imputer = SimpleImputer(strategy='mean')

# Fit the imputer on the DataFrame and perform imputation
df_imputed = pd.DataFrame(imputer.fit_transform(df), columns=df.columns)

print("\nDataFrame after imputation:")
print(df_imputed)
```

```
DataFrame after imputation
     Age     Salary
0    22.00   30000.0
1    26.25   50000.0
2    31.00   42750.0
3    18.00   40000.0
4    26.25   42750.0
5    34.00   51000.0
```

Output:

```
Original DataFrame:
     Age     Salary
0    22.0    30000.0
1    NaN     50000.0
2    31.0    NaN
3    18.0    40000.0
4    NaN     NaN
5    34.0    51000.0
DataFrame after imputation:
     Age     Salary
0    22.00   30000.0
1    26.25   50000.0
2    31.00   42750.0
3    18.00   40000.0
4    26.25   42750.0
5    34.00   51000.0
```

In this example, we used strategy='mean', which filled the missing values with the mean of the respective columns. If you want to use another strategy, such as filling with the median or most frequent value, you can specify it in the SimpleImputer constructor using the strategy parameter. For example, to fill missing values with the median, you can use strategy='median':

```
# Initialize the SimpleImputer with strategy='median' to fill missing values with the median
imputer_median = SimpleImputer(strategy='median')

# Fit the imputer on the DataFrame and perform imputation with median
df_imputed_median = pd.DataFrame(imputer_median.fit_transform(df), columns=df.columns)

print("\nDataFrame after imputation with median:")
print(df_imputed_median)
```

In [47]:
```
# Initialize the SimpleImputer with strategy='median' to fill missing values with the median
imputer_median = SimpleImputer(strategy='median')

# Fit the imputer on the DataFrame and perform imputation with median
df_imputed_median = pd.DataFrame(imputer_median.fit_transform(df), columns=df.
columns)

print("\nDataFrame after imputation with median:")
print(df_imputed_median)
```

```
DataFrame after imputation with median:
   Age    Salary
0  22.0   30000.0
1  26.5   50000.0
2  31.0   45000.0
3  18.0   40000.0
4  26.5   45000.0
5  34.0   51000.0
```

Output:

```
DataFrame after imputation with median:
   Age    Salary
0  22.0   30000.0
1  26.5   50000.0
2  31.0   45000.0
3  18.0   40000.0
4  26.5   45000.0
5  34.0   51000.0
```

In this case, the missing values were filled with the median values of their respective columns. You can use the same approach to fill with the most frequent value or any constant value of your choice.

(f) **Indicator Variables (Dummy Variables):** If missing values have a specific meaning or are non-random, you can create indicator variables (also known as dummy variables) to represent the presence or absence of missing values.

```
import pandas as pd

# Sample DataFrame with categorical data
data = {
    'Gender': ['Male', 'Female', 'Male', 'Male', 'Female'],
    'City': ['Delhi', 'Uttar Pradesh', 'Panjab', 'Delhi', 'Uttar Pradesh']
}

df = pd.DataFrame(data)

print("Original DataFrame:")
print(df)
```

```
In [48]:  import pandas as pd

          # Sample DataFrame with categorical data
          data = {
              'Gender': ['Male', 'Female', 'Male', 'Male', 'Female'],
              'City': ['Delhi', 'Uttar Pradesh', 'Panjab', 'Delhi', 'Uttar Pradesh']
          }

          df = pd.DataFrame(data)

          print("Original DataFrame:")
          print(df)

          Original DataFrame:
              Gender          City
          0     Male         Delhi
          1   Female  Uttar Pradesh
          2     Male        Punjab
          3     Male         Delhi
          4   Female  Uttar Pradesh
```

```
# Create indicator variables for the 'Gender' column
gender_dummies = pd.get_dummies(df['Gender'], prefix='Gender')

# Create indicator variables for the 'City' column
city_dummies = pd.get_dummies(df['City'], prefix='City')
```

```
# Concatenate the original DataFrame with the indicator variables
df_with_dummies = pd.concat([df, gender_dummies, city_dummies], axis=1)

print("\nDataFrame with Indicator Variables:")
print(df_with_dummies)
```

```
In [49]:  # Create indicator variables for the 'Gender' column
          gender_dummies = pd.get_dummies(df['Gender'], prefix='Gender')

In [50]:  # Create indicator variables for the 'City' column
          city_dummies = pd.get_dummies(df['City'], prefix='City')

          # Concatenate the original DataFrame with the indicator variables
          df_with_dummies = pd.concat([df, gender_dummies, city_dummies], axis=1)

          print("\nDataFrame with Indicator Variables:")
          print(df_with_dummies)
          DataFrame with Indicator Variables:

             Gender          City  Gender_Female  Gender_Male  City_Delhi  City_Punjab/
          0    Male         Delhi              0            1           1             0
          1  Female  Uttar Pradesh             1            0           0             0
          2    Male        Punjab              0            1           0             1
          3    Male         Delhi              0            1           1             0
          4  Female  Uttar Pradesh             1            0           0             0

             City_Uttar Pradesh
          0                   0
          1                   1
          2                   0
          3                   0
          4                   1
```

Output:

```
Original DataFrame:
     Gender          City
0      Male         Delhi
1    Female  Uttar Pradesh
2      Male        Panjab
3      Male         Delhi
4    Female  Uttar Pradesh
```

```
DataFrame with Indicator Variables:
   Gender          City  Gender_Female  Gender_Male  City_Delhi  City_Punjab/
0    Male         Delhi              0            1           1             0
1  Female  Uttar Pradesh             1            0           0             0
2    Male        Punjab              0            1           0             1
3    Male         Delhi              0            1           1             0
4  Female  Uttar Pradesh             1            0           0             0

   City_Uttar Pradesh
0                   0
1                   1
2                   0
3                   0
4                   1
```

'Gender' and 'City' are two categorical columns in the DataFrame used in this example. For each distinct category in both columns, indicator variables were made using pd.get_dummies(). The new indicator variable column names can have a prefix added using the prefix argument. As you can see in the result, new binary columns are added to the 'Gender' and 'City' columns for each category. A 1 indicates the presence of a category, and a 0 indicates its absence.

(g) **Data Imputation Using Machine Learning Models:** Using machine learning models to forecast missing values based on the existing data is a sophisticated technique. When working with enormous datasets and intricate patterns of missingness, this is extremely helpful.

```
import pandas as pd
from sklearn.datasets import load_iris
from sklearn.model_selection import train_test_split
from sklearn.preprocessing import StandardScaler
from sklearn.impute import KNNImputer

# Load the Iris dataset
data = load_iris()
iris_df = pd.DataFrame(data.data, columns=data.feature_names)

# Introduce some missing values in the first 10 rows of the first two features (sepal length and sepal width)
iris_df.iloc[:10, :2] = None

print("Original DataFrame with missing values:")
print(iris_df.head())
```

```
In [51]:  import pandas as pd
          from sklearn.datasets import load_iris
          from sklearn.model_selection import train_test_split
          from sklearn.preprocessing import StandardScaler
          from sklearn.impute import KNNImputer

          # Load the Iris dataset
          data = load_iris()
          iris_df = pd.DataFrame(data.data, columns=data.feature_names)

          # Introduce some missing values in the first 10 rows of the first two features (sepal length
          and sepal width)
          iris_df.iloc[:10, :2] = None

          print("Original DataFrame with missing values:")
          print(iris_df.head())

          Original DataFrame with missing values:
             sepal length (cm)   sepal width (cm)   petal length (cm)   petal_width (cm)
          0        NaN                 NaN                1.4                 0.2
          1        NaN                 NaN                1.4                 0.2
          2        NaN                 NaN                1.3                 0.2
          3        NaN                 NaN                1.5                 0.2
          4        NaN                 NaN                1.4                 0.2

# Split the data into features (X) and target (y) for imputation
X = iris_df.iloc[:, 2:]
y = iris_df.iloc[:, :2]

# Split the data into training and testing sets
X_train, X_test, y_train, y_test = train_test_split(X, y, test_size=0.2, random_state=42)

# Standardize the features
scaler = StandardScaler()
X_train_scaled = scaler.fit_transform(X_train)
X_test_scaled = scaler.transform(X_test)

# Initialize the KNNImputer
knn_imputer = KNNImputer(n_neighbors=5)

# Fit the imputer on the training data and perform imputation
y_train_imputed = knn_imputer.fit_transform(y_train)
```

In [52]:
```
# Split the data into features (X) and target (y) for imputation
X = iris_df.iloc[:, 2:]
y = iris_df.iloc[:, :2]
```

In [53]:
```
# Split the data into training and testing sets
X_train, X_test, y_train, y_test = train_test_split(X, y, test_size=0.2, random_state=42)
```

In [54]:
```
# Standardize the features
scaler = StandardScaler()
X_train_scaled = scaler.fit_transform(X_train)
X_test_scaled = scaler.transform(X_test)

# Initialize the KNNImputer
knn_imputer = KNNImputer(n_neighbors=5)

# Fit the imputer on the training data and perform imputation
y_train_imputed = knn_imputer.fit_transform(y_train)

# Transform the test data using the fitted imputer
y_test_imputed = knn_imputer.transform(y_test)

# Create a DataFrame with the imputed values
y_train_imputed_df = pd.DataFrame(y_train_imputed, columns=y.columns)
y_test_imputed_df = pd.DataFrame(y_test_imputed, columns=y.columns)

# Concatenate the imputed target variables with the original features
X_train_imputed = pd.concat([X_train, y_train_imputed_df], axis=1)
X_test_imputed = pd.concat([X_test, y_test_imputed_df], axis=1)

print("\nDataFrame with imputed missing values:")
print(X_train_imputed.head())
```

In [56]:
```
# Transform the test data using the fitted imputer
y_test_imputed = knn_imputer.transform(y_test)

# Create a DataFrame with the imputed values
y_train_imputed_df = pd.DataFrame(y_train_imputed, columns=y.columns)
y_test_imputed_df = pd.DataFrame(y_test_imputed, columns=y.columns)

# Concatenate the imputed target variables with the original features
X_train_imputed = pd.concat([X_train, y_train_imputed_df], axis=1)
X_test_imputed = pd.concat([X_test, y_test_imputed_df], axis=1)
```

```
print("\nDataFrame with imputed missing values:")
print(X_train_imputed.head())

DataFrame with imputed missing values:
    petal length (cm)  petal width (cm)  sepal length (cm)  sepal width (cm)
22                1.0               0.2                5.6               3.0
15                1.5               0.4                5.5               2.4
65                4.4               1.4                5.5               2.5
11                1.6               0.2                6.0               3.4
42                1.3               0.2                6.0               3.0
```

Output:

```
Original DataFrame with missing values:
   sepal length (cm)  sepal width (cm)  petal length (cm)  petal_width (cm)
0                NaN               NaN                1.4               0.2
1                NaN               NaN                1.4               0.2
2                NaN               NaN                1.3               0.2
3                NaN               NaN                1.5               0.2
4                NaN               NaN                1.4               0.2
DataFrame with imputed missing values:
    petal length (cm)  petal width (cm)  sepal length (cm)  sepal width (cm)
22                1.0               0.2                5.6               3.0
15                1.5               0.4                5.5               2.4
65                4.4               1.4                5.5               2.5
11                1.6               0.2                6.0               3.4
42                1.3               0.2                6.0               3.0
```

In this example, the "sepal length (cm)" and "sepal width (cm)" columns of the Iris dataset initially had some missing values. The missing values were then predicted using the KNNImputer based on the other characteristics in the training set. In order to obtain the DataFrame with imputed missing values, we finally joined the imputed target variables and the original features.

Please note that imputing missing values using machine learning models can be computationally expensive and may not always yield better results than simpler methods like mean or median imputation.

Based on the characteristics of the data and the analysis you intend to do, you can choose the best strategy for handling missing values. To maintain data integrity and openness in your analysis, always remember to carefully consider the impact of handling missing values and record your procedure.

OUTLIERS DETECTION

Data points known as outliers are those that stand out from the majority of the data in a dataset. Detecting outliers is an essential step in data analysis as they can distort statistical analyses and machine learning models. Python offers various methods and libraries to identify outliers effectively. Here are some common techniques for outlier detection:

Visualizations: Boxplots, histograms, and scatter plots are useful tools for visually identifying potential outliers. Matplotlib and Seaborn libraries can be used to create these visualizations in Python.

Z-Score Method: The Z-score calculates a data point's standard deviation from the mean. Data points with Z-scores beyond a certain threshold (e.g., 2 or 3) can be considered outliers. NumPy and SciPy libraries provide functions to calculate Z-scores.

```
import pandas as pd

# Sample data with some outliers
data = {
    'Value': [5, 8, 16, 11, 13, 18, 9, 30, 17, 19, 500]
}

df = pd.DataFrame(data)

print("Original DataFrame:")
print(df)
```

```
In [60]:  import pandas as pd

          # Sample data with some outliers
          data = {
              'Value': [5, 8, 16, 11, 13, 18, 9, 30, 17, 19, 500]
          }

          df = pd.DataFrame(data)

          print("Original DataFrame:")
          print(df)

          Original DataFrame:
               Value
          0      5
          1      8
          2     16
          3     11
          4     13
          5     19
          6      9
          7     30
          8     17
          9     19
          10   500
```

```
# Calculate the Z-score for each data point in the 'Value' column
z_scores = (df['Value'] - df['Value'].mean()) / df['Value'].std()

# Define a threshold for outlier detection (e.g., Z-score greater than 3 or less than -3)
threshold = 3

# Create a boolean mask to identify outliers
outliers_mask = (z_scores.abs() > threshold)

# Filter the DataFrame to get the outliers
outliers_df = df[outliers_mask]

print("\nDataFrame with outliers:")
print(outliers_df)
```

```
In [61]:  # Calculate the Z-score for each data point in the 'Value' column
          z_scores = (df['Value'] - df['Value'].mean()) / df['Value'].std()

In [62]:  # Define a threshold for outlier detection (e.g., Z-score greater than 3 or less than -3)
          threshold = 3

          # Create a boolean mask to identify outliers
          outliers_mask = (z_scores.abs() > threshold)

          # Filter the DataFrame to get the outliers
          outliers_df = df[outliers_mask]
          print("\nDataFrame with outliers:")
          print(outliers_df)

          DataFrame with outliers:
                Value
          10    500
```

Output:

```
Original DataFrame:
     Value
0      5
1      8
2     16
3     11
4     13
5     19
```

```
6     9
7     30
8     17
9     19
10    500
DataFrame with outliers:
      Value
10    500
```

In this example, we have a DataFrame with a 'Value' column containing some outliers (500 is an extreme outlier compared to the other values). Every data point in the 'Value' column is given a Z-score, and we utilize a 3 point threshold to identify outliers. An outlier is any data point with a Z-score larger than 3 or lower than -3.

The outliers_df DataFrame contains the detected outliers. You can choose a different threshold or use other methods for outlier detection based on your specific data and problem requirements.

Please be aware that the Z-score approach relies on the data's normal distribution and is sensitive to that distribution. Other techniques, such as the IQR (Interquartile Range) or the modified Z-score, might be more suitable for outlier discovery for non-normally distributed data.

Modified Z-Score Method (MAD): A reliable substitute for the standard deviation that is less susceptible to outliers is the median absolute deviation (MAD). Outliers are data points with MAD values greater than a predetermined threshold.

```
import pandas as pd

# Sample data with some outliers
data = {
    'Value': [5, 8, 16, 11, 13, 18, 9, 30, 17, 19, 500]
}

df = pd.DataFrame(data)

print("Original DataFrame:")
print(df)

# Calculate the median and Median Absolute Deviation (MAD) for the 'Value' column
median_value = df['Value'].median()
mad_value = (df['Value'] - median_value).abs().median()

# Define a threshold for outlier detection (e.g., Modified Z-score greater than 3.5)
threshold = 3.5

# Calculate the Modified Z-score for each data point in the 'Value' column
modified_z_scores = 0.6745 * (df['Value'] - median_value) / mad_value
```

```
# Create a boolean mask to identify outliers
outliers_mask = (modified_z_scores.abs() > threshold)

# Filter the DataFrame to get the outliers
outliers_df = df[outliers_mask]

print("\nDataFrame with outliers (detected using Modified Z-Score Method):")
print(outliers_df)
```

In [64]:
```
# Calculate the median and Median Absolute Deviation (MAD) for the 'Value' column
median_value = df['Value'].median()
mad_value = (df['Value'] - median_value).abs().median()
```

In [65]:
```
# Define a threshold for outlier detection (e.g., Modified Z-score greater than 3.5)
threshold = 3.5

# Calculate the Modified Z-score for each data point in the 'Value' column
modified_z_scores = 0.6745 * (df['Value'] - median_value) / mad_value

# Create a boolean mask to identify outliers
outliers_mask = (modified_z_scores.abs() > threshold)

# Filter the DataFrame to get the outliers
outliers_df = df[outliers_mask]

print("\nDataFrame with outliers (detected using Modified Z-Score Method):")
print(outliers_df)
```

```
DataFrame with outliers (detected using Modified Z-Score Method):
      Value
10    500
```

Output:

```
Original DataFrame:
    Value
0     5
1     8
2    16
3    11
4    13
5    19
6     9
7    30
```

```
8       17
9       19
10      500
DataFrame with outliers (detected using Modified Z-Score Method):
        Value
10      500
```

In this example, we have a DataFrame with a 'Value' column containing some outliers (500 is an extreme outlier compared to the other values). We calculate the median and MAD for the 'Value' column and use a threshold of 3.5 to identify outliers. Any data point with a Modified Z-score greater than 3.5 or less than -3.5 is considered an outlier. The outliers_df DataFrame contains the detected outliers. The Modified Z-Score Method is more robust to outliers compared to the standard Z-score method, making it suitable for datasets with skewed or heavy-tailed distributions.

Interquartile Range (IQR) Method: The interval between the 25th and 75th percentiles of the data (Q1 and Q3) is known as the IQR. Outliers are data points that fall outside the normal distribution (Q1 - 1.5 * IQR, Q3 + 1.5 * IQR). Pandas has the cut() method to identify outliers and the quantile() tool to determine percentiles.

```
import pandas as pd

# Sample data with some outliers
data = {
    'Value': [5, 8, 16, 11, 13, 18, 9, 30, 17, 19, 500]
}

df = pd.DataFrame(data)

print("Original DataFrame:")
print(df)

# Calculate the first quartile (Q1), third quartile (Q3), and IQR for the 'Value' column
Q1 = df['Value'].quantile(0.25)
Q3 = df['Value'].quantile(0.75)
IQR = Q3 - Q1
print(IQR)
```

```
In [70]:  Calculate the first quartile (Q1), third quartile (Q3), and IQR for the 'Value' column
          Q1 = df['Value'].quantile(0.25)
          Q3 = df['Value'].quantile(0.75)
          IQR = Q3 - Q1
          print(IQR)

          # Define the Lower bound and upper bound for outlier detection
          lower_bound = Q1 – 1.5 * IQR
```

```
upper_bound = Q3 + 1.5 * IQR
8.5
```

```
# Define the lower bound and upper bound for outlier detection
lower_bound = Q1 - 1.5 * IQR
upper_bound = Q3 + 1.5 * IQR

# Create a boolean mask to identify outliers
outliers_mask = (df['Value'] < lower_bound) | (df['Value'] > upper_bound)

# Filter the DataFrame to get the outliers
outliers_df = df[outliers_mask]

print("\nDataFrame with outliers (detected using IQR Method):")
print(outliers_df)
```

```
In [71]:  # Create a boolean mask to identify outliers
          outliers_mask = (df['Value'] < lower_bound) | (df['Value'] > upper_bound)

          # Filter the DataFrame to get the outliers
          outliers_df = df[outliers_mask]

          print("\nDataFrame with outliers (detected using IQR Method):")
          print(outliers_df)

          DataFrame with outliers (detection using IQR Method):
                Value
          10    500
```

Output:

```
Original DataFrame:
      Value
0     5
1     8
2     16
3     11
4     13
5     19
6     9
7     30
8     17
9     19
10    500
8.5
```

```
DataFrame with outliers (detected using IQR Method):
    Value
10  500
```

In this example, the 'Value' column of a DataFrame contains some outliers (500 is a particularly extreme outlier in comparison to the other values). For the 'Value' column, we compute the first quartile (Q1), third quartile (Q3), and IQR. Then, we establish Q1 - 1.5 * IQR and Q3 + 1.5 * IQR, respectively, as the lower bound and upper bound for outlier detection. An outlier is a data point that deviates from either the lower or upper bound.

The identified outliers are contained in the outliers_df DataFrame. In comparison to the Z-score method, the IQR Method is a reliable method for identifying outliers since it is less susceptible to extreme results.

Tukey's Fences: Tukey's method is similar to the IQR method but uses more stringent cutoffs (Q1 - 3 * IQR, Q3 + 3 * IQR) to identify outliers.

```
import pandas as pd

# Sample data with some outliers
data = {
    'Value': [5, 8, 16, 11, 13, 18, 9, 30, 17, 19, 500]
}

df = pd.DataFrame(data)

print("Original DataFrame:")
print(df)
```

```
In [72]:  import pandas as pd
          # Sample data with some outliers
          data = {
              'Value': [5, 8, 16, 11, 13, 18, 9, 30, 17, 19, 500]
          }

          df = pd.DataFrame(data)

          print("Original DataFrame:")
          print(df)

          Original DataFrame:
              Value
          0   5
          1   8
          2   16
          3   11
```

```
4    13
5    19
6    9
7    30
8    17
9    19
10   500
```

```
# Calculate the first quartile (Q1) and third quartile (Q3) for the 'Value' column
Q1 = df['Value'].quantile(0.25)
Q3 = df['Value'].quantile(0.75)
print(Q1)
print(Q3)
```

```
In [74]:  # Calculate the first quartile (Q1) and third quartile (Q3) for the 'Value' column
          Q1 = df['Value'].quantile(0.25)
          Q3 = df['Value'].quantile(0.75)
          print(Q1)
          print(Q3)
          10.0
          18.5
```

```
# Define the inner and outer fences for outlier detection
inner_fence_lower = Q1 - 1.5 * (Q3 - Q1)
inner_fence_upper = Q3 + 1.5 * (Q3 - Q1)
outer_fence_lower = Q1 - 3.0 * (Q3 - Q1)
outer_fence_upper = Q3 + 3.0 * (Q3 - Q1)

# Create a boolean mask to identify mild outliers (between inner fences) and extreme outliers (outside outer fences)
mild_outliers_mask = (df['Value'] < inner_fence_lower) | (df['Value'] > inner_fence_upper)
extreme_outliers_mask = (df['Value'] < outer_fence_lower) | (df['Value'] > outer_fence_upper)

# Filter the DataFrame to get mild outliers and extreme outliers
mild_outliers_df = df[mild_outliers_mask]
extreme_outliers_df = df[extreme_outliers_mask]

print("\nDataFrame with mild outliers (detected using Tukey's Fences):")
print(mild_outliers_df)

print("\nDataFrame with extreme outliers (detected using Tukey's Fences):")
print(extreme_outliers_df)
```

In [75]:
```
# Define the inner and outer fences for outlier detection
inner_fence_lower = Q1 - 1.5 * (Q3 - Q1)
inner_fence_upper = Q3 + 1.5 * (Q3 - Q1)
outer_fence_lower = Q1 - 3.0 * (Q3 - Q1)
outer_fence_upper = Q3 + 3.0 * (Q3 - Q1)
```

In [76]:
```
# Create a boolean mask to identify mild outliers (between inner fences) and extreme outliers (outside outer fences)
mild_outliers_mask = (df['Value'] < inner_fence_lower) | (df['Value'] > inner_fence_upper)
extreme_outliers_mask = (df['Value'] < outer_fence_lower) | (df['Value'] > outer_fence_upper)
```

In [77]:
```
# Filter the DataFrame to get mild outliers and extreme outliers
mild_outliers_df = df[mild_outliers_mask]
extreme_outliers_df = df[extreme_outliers_mask]
print("\nDataFrame with mild outliers (detected using Tukey's Fences):")
print(mild_outliers_df)
print("\nDataFrame with extreme outliers (detected using Tukey's Fences):")
print(extreme_outliers_df)
```

```
DataFrame with mild outliers (detected using Tukey's Fences):
    Value
10  500

DataFrame with extreme outliers (detected using Tukey's Fences):
    Value
10  500
```

Output:

Original DataFrame:

```
    Value
0     5
1     8
2    16
3    11
4    13
5    19
6     9
7    30
8    17
```

```
9       19
10      500
10.0
18.5
DataFrame with mild outliers (detected using Tukey's Fences):
      Value
10    500
DataFrame with extreme outliers (detected using Tukey's Fences):
      Value
10    500
```

In this example, the 'Value' column of a DataFrame contains some outliers (500 is a particularly extreme outlier in comparison to the other values). We determine the 'Value' column's first quartile (Q1) and third quartile (Q3). The inner and outer gates are therefore defined as Q1 - 1.5 * (Q3 - Q1) and Q3 + 1.5 * (Q3 - Q1), respectively, and Q1 - 3.0 * (Q3 - Q1) and Q3 + 3.0 * (Q3 - Q1).

Any data point outside the outer fences is regarded as a severe outlier, while any data point outside the lower inner fence or upper inner fence is regarded as a mild outlier.

Isolation Forest: Isolation Forest is a machine learning algorithm that separates outliers efficiently by building isolation trees. It's available in the scikit-learn library. Continue from previous data frame

```
from sklearn.ensemble import IsolationForest
# Initialize the Isolation Forest model
isolation_forest = IsolationForest(contamination=0.1)  # contamination represents the expected proportion of outliers

# Fit the model on the data
isolation_forest.fit(df)

# Predict outliers (1 represents inliers, -1 represents outliers)
outliers_prediction = isolation_forest.predict(df)

# Create a boolean mask to identify outliers
outliers_mask = (outliers_prediction == -1)

# Filter the DataFrame to get the outliers
outliers_df = df[outliers_mask]

print("\nDataFrame with outliers (detected using Isolation Forest):")
print(outliers_df)
```

In [79]:
```
from sklearn.ensemble import IsolationForest

# Initialize the Isolation Forest model
isolation_forest = IsolationForest(contamination=0.1) # contamination represents the
expected proportion of outliers

# Fit the model on the data
isolation_forest.fit(df)

# Predict outliers (1 represents inliers, -1 represents outliers)
outliers_prediction = isolation_forest.predict(df)

# Create a boolean mask to identify outliers
outliers_mask = (outliers_prediction == -1)

# Filter the DataFrame to get the outliers
outliers_df = df[outliers_mask]

print("\nDataFrame with outliers (detected using Isolation Forest):")
print(outliers_df)

DataFrame with outliers (detected using Isolation Forest):
      Value
10    500
```

Output:

DataFrame with outliers (detected using Isolation Forest):

```
    Value
10  500
```

In this example, we have a DataFrame with a 'Value' column containing some outliers (500 is an extreme outlier compared to the other values). We use the Isolation Forest algorithm to predict outliers. Setting the anticipated percentage of outliers in the data is done using the contamination parameter. In this case, we set it to 0.1 (10%), indicating that we expect approximately 10% of the data to be outliers. The outliers_df DataFrame contains the detected outliers.

Local Outlier Factor (LOF): A different machine learning approach called LOF uses the density of nearby data points to identify outliers. Additionally, Scikit-Learn has it. Assume we have a 2-dimensional point dataset:

Dataset:

(2, 3)

(3, 5)

(5, 8)

(7, 2)

(10, 12)

(12, 11)

(14, 15)

(16, 9)
(18, 13)

Step 1: Calculate the distance of each point to its k-nearest neighbors.
Let's choose k = 3 for this example.
Point (2, 3) has neighbors: (3, 5), (5, 8), (7, 2)
Point (3, 5) has neighbors: (2, 3), (5, 8), (7, 2)
Point (5, 8) has neighbors: (3, 5), (7, 2), (10, 12)
Point (7, 2) has neighbors: (2, 3), (3, 5), (5, 8)
Point (10, 12) has neighbors: (12, 11), (14, 15), (16, 9)
Point (12, 11) has neighbors: (10, 12), (14, 15), (16, 9)
Point (14, 15) has neighbors: (12, 11), (10, 12), (16, 9)
Point (16, 9) has neighbors: (18, 13), (14, 15), (12, 11)
Point (18, 13) has neighbors: (16, 9), (14, 15), (12, 11)

Step 2: Calculate the local reachability density (LRD) of each point.
LRD is the inverse of the average reachability distance of a point to its k-nearest neighbors.
LRD(2, 3) = 1 / ((3+4+8) / 3) ≈ 0.67
LRD(3, 5) = 1 / ((3+4+5) / 3) ≈ 0.75
LRD(5, 8) = 1 / ((3+5+9) / 3) ≈ 0.42
LRD(7, 2) = 1 / ((4+5+8) / 3) ≈ 0.40
LRD(10, 12) = 1 / ((3+7+9) / 3) ≈ 0.27
LRD(12, 11) = 1 / ((3+7+9) / 3) ≈ 0.27
LRD(14, 15) = 1 / ((3+7+9) / 3) ≈ 0.27
LRD(16, 9) = 1 / ((4+7+9) / 3) ≈ 0.25
LRD(18, 13) = 1 / ((4+7+9) / 3) ≈ 0.25

Step 3: Calculate the Local Outlier Factor (LOF) for each point.
LOF is the average ratio of the LRD of a point to the LRD of its k-nearest neighbors.
LOF(2, 3) = (0.67 / ((0.75+0.42+0.40) / 3)) ≈ 1.67
LOF(3, 5) = (0.75 / ((0.67+0.42+0.40) / 3)) ≈ 1.97
LOF(5, 8) = (0.42 / ((0.67+0.75+0.40) / 3)) ≈ 0.80
LOF(7, 2) = (0.40 / ((0.67+0.75+0.42) / 3)) ≈ 0.72
LOF(10, 12) = (0.27 / ((0.25+0.27+0.27) / 3)) ≈ 1.00
LOF(12, 11) = (0.27 / ((0.25+0.27+0.27) / 3)) ≈ 1.00
LOF(14, 15) = (0.27 / ((0.25+0.27+0.27) / 3)) ≈ 1.00
LOF(16, 9) = (0.25 / ((0.40+0.27+0.25) / 3)) ≈ 0.63
LOF(18, 13) = (0.25 / ((0.40+0.27+0.25) / 3)) ≈ 0.63

Step 4: Interpretation
Higher LOF values indicate that a data point is more likely to be an outlier. In this example, points (3, 5), (2, 3), and (10, 12) have higher LOF values, which means they are more likely to be outliers. Points (5, 8), (7, 2), (12, 11), (14, 15), (16, 9), and (18, 13) have LOF values close to 1, indicating that they are not outliers.

Keep in mind that the choice of k and the specific LOF threshold to consider a point as an outlier may vary depending on the dataset and the problem at hand

Robust Random Cut Forest (RRCF)

RRCF is a scalable, unsupervised algorithm for detecting outliers in streaming data. It's available through the rrcf library. RRCF is designed to detect anomalies in a more stable and reliable manner.

Step 1: Initialization

Set the number of trees (T) in the forest.

Set the tree size (T_size) for each tree.

Choose the desired threshold (threshold) for identifying outliers.

Step 2: Training

Suppose we have a streaming dataset of numerical data points:

Dataset:

[5, 7, 10]

[6, 8, 11]

[4, 7, 9]

[100, 95, 105] # Anomaly

[5, 9, 12]

[7, 8, 11]

[3, 6, 8]

[8, 10, 12]

Initialize the RRCF with the chosen parameters (T, T_size, threshold). Then, update the RRCF model with each new data point:

Train Tree 1 with the first T_size points (5, 7, 10, 100).

Train Tree 2 with the next T_size points (6, 8, 11, 95).

Train Tree 3 with the next T_size points (4, 7, 9, 105).

Train Tree 4 with the next T_size points (5, 9, 12, None).

Train Tree 5 with the next T_size points (7, 8, 11, None).

Train Tree 6 with the next T_size points (3, 6, 8, None).

Train Tree 7 with the next T_size points (8, 10, 12, None).

Step 3: Scoring and Detection

After training the RRCF with the specified number of trees, we can calculate the anomaly score for each data point using the RRCF model. The anomaly score represents how different a data point is compared to the majority of points in the forest.

To calculate the anomaly score of a new data point, we traverse the trees in the forest and measure the depth of the point in each tree. The average depth across all trees is used as the anomaly score. The deeper a point is in the trees, the more likely it is an outlier.

Let's assume the average depths of the anomaly (100, 95, 105) in each tree are as follows:

Tree 1: Depth 2

Tree 2: Depth 2

Tree 3: Depth 2
Tree 4: Depth 0
Tree 5: Depth 0
Tree 6: Depth 0
Tree 7: Depth 0
The average depth of the anomaly in the forest is (2 + 2 + 2 + 0 + 0 + 0 + 0) / 7 ≈ 0.57.

Step 4: Anomaly Detection

Compare the new data point's estimated anomaly score (100, 95, 105) to the selected threshold. The point is labeled as an outlier if the score is higher than the cutoff. If not, it is regarded as a typical data point.

In this example, let's assume the chosen threshold is 0.5. Since the average depth is 0.57, which is higher than the threshold, the point (100, 95, 105) is classified as an outlier.

Keep in mind that the actual implementation and fine-tuning of RRCF for a specific dataset may require adjusting hyperparameters and choosing an appropriate threshold based on domain knowledge and the characteristics of the data. The example provided above is simplified and intended to illustrate the general process of using RRCF for outlier detection.

When detecting outliers, it's essential to understand the context and domain knowledge. Not all outliers are necessarily errors; some could be valid data points representing unusual events or behaviors. Careful consideration and analysis are crucial before deciding to remove or handle outliers in any data analysis or modeling task.

MANAGING INDEXES IN PANDAS

In Pandas, indexes play a crucial role in data manipulation and analysis. The index in a DataFrame provides a label for each row and helps with fast data access, alignment, and merging operations. Pandas allows you to manage and manipulate indexes effectively using various methods and techniques. Here are some common operations for managing indexes in Pandas:

Setting a New Index: Using the set_index() method, you can choose a specific column to serve as the index. The specified column is used as the index in the new DataFrame that this function returns. Example: The function df.set_index('Column_Name', inplace=True) changes the index in the DataFrame df to be "Column_Name.".

Resetting the Index: The reset_index() method lets you return an index that has already been set to the integer-based default. An illustration is df.reset_index(inplace=True), which returns the default integer-based index in place for the DataFrame df.

Multi-Level Indexing: Pandas allows creating hierarchical or multi-level indexes using the MultiIndex class. This is useful for working with multi-dimensional data. Example: df.set_index(['Column1', 'Column2']) creates a multi-level index based on 'Column1' and 'Column2'.

Dropping the Index: You can remove the index and convert it back to a regular column using the reset_index() method with the drop=True parameter. Example: df.reset_index(drop=True, inplace=True) removes index and keeps original DataFrame intact.

Index Slicing and Selection: You can use the index to select rows or elements using the .loc[] and .iloc[] methods. Example: df.loc['index_label'] selects rows with the specified index label.

Conditional Indexing: You can use boolean conditions to perform conditional indexing on a DataFrame. Example: df[df['Column'] > 50] selects rows where value in 'Column' is greater than 50.

Sorting the Index: You can sort the DataFrame based on the index using the sort_index() method. Example: df.sort_index(ascending=False) sorts the DataFrame in descending order based on the index.

Managing indexes is essential for data alignment, joining, and merging operations in Pandas. By appropriately managing the index, you can improve the performance and efficiency of data manipulation and analysis tasks.

REVIEW QUESTIONS

Q.1. What is data manipulation, and what are some common techniques used in data manipulation?

Ans. Data manipulation refers to the process of transforming and restructuring data to make it more suitable for analysis or visualization. Common techniques used in data manipulation include:

Data Cleaning: This involves identifying and correcting errors or inconsistencies in the data, such as missing values, duplicate records, or outliers.

Data Transformation: Transformation techniques are used to modify the structure or format of the data. Examples include converting data types, scaling or normalizing variables, and encoding categorical variables.

Data Aggregation: Aggregation involves combining multiple data points into summary statistics or aggregating data across different groups or categories. This can include calculating means, sums, counts, or other summary statistics for groups of data.

Data Reshaping: Reshaping techniques are used to change the layout or structure of the data. This can involve pivoting data from long to wide format or vice versa, stacking or unstacking data, or merging datasets together.

Feature Engineering: Feature engineering involves creating new variables or features from existing ones to improve model performance or capture additional information. This can include creating interaction terms, polynomial features, or deriving new variables from existing ones.

Q.2. What are outliers in a dataset, and how can they be identified and handled?

Ans. Outliers are data points that significantly deviate from the rest of the dataset. They can occur due to errors in data collection, measurement errors, or genuine variability in the data. Outliers can have a disproportionate influence on statistical analyses or machine learning models, leading to biased results.

Identifying outliers typically involves visual inspection of the data using techniques such as box plots, histograms, or scatter plots. Statistical methods such as z-scores or interquartile range (IQR) can also be used to detect outliers based on their deviation from the mean or median of the dataset.

Once outliers are identified, they can be handled in several ways:

Removal: Outliers can be removed from the dataset if they are deemed to be the result of errors or anomalies. However, this approach should be used cautiously, as removing outliers can lead to loss of valuable information.

Transformation: Data transformation techniques such as log transformation or winsorization can be applied to mitigate the impact of outliers on the analysis.

Model-based Approaches: Some algorithms are robust to outliers or can handle them explicitly. For example, robust regression techniques or algorithms based on decision trees may be less sensitive to outliers.

Imputation: Outliers can be replaced with more representative values using imputation techniques such as mean, median, or predictive modeling.

Q.3. What is group summary in data analysis, and how is it performed?

Ans. Group summary, also known as group-wise summary or aggregation, involves calculating summary statistics for subsets or groups of data based on one or more grouping variables. This allows for the analysis of data at a more granular level and can reveal patterns or trends within different groups.

Group summary is typically performed using the following steps:

Grouping: The dataset is first divided into groups based on one or more categorical variables. This can be done using the groupby() function in libraries like pandas or by using SQL queries in databases.

Aggregation: Once the data is grouped, summary statistics are calculated for each group. Common summary statistics include means, medians, sums, counts, standard deviations, and percentiles.

Presentation: Finally, the aggregated results are presented in a format that is easy to interpret, such as tables, charts, or visualizations. This allows for comparisons between different groups and helps identify patterns or differences in the data.

Multiple Choice Questions

Q.1. What is data manipulation?

(*a*) The process of extracting data from a database
(*b*) The process of transforming and restructuring data to make it more suitable for analysis
(*c*) The process of visualizing data using charts and graphs
(*d*) The process of cleaning data to remove errors

Q.2. Which of the following is NOT a common technique used in data manipulation?

(*a*) Data cleaning
(*b*) Data transformation
(*c*) Data visualization
(*d*) Data aggregation

Q.3. What are outliers in a dataset?

(*a*) Data points that are close to the mean of the dataset
(*b*) Data points that significantly deviate from the rest of the dataset
(*c*) Data points that are missing from the dataset
(*d*) Data points that are duplicates

Q.4. How can outliers be identified in a dataset?

(*a*) By visual inspection using box plots or scatter plots
(*b*) By calculating the mean of the dataset
(*c*) By removing all data points with extreme values
(*d*) By sorting the dataset

Q.5. Which of the following is NOT a common method for handling outliers?

(*a*) Removing the outliers from the dataset
(*b*) Transforming the data using log transformation
(*c*) Replacing the outliers with the mean of the dataset
(*d*) Applying robust regression techniques

Q.6. What is group summary in data analysis?

(*a*) The process of summarizing data using descriptive statistics
(*b*) The process of identifying outliers in the data
(*c*) The process of grouping data based on categorical variables and calculating summary statistics for each group
(*d*) The process of visualizing data using charts and graphs

Q.7. How is group summary performed?

(*a*) By removing outliers from the dataset
(*b*) By calculating the mean of the entire dataset
(*c*) By grouping the data based on categorical variables and calculating summary statistics for each group
(*d*) By visual inspection using box plots

Q.8. Which of the following is a common summary statistic used in group summary?

(*a*) Mean (*b*) Median (*c*) Mode (*d*) All of the above

Q.9. Which Python library is commonly used for data manipulation?

(*a*) NumPy (*b*) TensorFlow (*c*) PyTorch (*d*) OpenCV

Q.10. Which Python library is commonly used for data visualization?

(*a*) NumPy (*b*) TensorFlow (*c*) Matplotlib (*d*) Scikit-learn

Q.11. Which Python library is commonly used for outlier detection?

(*a*) NumPy (*b*) Pandas (*c*) Scikit-learn (*d*) Seaborn

Q.12. Which Python library is commonly used for group summary?

(*a*) NumPy (*b*) Pandas (*c*) Matplotlib (*d*) Scikit-learn

Q.13. What does the term "transforming data" refer to?

(*a*) Changing the data type of the dataset
(*b*) Reshaping the dataset into a different format
(*c*) Scaling or normalizing the dataset
(*d*) All of the above

Q.14. Which of the following is a common method for scaling or normalizing data?

(*a*) Standardization (*b*) Normalization (*c*) Min-Max Scaling (*d*) All of the above

Q.15. What is the primary purpose of data aggregation?

(*a*) To clean the data (*b*) To visualize the data
(*c*) To summarize the data (*d*) To transform the data

Q.16. Which of the following is NOT a common technique used in data aggregation?

(*a*) Calculating the mean (*b*) Calculating the standard deviation
(*c*) Calculating the range (*d*) Calculating the mode

Q.17. What does the term "data cleaning" refer to?

(*a*) Removing outliers from the dataset
(*b*) Transforming the data into a different format
(*c*) Identifying and correcting errors or inconsistencies in the data
(*d*) Grouping the data based on categorical variables

Q.18. Which of the following is a common technique used in data transformation?

(*a*) Encoding categorical variables (*b*) Imputing missing values
(*c*) Scaling or normalizing variables (*d*) All of the above

Q.19. What is the purpose of encoding categorical variables?

(*a*) To remove outliers from the dataset

(*b*) To convert categorical variables into numerical format

(*c*) To calculate summary statistics for the dataset

(*d*) To group the data based on categorical variables

Q.20. Which of the following is NOT a common method for handling missing values?

(*a*) Removing the rows with missing values

(*b*) Imputing the missing values using the mean or median

(*c*) Encoding the missing values as a separate category

(*d*) Ignoring the missing values

Answer to Multiple Choice Questions

1. (*b*)	**2.** (*c*)	**3.** (*b*)	**4.** (*a*)	**5.** (*c*)	**6.** (*c*)	**7.** (*c*)	**8.** (*d*)	**9.** (*a*)
10. (*c*)	**11.** (*c*)	**12.** (*b*)	**13.** (*d*)	**14.** (*d*)	**15.** (*c*)	**16.** (*d*)	**17.** (*c*)	**18.** (*d*)
19. (*b*)	**20.** (*d*)							

❑❑❑

6

MODELING TECHNIQUES

SIMPLE LINEAR REGRESSION

A dependent variable (also known as the target or response variable) and an independent variable (also known as the predictor or feature variable) are intended to be linearly related in the Simple Linear Regression model. A straight line is used to depict the relationship and is fitted to the data points in order to reduce the sum of squared discrepancies between the actual value and the anticipated value. The straightforward linear regression equation appears as:

$$y = mx+b$$

where:

y is the dependent variable (target)

x is the independent variable (feature)

m is the slope of the line (also known as the coefficient or weight)

b is the y-intercept of the line (the value of y when x is 0)

Finding the best m and b values that reduce the discrepancy between the observed y values and those predicted by the linear equation is the objective of simple linear regression. Ordinary Least Squares (OLS), a common technique for accomplishing this, identifies the values of m and b that minimize the sum of squared residuals, or the vertical distances between the data points and the line.

Simple linear regression can be done using tools in Python's scikit-learn module. Here is a straightforward example of fitting a straightforward linear regression model to some sample data using Scikit-Learn.:

```
import numpy as np
from sklearn.linear_model import LinearRegression

# Sample data
X = np.array([1, 2, 3, 4, 5]).reshape(-1, 1)  # Independent variable (reshaped as a column vector)
y = np.array([3, 4, 2, 5, 6])            # Dependent variable

# Create a Linear Regression model
model = LinearRegression()
```

```
# Fit the model to the data
model.fit(X, y)

# Get the slope (coefficient) and y-intercept of the line
slope = model.coef_[0]
intercept = model.intercept_

# Predicting a new value
new_x = 6
predicted_y = model.predict(np.array(new_x).reshape(-1, 1))

print(f"Slope: {slope}")
print(f"Intercept: {intercept}")
print(f"Predicted value for {new_x}: {predicted_y[0]}")
```

In [1]:

```
import numpy as np
from sklearn.linear_model import LinearRegression

# Sample data
X = np.array([1, 2, 3, 4, 5]).reshape(-1, 1)  # Independent variable (reshaped as a column
vector)
y = np.array([3, 4, 2, 5, 6])          # Dependent variable

# Create a Linear Regression model
model = LinearRegression()

# Fit the model to the data
model.fit(X, y)

# Get the slope (coefficient) and y-intercept of the line
slope = model.coef_[0]
intercept = model.intercept_

# Predicting a new value
new_x = 6
predicted_y = model.predict(np.array(new_x).reshape(-1, 1))

print(f"Slope: {slope}")
print(f"Intercept: {intercept}")
print(f"Predicted value for {new_x}: {predicted_y[0]}")
```

```
C;\ProgramData\Anacondas\11b\site-packages\scipy\_init__.py:146: Userwarning:
A Numpy version >=1.16.5 and <1.23.9 is required for this version of Scipy (detected
version 1.25.0
    warning.warn(f"A NumPy version >=(np_minversion) and <(np_maxversion)"

Slope: 0.7000000000000002
Intercept: 1.8999999999999995
Predicted value for 6: 6.1000000000000005
```

Output:

Slope: 0.7000000000000002

Intercept: 1.8999999999999995

Predicted value for 6: 6.1000000000000005

A linear relationship between the variables is assumed by linear regression, which may not be appropriate for all types of data. You may need to investigate additional regression approaches, such as polynomial regression, multiple linear regression, or non-linear regression, if the relationship between the variables is more complex.

MULTIPLE LINEAR REGRESSION

As an extension of simple linear regression, multiple linear regression enables the modeling of the correlation between a dependent variable and a number of independent variables. When more than one predictor variable is influencing the target variable, it is employed. Finding the best-fit hyperplane, or higher-dimensional line, that minimizes the discrepancy between the actual and predicted values, is the objective of multiple linear regression. The formula for the multiple linear regression is:

$$y = b0 + b1 \cdot x1 + b2 \cdot x2 + \ldots + bn \cdot xn$$

$$y - b0 + b1 \cdot x1 + b2 \cdot x2 + \ldots + bn \cdot xn$$

where:

y is the dependent variable (target).

1, 2, …,x1,x2,…,xn are the independent variables (features).

b0 is the y intercept (the value of y when all x's are 0).

b1, b2, …,bn are the coefficients (slopes) representing the impact of each independent variable on the dependent variable.

A technique like Ordinary Least Squares (OLS), which reduces the sum of squared differences between the actual y values and the predicted y values from the linear equation, is used to estimate the coefficients b1, b2,...,bn in multiple linear regression.

Multiple linear regression can be done using simple functions from the scikit-learn package of Python. Here is a straightforward demonstration of how to train a multiple linear regression model to some sample data using Scikit-Learn.:

```
import numpy as np
from sklearn.linear_model import LinearRegression
```

```
# Sample data
X = np.array([[1, 2], [2, 3], [3, 4], [4, 5], [5, 6]]) # Independent variables (features)
y = np.array([3, 4, 2, 5, 6])                          # Dependent variable

# Create a Multiple Linear Regression model
model = LinearRegression()

# Fit the model to the data
model.fit(X, y)

# Get the coefficients (slopes) and y-intercept of the line
coefficients = model.coef_
intercept = model.intercept_

# Predicting a new value
new_x = np.array([6, 7]).reshape(1, -1)
predicted_y = model.predict(new_x)

print(f"Coefficients: {coefficients}")
print(f"Intercept: {intercept}")
print(f"Predicted value for {new_x}: {predicted_y[0]}")
```

```
In [2]:   import numpy as np
          from sklearn.linear_model import LinearRegression

          # Sample data
          X = np.array([[1, 2], [2, 3], [3, 4], [4, 5], [5, 6]]) # Independent variables (features)
          y = np.array([3, 4, 2, 5, 6])                          # Dependent variable

          # Create a Multiple Linear Regression model
          model = LinearRegression()

          # Fit the model to the data
          model.fit(X, y)

          # Get the coefficients (slopes) and y-intercept of the line
          coefficients = model.coef_
          intercept = model.intercept_

          # Predicting a new value
          new_x = np.array([6, 7]).reshape(1, -1)
          predicted_y = model.predict(new_x)
```

```
print(f"Coefficients: {coefficients}")
print(f"Intercept: {intercept}")
print(f"Predicted value for {new_x}: {predicted_y[0]}")
```

```
Coefficients: [0.35 0.35]
Intercept: 1.5499999999999998
Predicted value for [[6 7]]: 6.1000000000000005
```

Output:

Coefficients: [0.35 0.35]

Intercept: 1.5499999999999998

Predicted value for [[6 7]]: 6.1000000000000005

Multiple linear regression is a versatile and powerful regression technique used in various fields, including economics, social sciences, and engineering, to analyze the relationships between multiple variables and make predictions. It is essential to carefully interpret the coefficients and perform proper feature selection and data preprocessing to ensure the model's accuracy and validity.

LIBRARIES - SKLEARN, STATSMODELS

Both scikit-learn (sklearn) and statsmodels are popular Python libraries used for statistical modeling, machine learning, and data analysis. While they share some similarities, they serve different purposes and have distinct features. Here's a brief overview of each library:

scikit-learn (sklearn): Python has a robust and popular machine learning library called scikit-learn. It offers a variety of tools for preprocessing data, supervised and unsupervised machine learning methods, evaluating models, and more.

Focus: Machine learning tasks like classification, regression, clustering, dimensionality reduction, and model selection are the main focus of scikit-learn.

API Design: It has a consistent and user-friendly API design, making it easy to use and understand, especially for beginners.

Model Evaluation: Numerous indicators and tools are available in scikit-learn for assessing model performance.

Integration: Other scientific computing libraries like NumPy, Pandas, and Matplotlib are nicely integrated with it.

Statsmodels: A library devoted to statistical modeling and hypothesis testing is called statsmodels. It provides a variety of statistical techniques for developing and analyzing models for data analysis.

Focus: Classical statistical techniques like linear regression, logistic regression, time series analysis, and hypothesis testing are particularly suited to statsmodels.

Detailed Statistics: It provides detailed statistical outputs, including p-values, t-values, confidence intervals, and more, which are valuable for statistical inference and interpretation.

Integration: While statsmodels can work with NumPy and Pandas, its primary focus is on statistical modeling, rather than machine learning.

Choosing between scikit-learn and statsmodels depends on the nature of your analysis and the tasks you want to perform:

Use scikit-learn when you need to apply machine learning algorithms for tasks like classification, regression, clustering, etc.

Use statsmodels when your focus is on statistical modeling and you require detailed statistical analysis and hypothesis testing.

In some cases, you might use both libraries together, leveraging the strengths of each, for comprehensive data analysis and modeling. For example, you could use statsmodels to perform a detailed statistical analysis of your data and then use scikit-learn to build predictive models based on the insights gained from statsmodels.

PREDICT DV ON IV

To predict the dependent variable (DV) based on independent variables (IVs), you can use various regression models. In Python, both scikit-learn and statsmodels offer functionalities for building regression models. Here's a step-by-step guide on how to predict the DV using IVs:

Data Preparation: Prepare your data by organizing the dependent variable and independent variables into separate arrays or columns. Make sure the data is in a format that can be used by the chosen library.

Choose a Regression Model: Based on the characteristics of the DV and IVs, select the best regression model for your data. Use LinearRegression from scikit-learn or OLS (Ordinary Least Squares) from statsmodels for simple linear regression (one DV and one IV). Use the appropriate multiple regression algorithms from scikit-learn or statsmodels for multiple linear regression (one DV and multiple IVs).

Split Data into Training and Testing Sets (Optional): Consider creating a training set and a testing set from a large dataset if you want to accurately assess the model's performance.

Fit the Regression Model: Fit the selected regression model to the practice data using the fit() function.

Make Predictions: To make predictions on the testing set or any fresh data, use the fitted model's predict() method.

Evaluate Model Performance (Optional): Metrics like mean squared error, R-squared, etc. can be used to gauge the model's performance if you have a testing set. You can use classification accuracy or other classification metrics for jobs requiring categorization. Here is a scikit-learn example of straightforward linear regression:

```
import numpy as np
from sklearn.linear_model import LinearRegression

# Sample data
X = np.array([1, 2, 3, 4, 5]).reshape(-1, 1) # Independent variable (reshaped as a column vector)
y = np.array([3, 4, 2, 5, 6])          # Dependent variable

# Create a Linear Regression model
model = LinearRegression()

# Fit the model to the data
model.fit(X, y)
```

```
# Make predictions on new data
new_X = np.array([6, 7]).reshape(-1, 1)
predictions = model.predict(new_X)

print("Predictions:", predictions)
```

```
In [3]:   import numpy as np
          from sklearn.linear_model import LinearRegression

          # Sample data
          X = np.array([1, 2, 3, 4, 5]).reshape(-1, 1) # Independent variable (reshaped as a column
          vector)
          y = np.array([3, 4, 2, 5, 6])          # Dependent variable

          # Create a Linear Regression model
          model = LinearRegression()

          # Fit the model to the data
          model.fit(X, y)

          # Make predictions on new data
          new_X = np.array([6, 7]).reshape(-1, 1)
          predictions = model.predict(new_X)

          print("Predictions:", predictions)
          Predictions: [6.1  6.8]
```

Output:

Predictions: [6.1 6.8]

To predict the dependent variable (y) in this example given the independent variable (X), we utilized simple linear regression. a model.The predict() method returns the values based on the fitted model's predicted values.

Remember that the choice of regression model and evaluation metrics may vary depending on your specific data and solve problem. Additionally, ensure that your data meets the assumptions of the regression model you are using for accurate predictions and interpretation.

METRICS OF LINEAR REGRESSION (R2, RMSE, P-VALUES)

To assess the model's effectiveness and statistical significance, linear regression metrics are used. Here are three regularly employed linear regression measurements:

R-squared (R2): A measure of how well a model fits the data is R-squared. It shows the percentage of the dependent variable's (DV) variation that can be predicted from the model's independent variables (IVs). R-squared has a range of 0 to 1, with 0 denoting that the model explains no variance and 1 denoting a perfect fit to the data. A higher R-squared value indicates that the model fits the data more accurately. The model's goodness-of-fit cannot, however, be determined just by R-squared, particularly when working with complex data or several variables.

Root Mean Squared Error (RMSE): RMSE calculates the average difference between the actual and anticipated values. The mean of the squared discrepancies between the expected and actual values is calculated. A lower RMSE indicates greater performance because it shows how well the model's predictions match the actual values. RMSE provides a measurement of the amount of error in the model's predictions.

p-values (for Coefficients): P-values evaluate the statistical significance of the model's coefficients (slopes) in statistical hypothesis testing. There is a p-value assigned to each coefficient in the model, which represents the likelihood that the coefficient would have been equal to zero by chance if the null hypothesis were true. If the coefficient has a low p-value (usually less than 0.05), it is statistically significant, and the null hypothesis that it is zero can be rejected. We are unable to reject the null hypothesis since the coefficient has a high p-value (higher than 0.05), which indicates that it is not statistically significant.

To obtain these metrics, you can use statsmodels or scikit-learn library in Python. Here's an illustration of how to use statsmodels to obtain these metrics:

```
import numpy as np
import statsmodels.api as sm
# Sample data
X = np.array([1, 2, 3, 4, 5])
y = np.array([3, 4, 2, 5, 6])

# Add a constant term to the independent variable (for intercept in the model)
X = sm.add_constant(X)

# Create a linear regression model
model = sm.OLS(y, X)

# Fit the model to the data
results = model.fit()

# Get R-squared
r_squared = results.rsquared

# Get RMSE
y_pred = results.predict(X)
rmse = np.sqrt(((y_pred - y) ** 2).mean())

# Get p-values of coefficients
p_values = results.pvalues

print("R-squared:", r_squared)
print("RMSE:", rmse)
print("P-values:", p_values)
```

In [4]:
```
import numpy as np
import statsmodels.api as sm

# Sample data
X = np.array([1, 2, 3, 4, 5])
y = np.array([3, 4, 2, 5, 6])

# Add a constant term to the independent variable (for intercept in the model)
X = sm.add_constant(X)

# Create a linear regression model
model = sm.OLS(y, X)

# Fit the model to the data
results = model.fit()

# Get R-squared
r_squared = results.rsquared

# Get RMSE
y_pred = results.predict(X)
rmse = np.sqrt(((y_pred - y) ** 2).mean())

# Get p-values of coefficients
p_values = results.pvalues

print("R-squared:", r_squared)
print("RMSE:", rmse)
print("P-values:", p_values)
```

Output:

```
R-squared: 0.4900000000000001
RMSE: 1.0099504938362076
P-values: [0.25887024 0.1881204 ]
```

Keep in mind that these metrics provide valuable information about the model's performance and significance of the coefficients, but they should be interpreted in conjunction with other analysis and domain knowledge to draw meaningful conclusions about the model's validity and predictive capabilities.

APPLICATIONS OF LINEAR REGRESSION

The statistical technique of linear regression is flexible and popular, and it has many uses in a wide range of industries. Typical uses of linear regression include the following:

- **Economics**: In order to simulate the relationship between economic variables, linear regression is often utilized. It aids in comprehending how various economic indicators are affected by variables including inflation, interest rates, GDP, and unemployment.

- **Finance**: The relationship between stock prices, interest rates, and other financial measures is examined in finance using linear regression. It aids in forecasting and risk assessment for investment portfolios.
- **Marketing**: The relationship between marketing costs and sales can be investigated in marketing using linear regression. It aids in assessing the success of marketing initiatives and improving marketing tactics.
- **Healthcare**: Healthcare organizations use linear regression to examine the relationship between various health-related variables and patient outcomes. It can be used to forecast the course of an illness, a patient's recovery, and the efficacy of a treatment.
- **Social Sciences**: Many different associations are studied using linear regression in the social sciences, including those between wealth and education level, crime rates and societal issues, etc.
- **Environmental Science**: In environmental research, linear regression is employed to investigate the link between various environmental variables, such as pollution, temperature, and other climate indicators.
- **Manufacturing and Quality Control**: In the manufacturing sector, linear regression can be used to investigate the connection between product quality and process characteristics. It aids in process optimization and quality assurance.
- **Sports Analytics**: In sports analytics, linear regression is used to examine the connection between player performance, team tactics, and game outcomes. Making data-driven decisions for team management and player selection is facilitated by this.
- **Insurance**: In the insurance sector, linear regression is used to examine the connection between risk factors and insurance claims. It aids in determining insurance policy prices and risk assessment.
- **Real Estate**: To simulate the relationship between property prices and several criteria including location, size, and amenities in real estate.

These are but a few of the numerous uses for which linear regression can be put. It is a fundamental and effective tool for statistics and data analysis, offering insightful information about the connections between variables and creating predictions based on data that has already been collected.

ASSUMPTIONS OF LINEAR REGRESSION

In order to get accurate and trustworthy findings, linear regression is predicated on a number of premises. The validity of the model and the interpretations of the coefficients may be impacted by breaking these suppositions. The main tenets of linear regression are listed below:

Linearity: The independent variables (IVs) and the dependent variable (DV) should have a linear relationship. The model posits that variations in the DV are inversely correlated with variations in the IVs.

Independence: The observations should be independent of each other. In time series data, this assumption can be violated if there is autocorrelation between consecutive observations.

Homoscedasticity: Homoscedasticity is the property that all IV levels have a consistent variance of residuals (the discrepancies between actual and anticipated values). To put it another way, the spread of the residuals ought to be uniform across the range of the IVs.

Normality of Residuals: A normal distribution should be observed for the residuals. This presumption is crucial for developing confidence intervals for the coefficients and doing hypothesis testing.

No Multicollinearity: When two or more IVs have a high correlation with one another, multicollinearity occurs. It can be difficult to separate the unique effects of each IV on the DV.

No Autocorrelation: Autocorrelation happens when the residuals exhibit correlation with themselves over time (in time series data). This assumption is crucial for time series regression models.

No Outliers: Extreme data points known as outliers diverge greatly from the trend of the data as a whole. They may alter the model's performance and the calculated coefficients.

Zero Conditional Mean: The error term (residual) should have a mean of zero given a specific set of IVs. This assumption ensures that the model is correctly specified.

When using linear regression, it's essential to assess these assumptions and take corrective actions if any assumptions are violated. Techniques like residual analysis, checking normality of residuals, identifying outliers, and dealing with multicollinearity can help ensure that the model is valid and the results are reliable. Additionally, there are advanced regression techniques like robust regression and generalized linear models that can be used to handle violations of certain assumptions.

REVIEW QUESTIONS

Multiple Choice Questions

Q.1. What is the purpose of modeling techniques in data analysis?

(*a*) To collect data
(*b*) To visualize data
(*c*) To transform data
(*d*) To build predictive or descriptive models

Q.2. Which of the following is a common type of modeling technique used in data analysis?

(*a*) Data cleaning
(*b*) Data transformation
(*c*) Linear regression
(*d*) Data aggregation

Q.3. What is the primary goal of predictive modeling?

(*a*) To describe patterns and relationships in the data
(*b*) To forecast future outcomes or behaviors
(*c*) To summarize data using descriptive statistics
(*d*) To visualize data using charts and graphs

Q.4. Which modeling technique is used for predicting a continuous outcome variable based on one or more predictor variables?

(*a*) Logistic regression
(*b*) Decision trees
(*c*) Linear regression
(*d*) K-nearest neighbors

Q.5. What is logistic regression used for?

(*a*) Predicting a continuous outcome variable
(*b*) Predicting a binary outcome variable
(*c*) Clustering data points
(*d*) Visualizing data

Q.6. Which modeling technique is a non-parametric method used for classification and regression?

(*a*) Support Vector Machines (SVM)
(*b*) K-nearest neighbors (KNN)
(*c*) Decision trees
(*d*) Linear regression

Q.7. What is the primary goal of classification modeling?

(*a*) To forecast future outcomes or behaviors
(*b*) To describe patterns and relationships in the data
(*c*) To predict categorical outcomes or classes
(*d*) To summarize data using descriptive statistics

Q.8. Which modeling technique is used for predicting the probability of a binary outcome variable?

(*a*) Linear regression
(*b*) Logistic regression
(*c*) Decision trees
(*d*) K-means clustering

Q.9. Which modeling technique creates a decision tree to predict the value of a target variable by learning simple decision rules inferred from the data features?

(*a*) Linear regression
(*b*) Logistic regression
(*c*) Decision trees
(*d*) K-means clustering

Q.10. What is ensemble learning?

(*a*) A type of machine learning algorithm that uses multiple models to make predictions
(*b*) A technique for visualizing high-dimensional data
(*c*) A method for imputing missing values in a dataset
(*d*) A process for transforming data

Q.11. Which modeling technique combines multiple weak models to create a stronger model with improved predictive performance?

(*a*) Decision trees
(*b*) K-means clustering
(*c*) Ensemble learning
(*d*) Logistic regression

Q.12. Which ensemble learning technique combines multiple decision trees to create a more robust model?

(*a*) Random forests
(*b*) Gradient boosting
(*c*) AdaBoost
(*d*) Bagging

Q.13. Which ensemble learning technique builds a sequence of weak learners, where each subsequent learner corrects the errors of the previous one?

(*a*) Random forests
(*b*) Gradient boosting
(*c*) AdaBoost
(*d*) Bagging

Q.14. What is the primary goal of clustering modeling?

(*a*) To forecast future outcomes or behaviors
(*b*) To describe patterns and relationships in the data
(*c*) To predict categorical outcomes or classes
(*d*) To group similar data points together

Q.15. Which clustering technique partitions data points into distinct groups based on similarity?

(*a*) K-means clustering
(*b*) Hierarchical clustering
(*c*) DBSCAN
(*d*) Spectral clustering

Q.16. Which clustering technique builds a hierarchy of clusters by recursively merging or splitting clusters based on similarity?

(*a*) K-means clustering
(*b*) Hierarchical clustering
(*c*) DBSCAN
(*d*) Spectral clustering

Q.17. Which modeling technique is used for dimensionality reduction?

(*a*) Principal Component Analysis (PCA)
(*b*) Support Vector Machines (SVM)
(*c*) Linear regression
(*d*) K-means clustering

Q.18. What is the primary goal of dimensionality reduction?

(*a*) To summarize data using descriptive statistics
(*b*) To group similar data points together
(*c*) To visualize high-dimensional data
(*d*) To reduce the number of features while preserving the most important information

Q.19. Which modeling technique is used for anomaly detection?

(*a*) Principal Component Analysis (PCA)
(*b*) Support Vector Machines (SVM)
(*c*) K-means clustering
(*d*) Isolation Forest

Q.20. What is the primary goal of anomaly detection modeling?

(*a*) To summarize data using descriptive statistics
(*b*) To group similar data points together
(*c*) To identify unusual patterns or outliers in the data
(*d*) To reduce the number of features while preserving the most important information

Answer to Multiple Choice Questions

1. (*d*)	**2.** (*c*)	**3.** (*b*)	**4.** (*c*)	**5.** (*b*)	**6.** (*b*)	**7.** (*c*)	**8.** (*b*)	**9.** (*c*)
10. (*a*)	**11.** (*c*)	**12.** (*a*)	**13.** (*c*)	**14.** (*d*)	**15.** (*a*)	**16.** (*b*)	**17.** (*a*)	**18.** (*d*)
19. (*d*)	**20.** (*c*)							

❑❑❑

7

DATA VISUALIZATION

INTRODUCTION

The graphical display of data for the purpose of understanding patterns, trends, and insights within the data is known as data visualization. It is simpler for people to understand and evaluate data when it is presented in a clear and concise manner through the use of visualization. There are several sorts of data visualizations, and each is appropriate for specific types of data and research objectives.

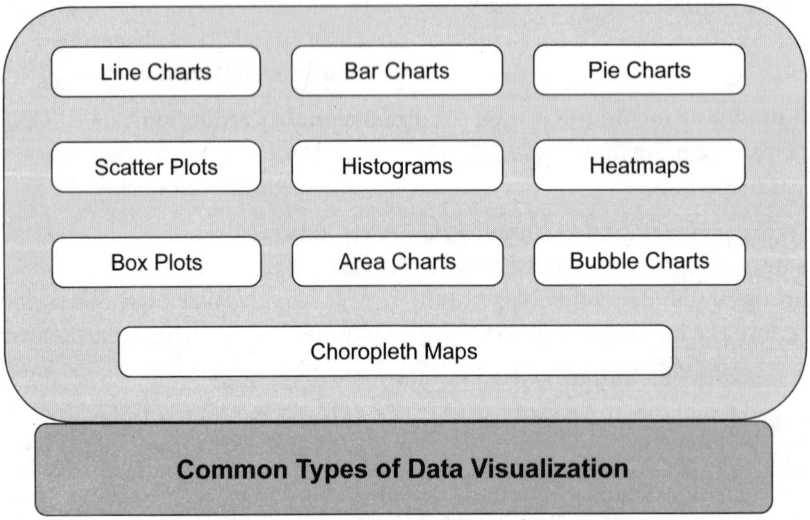

Fig. 7.1: Data Visualization Types (Common)

Line Charts: Line charts are used to display trends and patterns over time. They are effective for showing how a variable changes over a continuous period.

In [5]:
```
import matplotlib.pyplot as plt
# Sample data
x_values = [1, 2, 3, 4, 5]
y_values = [5, 2, 7, 4, 6]
```

```
# Create the Line chart
plt.plot(x_values, y_values, marker='o', linestyle='-')

# Add Labels and title
plt.xlabel('X-axis Label')
plt.ylabel('Y-axis Label')
plt.title('Simple Line Chart Example')

# Show the plot
plt.show()
```

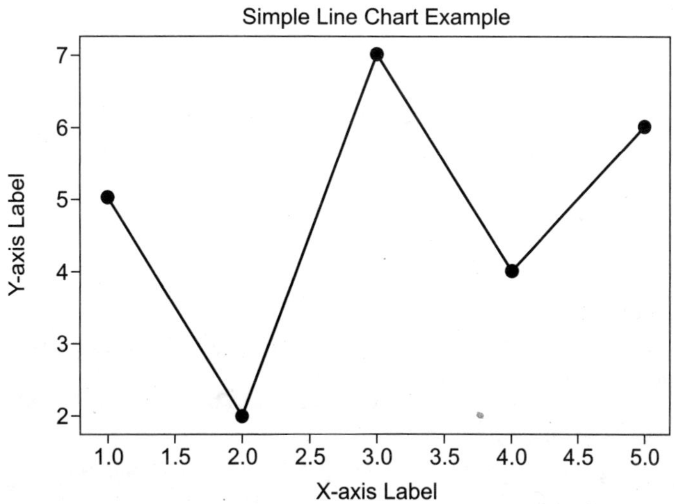

Bar Charts: Bar charts use rectangular bars to compare data across different categories. They are suitable for visualizing discrete data and comparing values.

In [6]:
```
import matplotlib.pyplot as plt

# Sample data
categories = ['Category A', 'Category B', 'Category C', 'Category D', 'Category E']
values = [15, 23, 7, 32, 18]

# Create the bar chart
plt.bar(categories, values)

# Add Labels and title
plt.xlabel('Categores')
plt.ylabel('Values')
plt.title('Simple Bar Chart Example')

# Show the plot
plt.show()
```

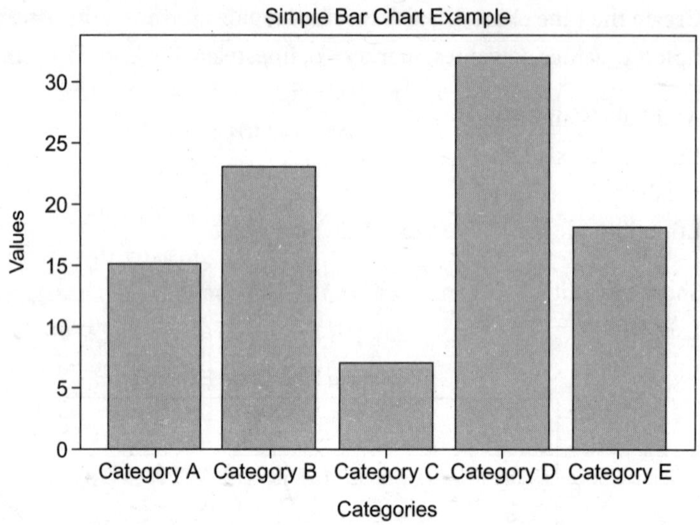

Pie Charts: Pie charts display the proportion of different categories as slices of a circle. They are helpful for showing relative proportions of parts to a whole.

In [7]:
```
import matplotlib.pyplot as plt

# Sample data
categories = ['Category A', 'Category B', 'Category C', 'Category D', 'Category E']
values = [25, 15, 10, 30, 20]

# Create the pie chart
plt.pie(values, labels=categores, autopct='%1.1f%', startangle=90)

# Add title
plt.title('Simple Pie Chart Example')

# Show the plot
plt.axis('equal') # This ensure the pie chart is drawn as a circle.
plt.show ()
```

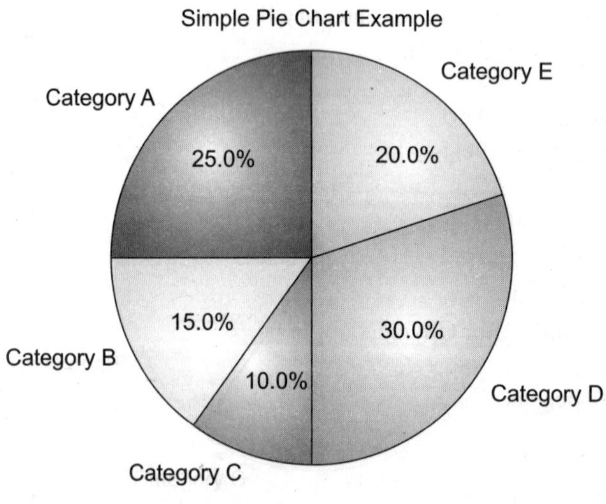

Scatter Plots: The link between two numerical variables is displayed on scatter plots. They help visualize correlations and identify patterns or outliers.

In [8]:
```
import matplotlib.pyplot as plt

# Sample data
x_values = [1, 2, 3, 4, 5]
y_values = [5, 2, 7, 4, 6]

# Create the scatter plot
plt.scatter(x_values, y_values, marker='o', color='blue')

# Add labels and title
plt.xlabel('X-axis Label')
plt.ylabel('Y-axis Label')
plt.title('Simple Scatter Plot Example')

# Show the plot
plt.show()
```

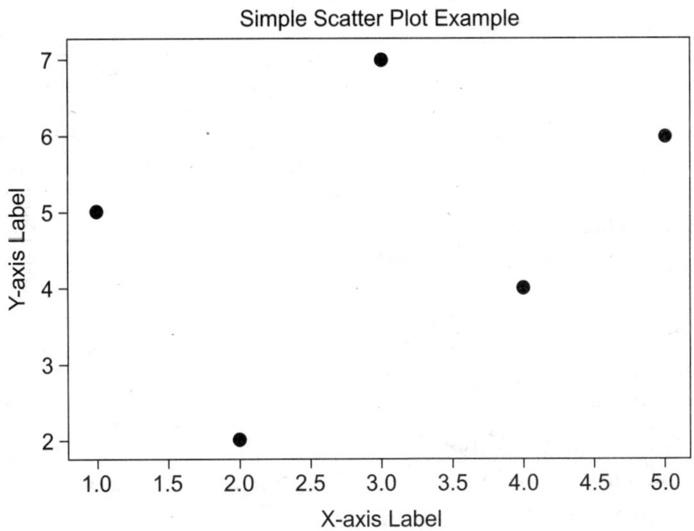

Histograms: The distribution of a single numerical variable is shown using histograms. They divide the data into bins and display how frequently each bin contains observations.

In [9]:
```
import matplotlib.pyplot as plt

# Sample data
data = [5, 2, 7, 4, 6, 3, 5, 8, 4, 9, 5, 6, 7, 3, 4, 5, 6, 4, 8, 7]

# Create the histogram
plt.hist(data, bins=10, edgecolor='black')
```

```
# Add labels and title
plt.xlabel('Value')
plt.ylable('Frequency')
plt.title('Simple Histogram Example')

# Show the plot
plt.show()
```

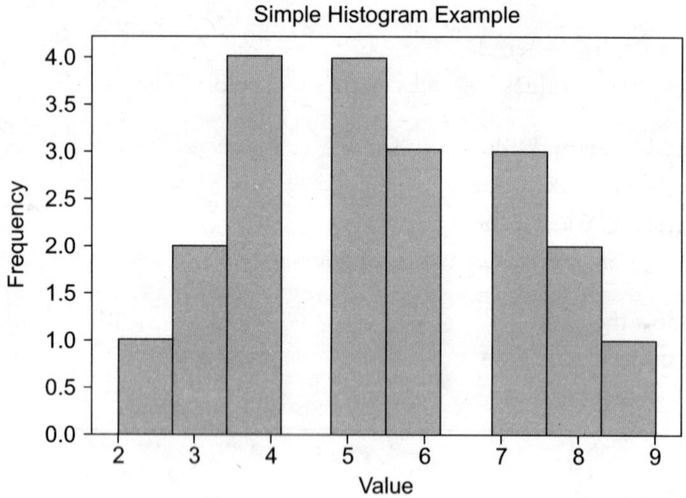

Heatmaps: Heatmaps use color intensity to represent data in a two-dimensional matrix. They are useful for visualizing correlations or relationships between two categorical variables.

```
In [10]:  import seborn as sns
          import matplotlib.pyplot as plt

          # Sample data (2D matrix)
          data = [
                [0.2, 0.5, 0.8, 0.3],
                [0.4, 0.7, 0.1, 0.6],
                [0.9, 0.2, 0.5, 0.3],
                [0.6, 0.8, 0.2, 0.4]
          ]

          # Create the heatmap using seaborn
          sns.heatmap(data, annot=True, cmap='coolwarm')

          # Add title
          plt.title('Simple Heatmap Example')

          Show the plot
          plt.show()
```

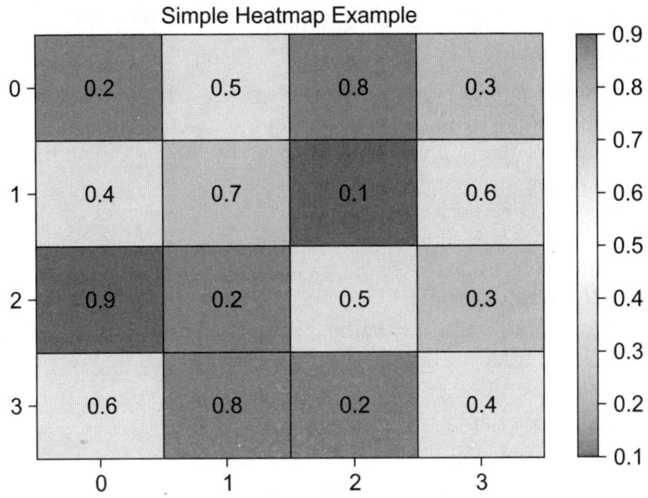

Box Plots: Box plots offer a summary of the quartile-based distribution of numerical data. The median, interquartile range, and any outliers are displayed.

In [11]:
```
import matplotlib.pyplot as plt

# Sample data
data = [5, 2, 7, 4, 6, 3, 5, 8, 4, 9, 5, 6, 7, 3, 4, 5, 6, 4, 8, 7]

# Create the box plot
plt.boxplot(data)

# Add title
plt.title('Simple Box Plot Example')

# Show the plot
plt.show()
```

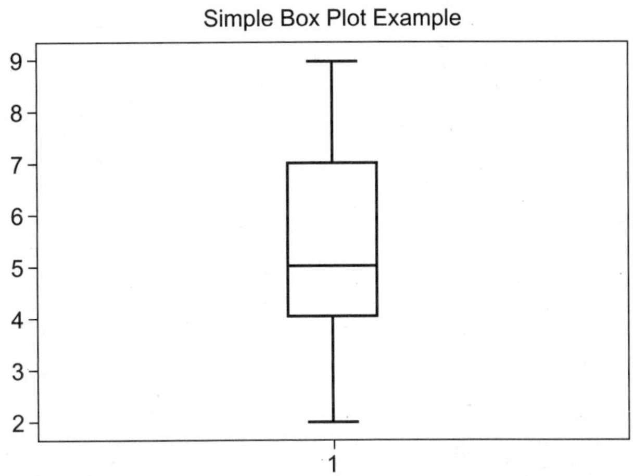

Area Charts: Area charts are similar to line charts but filled with color, representing the cumulative total of the data over time.

In [12]:
```
import matplotlib.pyplot as plt

# Sample data
x_values = [1, 2, 3, 4, 5]
y_values = [5, 2, 7, 4, 6]

# Create the area chart
plt.fill_between(x_values, y_values, color='skyblue', alpha=0.6)

# Add labels and title
plt.xlabel('X-axis Label')
plt.ylabel('Y-axis Label')
plt.title('Simple Area Chart Example')

# Show the plot
plt.show()
```

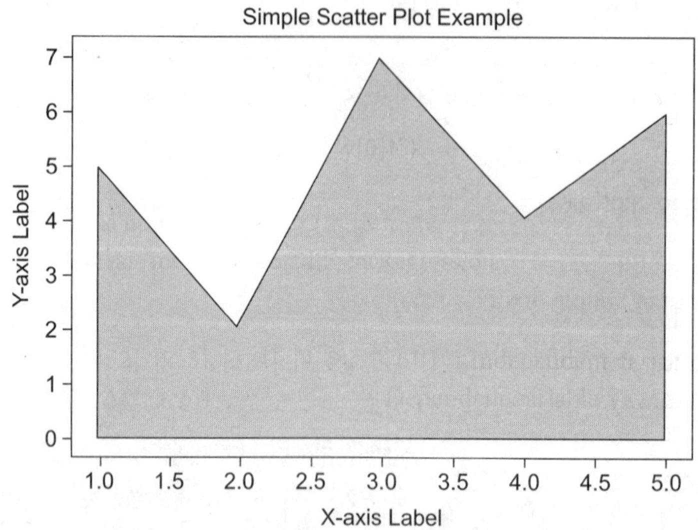

Bubble Charts: Bubble charts are a variation of scatter plots, where the size of the markers represents a third variable.

In [13]:
```
import matplotlib.pyplot as plt

# Sample data
x_values = [1, 2, 3, 4, 5]
y_values = [5, 2, 7, 4, 6]
bubble_sizes = [30, 60, 90, 120, 150]

# Create the bubble chart
plt.scatter(x_values, y_values, s=bubble_sizes, alpha=0.7, c='blue', edgecolors='black')
```

```
# Add labels and title
plt.xlabel('X-axis Label')
plt.ylabel('Y-axis Label')
plt.title('Simple Bubble Chart Example')

# Show the plot
plt.show()
```

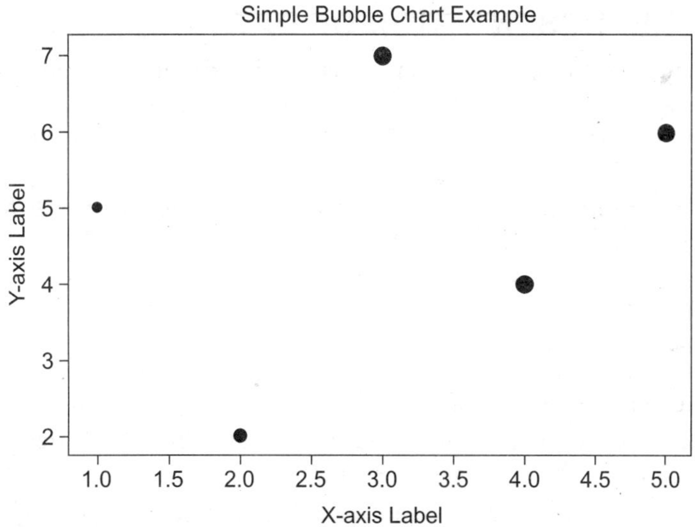

Choropleth Maps: Choropleth maps use colors or patterns to represent data values across different geographic areas.

```
In [11]:  # import plotly library
          import plotly

          # import plotly.express module
          import plotly.express as px

          # creating choropleth map of India state
          fig = px.choropleth(locationmode="USA-states", color=[1], scope="usa")
          fig.show()
```

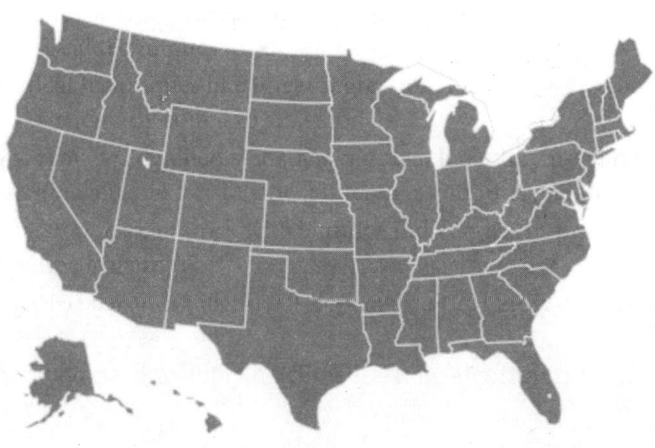

Python offers a number of libraries for displaying data, including Pandas (built-in plotting capabilities), Seaborn, Plotly, and Matplotlib. For the creation of visually appealing and educational data visualizations, these libraries offer a wide range of features and options. Depending on the features of the data and the insights you want to share with your audience, you should choose the right type of visualization. Always think about the appropriate visualization technique to tell your data-driven story clearly.

GRAPHICAL REPRESENTATION OF DATA

Using visual elements like maps, graphs, and charts to represent and communicate data in a graphical style is known as "graphical representation of data." Data exploration, analysis, and presentation are made easier and more meaningful with the aid of data visualization. Here are some popular types of data visualization graphics:

Line Charts (Time Series): Line charts show data points connected by straight lines. They are useful for representing trends and patterns over time.

In [19]:
```
import matplotlib.pyplot as plt
import pandas as pd

# Sample time series data
dates = pd.date_range(start='2023-01-01', end='2023-12-31', freq='M')
values = [10, 15, 20, 25, 30, 28, 22, 18, 16, 12, 8, 5]

# Create a pandas DataFrame with the time series data
df = pd.DataFrame({'Date': dates, 'Value': values})

# Create the line chart
plt.plot(df['Date'], df['Value'], marker='o', linestyle='-')

# Add labels and title
plt.xlabel('Date')
plt.ylabel('Value')
plt.title('Time Series Line Chart Example')

# Rotate x-axis labels for better readability (optional)
plt.xticks(rotation=45)

# Show the plot
plt.tight_layout()   # Adjusts the layout to prevent overlapping labels
plt.show()
```

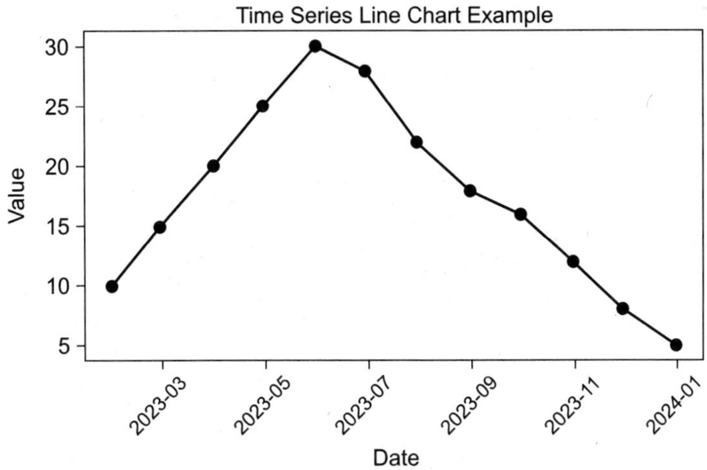

Bar Charts, Pie Charts, Scatter Plots, Histograms, Box Plots (Box-and-Whisker Plots), Area Charts, Bubble Charts, heatmaps, Choropleth Maps, Stacked Bar Charts are akso used for Graphical representation of data.

Polar Charts (Radial Charts): Polar charts use a circular grid to represent data, suitable for displaying cyclical or periodic data.

In [20]:
```
import matplotlib.pyplot as plt
import numpy as np

# Sample data
categories = ['Category A', 'Category B', 'Category C', 'Category D', 'Category E']
values = [20, 12, 18, 25, 15]

# Calculate the angles for each category
angles = np. linspace(0, 2 * np.pe, len(categores), endpoint=False)

# Close the plot by repeating the first value
values = np.append(values, values[0])
angles = np.append(angles, angles[0])

# Create the polar chart
plt.polar(angles, values, marker='o', linestyle='-')

# Add labels and title
plt.xticks(angles[:-1], categores)
plt.title('Polar Chart (Radial Chart) Example')

# Show the plot
plt.show()
```

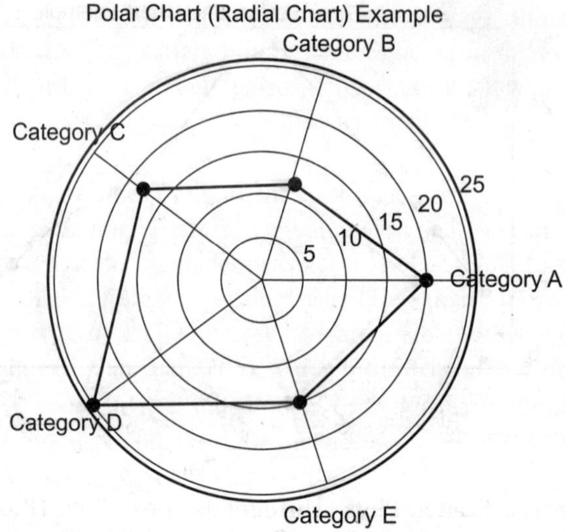

Python libraries like Matplotlib, Seaborn, Plotly, Pandas (built-in plotting capabilities), and others offer powerful tools for creating various types of data visualizations. The type of data, the goal of visualization, and the insights you wish to convey to your audience all affect the choice of graphical representation. Properly designed visualizations can provide a more intuitive understanding of complex data and help in making data-driven decisions.

SELECTION OF GRAPH

Depending on the type of data and the precise insights you want to express, you should choose the right graph or chart for data visualization. Here are some recommendations to assist you in selecting the ideal graph for your data:

Comparison of Data:

Use **Bar Charts** when comparing discrete data or categories.

Use **Line Charts** when comparing trends or patterns over time or continuous data.

Proportions and Percentages:

Use **Pie Charts** to represent proportions of different categories in a whole.

Correlations and Relationships:

To see the connection between two numerical variables and find correlations, use **scatter plots.**

Use **Bubble Charts** to add a third dimension to a scatter plot, where the size of the markers represents a third variable.

Distribution of Data:

To see the distribution of a single numerical variable and spot patterns, use **histograms.**

Use **Box Plots** to display the summary statistics and identify outliers in a numerical dataset.

Time Series Data:

Use **Line Charts** for time series data to visualize trends and changes over time.

Spatial Data:

Use **Choropleth Maps** to visualize data that is geographically distributed, showing values on a map.

Composition of Data:

Use **Stacked Bar Charts** to show the composition of a whole broken down into different categories.

Comparison and Ranking:

Use **Bar Charts** or Dot Plots to compare values and ranks across categories.

Cyclical or Periodic Data:

Use **Polar Charts** (Radial Charts) for cyclical data, such as time of day or months of the year.

Correlation Matrix:

Use **Heatmaps** to visualize the correlation matrix of variables.

Keep in mind that the appropriateness of a particular graph may also depend on the complexity of the data and the level of detail you want to convey. Additionally, consider the audience for whom the visualization is intended; choose a graph that best communicates the insights to them effectively.

Experiment with different visualizations, and if needed, combine multiple graphs to tell a comprehensive and meaningful data-driven story. Python libraries like Matplotlib, Seaborn, Plotly, and Pandas offer a wide range of options for creating various types of visualizations.

BASIC GRAPHS (HISTOGRAM, BARPLOT, BOXPLOT, PIE, ETC)

Some basic types of graphs along with Python code examples using the popular data visualization libraries Matplotlib and Seaborn.

Histogram: To see how a continuous variable is distributed, use a histogram. It displays the data's frequency within particular intervals (bins).

```
import numpy as np
import matplotlib.pyplot as plt

# Sample data
data = np.random.normal(loc=0, scale=1, size=1000)

# Plot histogram
plt.hist(data, bins=20, color=‘skyblue’, edgecolor=‘black’)
plt.xlabel(‘Value’)
plt.ylabel(‘Frequency’)
plt.title(‘Histogram’)
plt.show()
```

```
In [21]:  import numpy as np
          import matplotlib.pyplot as plt

          # Sample data
          data = np.random.normal(loc=0, scale=1, size=1000)

          # Plot histogram
          plt.hist(data, bins=20, color=‘skyblue’, edgecolor=‘black’)
          plt.xlabel(‘Value’)
```

```
plt.ylabel('Frequency')
plt.title('Histogram')
plt.show()
```

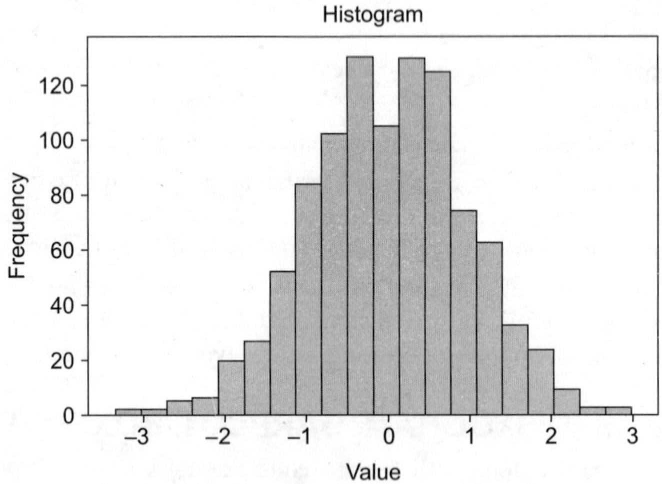

Bar Plot: A bar plot is used to compare data across different categories or groups. It displays data as rectangular bars of varying heights or lengths.

```
import pandas as pd
import matplotlib.pyplot as plt

# Sample data
data = {'Category': ['A', 'B', 'C', 'D'],
    'Value': [15, 30, 10, 25]}
df = pd.DataFrame(data)

# Plot bar plot
plt.bar(df['Category'], df['Value'], color='lightcoral')
plt.xlabel('Category')
plt.ylabel('Value')
plt.title('Bar Plot')
plt.show()
```

```
In [22]:  import pandas as pd
          import matplotlib.pyplot as plt

          # Sample data
          data = {'Category': ['A', 'B', 'C', 'D'],
              'Value': [15, 30, 10, 25]}
          df = pd.DataFrame(data)
```

```
# Plot bar plot
plt.bar(df['Category'], df['Value'], color='lightcoral')
plt.xlabel('Category')
plt.ylabel('Value')
plt.title('Bar Plot')
plt.show()
```

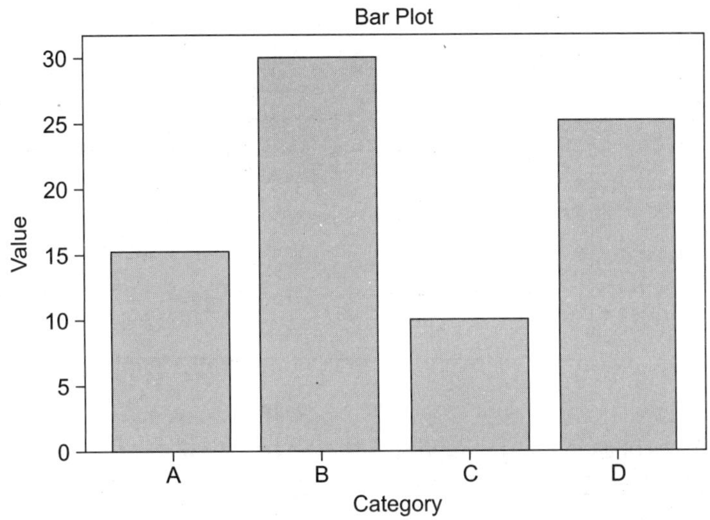

Box Plot: A box plot (box-and-whisker plot) shows how a numerical variable is distributed. It displays the data's median, quartiles, and any outliers.

```
import numpy as np
import matplotlib.pyplot as plt

# Sample data
data = np.random.normal(loc=0, scale=1, size=100)

# Plot box plot
plt.boxplot(data, vert=False, patch_artist=True)
plt.xlabel('Value')
plt.title('Box Plot')
plt.show()
```

```
In [23]:  import numpy as np
          import matplotlib.pyplot as plt

          # Sample data
          data = np.random.normal(loc=0, scale=1, size=100)

          # Plot box plot
          plt.boxplot(data, vert=False, patch_artist=True)
```

```
plt.xlabel('Value')
plt.title('Box Plot')
plt.show()
```

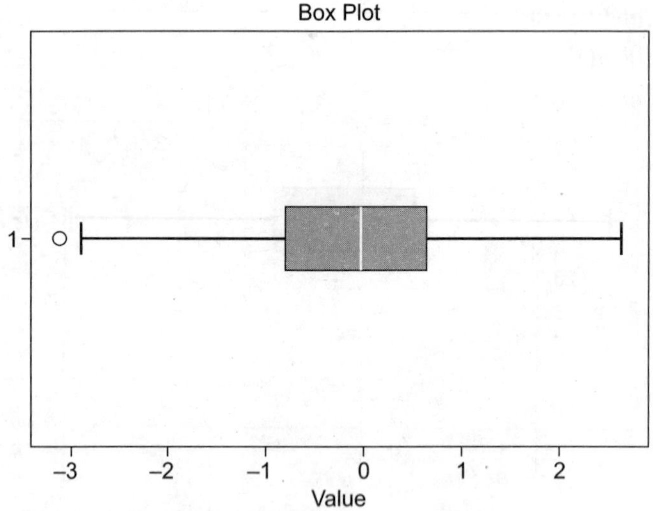

Pie Chart: Slices of a circular pie represent the percentage of each category in a pie chart.

```
import matplotlib.pyplot as plt

# Sample data
sizes = [20, 30, 10, 40]
labels = ['A', 'B', 'C', 'D']
colors = ['lightblue', 'lightcoral', 'lightgreen', 'lightsalmon']

# Plot pie chart
plt.pie(sizes, labels=labels, colors=colors, autopct='%1.1f%%', shadow=True)
plt.title('Pie Chart')
plt.axis('equal')  # Equal aspect ratio ensures the pie is drawn as a circle.
plt.show()
```

```
In [24]:  import matplotlib.pyplot as plt

          # Sample data
          sizes = [20, 30, 10, 40]
          labels = ['A', 'B', 'C', 'D']
          colors = ['lightblue', 'lightcoral', 'lightgreen', 'lightsalmon']

          # Plot pie chart
          plt.pie(sizes, labels=labels, colors=colors, autopct='%1.1f%%', shadow=True)
          plt.title('Pie Chart')
          plt.axis('equal')  # Equal aspect ratio ensures the pie is drawn as a circle.
          plt.show()
```

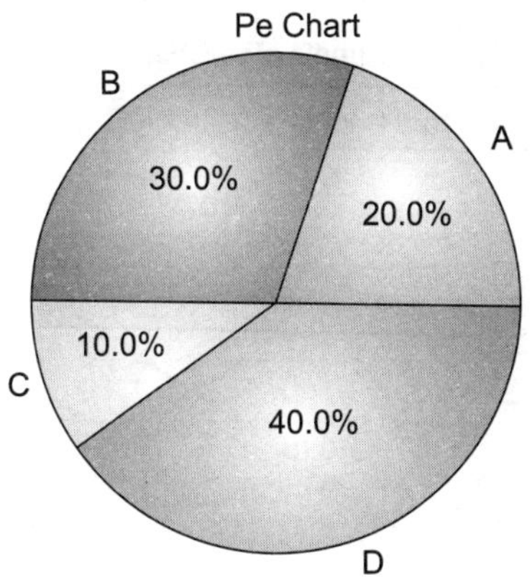

The data visualization modules for Python can be used to construct several fundamental types of graphs. Seaborn offers a higher-level interface with chic default settings, while Matplotlib is a potent toolkit for building customised plots. Select the graph type and library that best represent your data and the insights you wish to communicate.

LIBRARIES (MATPLOTLIB, SEABORN, PLOTLINE)

It seems there might be a misunderstanding regarding the library names. As of my last update in September 2021, there is no widely known Python library called "plotline." However, based on your question, I will assume you meant "Plotly" instead of "plotline." Let's explore these three popular data visualization libraries in Python:

Matplotlib: One of the most popular Python packages for data visualization is Matplotlib. It provides a flexible and comprehensive set of functions for creating a wide range of static, interactive, and animated plots. Matplotlib serves as the foundation for many other data visualization libraries. While powerful, it can sometimes require more code for complex visualizations.

```
In [25]: import matplotlib.pyplot as plt

         # Sample data
         x = [1, 2, 3, 4, 5]
         y = [2, 4, 6, 8, 10]

         # Plot a simple line chart using Matplotlib
         plt.plot(x, y, marker='o', linestyle='-', color='blue', label='Data Points')
         plt.xlabel('X-axis')
         plt.ylabel('Y-axis')
         plt.title('Simple Line Chart using Matplotlib')
         plt.legend()
         plt.grid(True)
         plt.show()
```

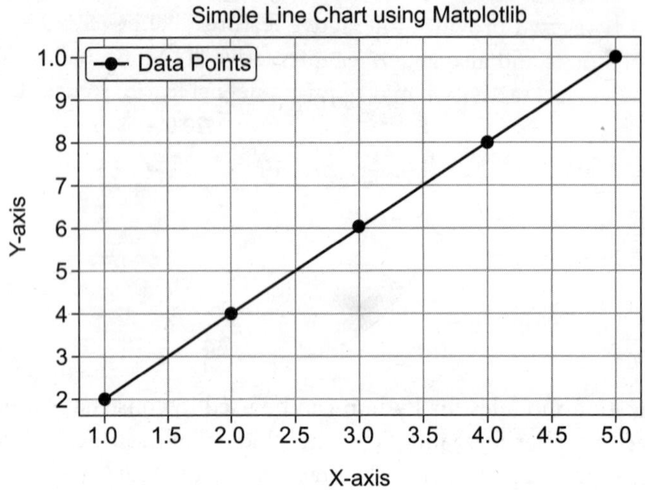

Seaborn: On top of Matplotlib, Seaborn offers a higher-level interface for producing beautiful statistical visuals. It makes the process of creating intricate visualizations simpler and is made to work well with Pandas DataFrames. Numerous statistical plots, including scatter plots, box plots, violin plots, etc., are supported by Seaborn. It is a fantastic option for rapid and lovely visualizations.

In [26]:
```
import seaborn as sns
# Sample data
data = sns.loac_dataset('tips')
# Plot a scatter plot using Seaborn
sns.scatterplot(x='total_bill', y='tip', data=data, hue='day', style='time', size='size',
palette='Set1')
plt.xlabel('Total Bill')
plt.ylabel('Tip')
plt.title('Scatter Plot using Seaborn')
plt.show()
```

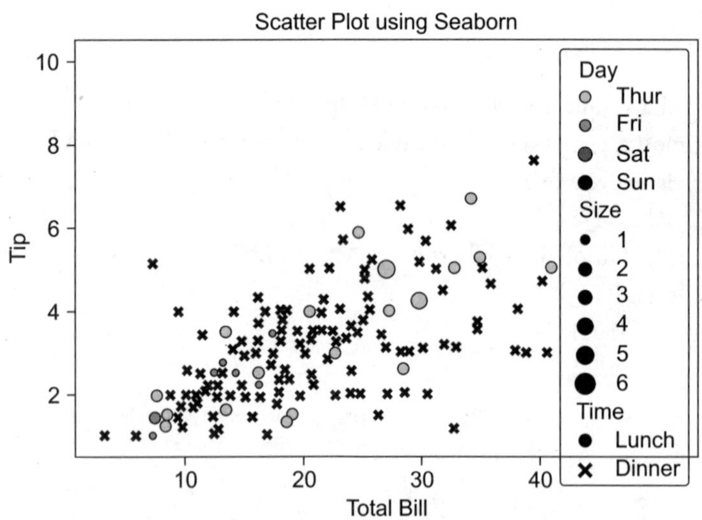

Plotly: Plotly is a powerful library for creating interactive and web-based visualizations. It supports a wide range of chart types and provides interactive features like hover, zoom, and pan. Plotly can be used with Jupyter Notebooks and also generates interactive HTML visualizations for web applications. Although it offers excellent interactivity, it may require a steeper learning curve for complex visualizations.

In [27]:
```
import plotly.express as px

# Sample data
data = px.data.iris()

# Plot a scatter plot using Plotly
fig = px.scatter(data, x='sepal_width', y='sepal_length', color='species', size='petal_length',
      hover_data=['petal_width'])
fig.update_layout(title='Scatter Plot using Plotly', xaxis_title='Sepal Width', yaxis_
title='Sepal Length')
fig.show()
```

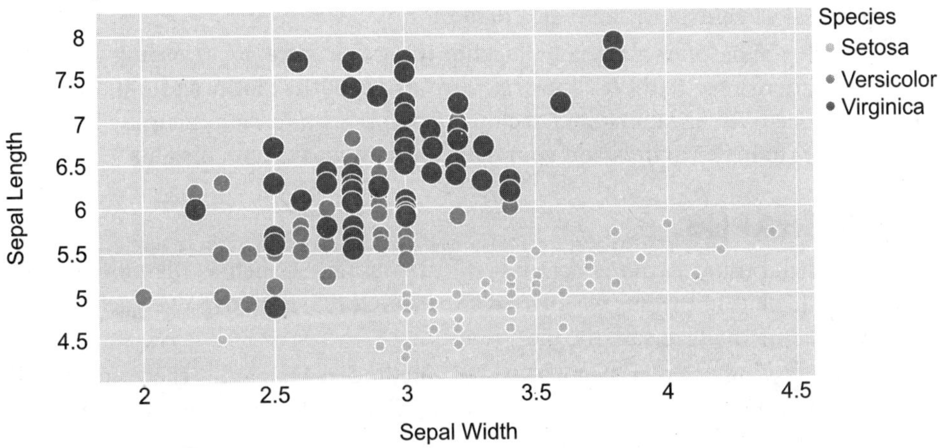

These libraries, Matplotlib, Seaborn, and Plotly, each have their strengths and are well-suited for various visualization needs. Depending on your project requirements, data complexity, and desired level of interactivity, you can choose the library that best meets your needs.

MANAGING PLOT PARAMETERS (SIZE, TITLE, AXIS, LEGEND, ETC)

Managing plot parameters such as size, title, axis labels, legend, etc., is crucial for creating clear and visually appealing data visualizations.

In Python, you can use libraries like Matplotlib, Seaborn, and Plotly to customize these plot parameters. Above three library example of Matplotlib, Seaborn, and Plotly is visualized.

In the examples above, you can see how to set the size of the plot (figsize in Matplotlib and width and height in Plotly), set titles for the plot (title), x-axis (xlabel), and y-axis (ylabel), customize the legend (legend), and more.

Each library provides specific functions and attributes to control various plot parameters. Refer to the documentation of the respective library for a comprehensive list of customization options. With these customization capabilities, you can create visually appealing and informative data visualizations tailored to your needs.

ADVANCED GRAPHS (CORRELATION, HEATMAP, MOSAIC, ETC)

Advanced graphs go beyond basic plots to provide more sophisticated visualizations that allow for in-depth data analysis. These advanced graphs are especially useful for understanding complex relationships and patterns within the data. Let's explore some advanced graphs using Python's data visualization libraries:

Correlation Plot: The correlation matrix of numerical variables in a dataset is displayed using a correlation plot. It aids in determining the strength of correlations between various variables.

Heatmap: A heatmap is used to visualize the distribution of data values in a 2D matrix. It uses colors to represent the values, making it easier to identify patterns or trends.

Mosaic Plot: The association between two categorical variables is shown via a mosaic plot. The percentage of observations in each combination of categories is shown.

Pair Plot: To see the connections between various numerical variables, utilize a pair plot. It displays scatter plots of all possible pairs of variables in a dataset.

These advanced graphs offer powerful insights into your data by revealing hidden patterns, correlations, and relationships. Python's libraries, such as Seaborn, Plotly, and Pandas, make it easy to create these advanced visualizations and facilitate comprehensive data analysis. Experiment with different visualizations to better understand your data and gain meaningful insights.

EXPORTING GRAPHS

To export graphs created using Python's data visualization libraries, such as Matplotlib, Seaborn, and Plotly, you can save the plots in various file formats like PNG, JPEG, PDF, or SVG. Each library provides different functions and methods to save the plots to files.

In these examples, we used the respective savefig() method in Matplotlib, the write_html() method in Plotly, and the standard Python file handling to save the plots as files. You can specify the filename and file format according to your preference.

By exporting the graphs, you can share them with others, include them in reports or presentations, or use them in web applications to make your data visualizations accessible to a wider audience.

REVIEW QUESTIONS

Multiple Choice Questions

Q.1. What is data visualization?

(*a*) Storing data in a database (*b*) Analyzing data using statistical techniques
(*c*) Presenting data in graphical or visual formats
(*d*) Transforming data into numerical format

Q.2. What is the primary goal of data visualization?

(*a*) To summarize data using descriptive statistics
(*b*) To identify patterns or trends in the data (*c*) To clean and preprocess data
(*d*) To transform data into a different format

Q.3. Which of the following is NOT a common type of data visualization?

(*a*) Bar chart (*b*) Scatter plot (*c*) Linear regression (*d*) Histogram

Q.4. What type of data visualization is best suited for displaying the distribution of a single numerical variable?

(*a*) Bar chart (*b*) Histogram (*c*) Scatter plot (*d*) Pie chart

Q.5. Which data visualization technique is commonly used for showing the relationship between two numerical variables?

(*a*) Bar chart (*b*) Histogram (*c*) Scatter plot (*d*) Box plot

Q.6. What does a box plot visualize?

(*a*) The distribution of a single numerical variable
(*b*) The relationship between two numerical variables
(*c*) The summary statistics of a numerical variable
(*d*) The distribution of a categorical variable

Q.7. Which type of data visualization is suitable for comparing the proportions of different categories?

(*a*) Bar chart (*b*) Histogram (*c*) Scatter plot (*d*) Line chart

Q.8. What does a pie chart represent?

(*a*) The distribution of a single numerical variable
(*b*) The relationship between two numerical variables
(*c*) The proportions of different categories within a dataset
(*d*) The summary statistics of a numerical variable

Q.9. Which data visualization technique is commonly used for time series data?

(*a*) Bar chart (*b*) Histogram (*c*) Scatter plot (*d*) Line chart

Q.10. What is a heatmap used for?

(*a*) Showing the distribution of a single numerical variable
(*b*) Comparing the proportions of different categories
(*c*) Visualizing the relationship between two numerical variables
(*d*) Displaying the correlation matrix between variables

Q.11. Which data visualization technique is used to visualize the relationship between three variables?

(*a*) Scatter plot (*b*) Histogram (*c*) Pie chart (*d*) 3D plot

Q.12. What is the purpose of color in data visualization?

(*a*) To make the visualization more visually appealing
(*b*) To encode additional information or variables
(*c*) To reduce the complexity of the visualization
(*d*) To transform the data into a different format

Q.13. Which of the following is a disadvantage of using pie charts?

(*a*) They can only represent categorical data
(*b*) They cannot show the relationship between variables
(*c*) They are difficult to interpret for large datasets
(*d*) All of the above

Q.14. What is the purpose of data visualization libraries such as Matplotlib and Seaborn?

(*a*) To store and manage data (*b*) To analyze data using statistical techniques
(*c*) To create interactive data visualizations (*d*) To create static and dynamic visualizations

Q.15. Which data visualization technique is commonly used for visualizing geographical data?

(*a*) Bar chart (*b*) Scatter plot (*c*) Choropleth map (*d*) Line chart

Q.16. What does a bar chart visualize?

(*a*) The distribution of a single numerical variable
(*b*) The relationship between two numerical variables
(*c*) The summary statistics of a numerical variable
(*d*) The proportions of different categories

Q.17. What does a scatter plot visualize?

(*a*) The distribution of a single numerical variable
(*b*) The relationship between two numerical variables
(*c*) The summary statistics of a numerical variable
(*d*) The proportions of different categories

Q.18. Which data visualization technique is commonly used for comparing groups or categories?

(*a*) Histogram (*b*) Scatter plot (*c*) Box plot (*d*) Line chart

Q.19. What is the purpose of data storytelling in data visualization?

(*a*) To create visually appealing visualizations
(*b*) To communicate insights and findings effectively

(*c*) To encode additional information or variables
(*d*) To transform the data into a different format

Q.20. Which of the following is NOT a characteristic of effective data visualization?
(*a*) Clarity (*b*) Simplicity (*c*) Complexity (*d*) Relevance

Answer to Multiple Choice Questions

1. (*c*)	**2.** (*b*)	**3.** (*c*)	**4.** (*b*)	**5.** (*c*)	**6.** (*c*)	**7.** (*a*)	**8.** (*c*)	**9.** (*d*)
10. (*d*)	**11.** (*d*)	**12.** (*b*)	**13.** (*d*)	**14.** (*d*)	**15.** (*c*)	**16.** (*d*)	**17.** (*b*)	**18.** (*c*)
19. (*b*)	**20.** (*c*)							

❑❑❑

8

Data Analytics

BASICS

Data analytics is process of examining, cleaning, transforming, and interpreting data to extract valuable insights and make data-driven decisions. It involves using various techniques and tools to analyze large datasets and uncover patterns, trends, correlations, and other meaningful information. Data analytics is an essential part of the broader field of data science and is used across various industries to drive business strategies, improve processes, and optimize performance.

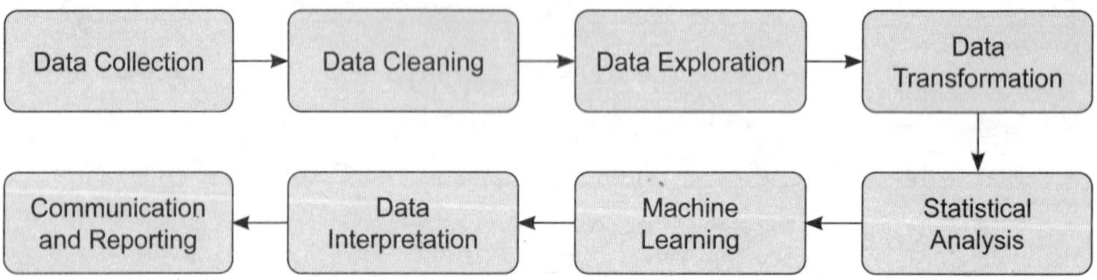

Fig. 8.1: Data Analytics key steps

Key Steps in Data Analytics

Data Collection: Gathering pertinent data from numerous sources, such as databases, APIs, files, or web scraping, is the initial stage in data analytics.

Data Cleaning: Raw data often contains errors, missing values, and inconsistencies. Data cleaning involves preprocessing and transforming the data to ensure it is accurate and reliable.

Data Exploration and Visualization: Data exploration involves summarizing and visualizing the data to gain a better understanding of its characteristics, distributions, and relationships. Data visualization tools help in creating meaningful visual representations of the data.

Data Transformation and Feature Engineering: Data may need to be transformed or features engineered to make it suitable for analysis. This step involves scaling, encoding categorical variables, and creating new relevant features.

Statistical Analysis: To find patterns, trends, and relationships in the data, statistical approaches are used. Techniques including grouping, regression analysis, and hypothesis testing are frequently employed.

Machine Learning: ML algorithms are used to build predictive models & make data-driven predictions based on historical data.

Data Interpretation: The insights gained from data analysis are interpreted to draw meaningful conclusions and make wise decisions.

Communication and Reporting: The results of data analytics are communicated to stakeholders through reports, dashboards, or presentations.

Data analytics can be applied to various domains, including marketing, finance, healthcare, manufacturing, e-commerce, and more. It plays a crucial role in extracting value from data and enabling organizations to make data-driven decisions to stay competitive in today's data-rich world. Python and other programming languages, along with specialized data analytics tools and libraries, are widely used to perform data analytics tasks efficiently and effectively.

DATA ANALYTICS AND BUSINESS APPLICATION

Data analytics has numerous business applications across various industries. It helps businesses extract valuable insights from data to improve decision-making, optimize processes, and drive growth. Here are some key business applications of data analytics:

Customer Analytics: Analysis of consumer behavior, preferences, and purchasing trends is done using data analytics. It helps businesses understand customer needs, segment customers, and personalize marketing efforts to improve customer satisfaction and retention.

Market Analysis: Data analytics is utilized to analyze market trends, competitor performance, and consumer sentiment. It helps businesses identify opportunities and threats in the market and make strategic decisions.

Supply Chain Optimization: Data analytics is applied to optimize the supply chain by predicting demand, improving inventory management, and reducing logistics costs.

Fraud Detection: Data analytics is used to detect fraudulent activities in financial transactions and insurance claims, helping businesses prevent financial losses.

Risk Management: Data analytics helps businesses identify and manage risks by analyzing historical data and predicting future risks.

Predictive Maintenance: Data analytics is employed to predict equipment failures and maintenance needs, reducing downtime and improving operational efficiency.

Human Resources Analytics: Data analytics is used to analyze employee performance, engagement, and turnover to optimize workforce management and improve productivity.

Healthcare Analytics: Data analytics is applied in healthcare to improve patient outcomes, optimize hospital operations, and identify disease patterns.

Marketing and **Advertising**: Data analytics helps businesses optimize marketing campaigns, measure the effectiveness of advertising efforts, and target the right audience.

E-commerce Personalization: Data analytics is used to recommend products, personalize content, and improve the overall user experience in e-commerce platforms.

Energy and Utilities Management: Data analytics helps optimize energy consumption, predict power demand, and improve energy efficiency.

Social Media Analytics: Data analytics is used to analyze social media data to understand customer sentiment, track brand reputation, and identify trends.

Data analytics empowers businesses to make data-driven decisions, identify new opportunities, and enhance overall performance. It provides a competitive advantage by enabling businesses to stay agile and responsive to changing market conditions and customer preferences. Implementing effective data analytics strategies requires skilled data analysts, data scientists, and the use of appropriate tools and technologies to process and analyze data efficiently. Python and other programming languages, along with advanced data analytics libraries and platforms, are commonly used to conduct data analysis and gain valuable insights for business applications.

BUSINESS ANALYTICS

Business analytics is a subset of data analytics that focuses on applying analytical techniques and methodologies to business-related data to gain insights, make data-driven decisions, and drive business performance. It involves using data and statistical methods to identify trends, patterns, and correlations that can provide valuable information for improving business operations, strategies, and outcomes.

Key Objectives of Business Analytics

Business Intelligence: By examining historical data to comprehend past performance and patterns, business analytics offers useful business intelligence.

Data Exploration and Visualization: It involves exploring and visualizing data to gain a better understanding of business metrics and KPIs.

Performance Measurement: Business analytics helps measure and track business performance against predefined goals and targets.

Predictive Analytics: By building predictive models, business analytics can forecast future outcomes and trends, enabling proactive decision-making.

Prescriptive Analytics: It provides recommendations and actions to optimize business processes and achieve desired outcomes.

Customer Insights: Analyzing customer data helps in understanding customer behavior, preferences, and needs, leading to better customer targeting and personalized marketing.

Risk Management: Business analytics aids in identifying and managing risks, such as financial risks, operational risks, and supply chain risks.

Marketing and Sales Optimization: By analyzing marketing and sales data, businesses can optimize their marketing campaigns and sales strategies to increase revenue and customer acquisition.

Supply Chain Management: Business analytics optimizes supply chain operations by predicting demand, improving inventory management, and reducing costs.

Financial Analytics: Analyzing financial data supports budgeting, financial forecasting, and investment decision-making.

Business analytics leverages a combination of tools, technologies, and methodologies, including statistical analysis, machine learning, data mining, data visualization, and optimization techniques. It relies on data from various sources, such as transactional systems, customer databases, web analytics, social media, and more.

By leveraging business analytics, organizations can gain a competitive advantage by making informed decisions, optimizing processes, and identifying new opportunities for growth and improvement. It enables businesses to transform raw data into valuable insights and actionable knowledge, facilitating strategic decision-making and ensuring long-term success. As data becomes more central to business operations, business analytics continues to play a crucial role in shaping the future of organizations across industries.

Analytics, Business Intelligence (BI), Business Analytics (BA), and the different levels of analytics play interconnected roles in the data-driven decision-making process within an organization. Let's explore these concepts in more detail:

Analytics: In order to find patterns, insights, and trends within large data sets, analytics is the process of using data, statistical approaches, and computing techniques. To support corporate goals and make data-driven decisions, it entails gathering, preparing, analyzing, and interpreting data

Business Intelligence (BI): BI is a subset of analytics that focuses on using data to provide meaningful insights and reports for business operations. BI tools and systems aggregate and analyze data from various sources to create dashboards, reports, and visualizations that aid in monitoring business performance and identifying trends.

Business Analytics (BA): Business Analytics (BA) is a broader term that encompasses the use of data analytics techniques and methodologies to inform business decision-making. BA involves descriptive, predictive, and prescriptive analytics to explore historical data, predict future outcomes, and provide actionable recommendations.

LEVELS OF ANALYTICS

Level of analytics" refers to the depth and complexity of data analysis being performed within an organization or context. It typically refers to different stages or categories of analytical processes, each building upon the previous one to provide deeper insights and value. The concept is often presented in a hierarchical manner, with each level representing a higher degree of sophistication and business impact.

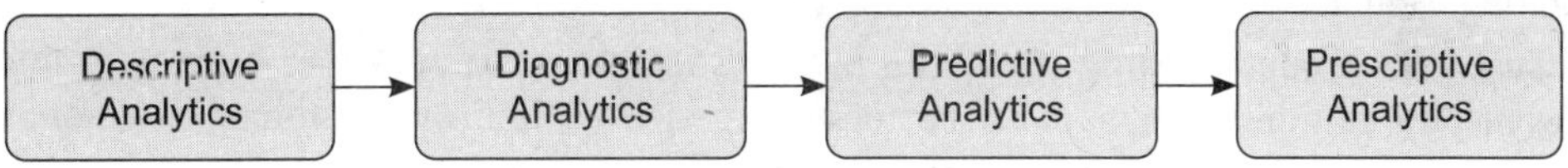

Fig. 8.2: Level of Analytics

Descriptive Analytics: At this level, you must perform a rudimentary historical data analysis to comprehend what happened in the past. It includes activities such as data summarization, reporting, and visualization. Descriptive analytics provides a foundational understanding of trends, patterns, and key performance indicators (KPIs).

Diagnostic Analytics: Going beyond the "what," diagnostic analytics seeks to uncover the reasons behind past events or trends. It involves deeper exploration of data to identify root causes and factors that contributed to specific outcomes. This level often involves correlation analysis and advanced querying to understand relationships between variables.

Predictive Analytics: Predictive analytics focuses on forecasting future events or outcomes based on historical data and patterns. ML algorithms are commonly used at this level to build predictive models that can anticipate future trends, behaviors, or events. Businesses can use predictive analytics to make informed decisions and plan for various scenarios.

Prescriptive Analytics: This level involves recommending specific actions or strategies based on predictive models and business goals. Prescriptive analytics provides actionable insights by suggesting what should be done to achieve desired outcomes. It takes into account different scenarios and constraints to guide decision-making.

Cognitive Analytics (or Advanced Analytics): This level involves more advanced techniques like machine learning, natural language processing, and artificial intelligence to gain deeper insights from complex and unstructured data sources. Cognitive analytics aims to mimic human thinking processes to uncover hidden patterns, sentiments, and relationships in data.

It's vital to keep in mind that the idea of analytics levels is not always strictly hierarchical and that various businesses may use different models or categorizations. The ultimate goal of progressing through these levels is to transform data into meaningful insights that drive better decision-making and business outcomes.

The relationship between BI and BA is often complementary, where BI tools and systems provide the foundation for visualizing and reporting on data, while BA leverages advanced analytical techniques to gain deeper insights and inform strategic decision-making. Organizations that effectively leverage analytics, BI, and BA can gain a competitive advantage by making data-driven decisions, improving operational efficiency, and identifying new opportunities for growth and innovation.

Why Analytics Required

Analytics is a potent tool with numerous uses across a variety of fields and industries. Here are some reasons why analytics is crucial and its applications across different domains:

Data-Driven Decision Making: Analytics allows organizations to make informed decisions based on data rather than intuition or guesswork. It helps businesses identify patterns, trends, and correlations in data, enabling more accurate and effective decision-making.

Business Optimization: In business domains, analytics is applied to optimize various processes, such as supply chain management, inventory control, resource allocation, pricing strategies, and marketing campaigns.

Customer Understanding: Analytics provides insights into customer behavior, preferences, and needs, helping businesses personalize customer experiences, improve customer retention, and increase customer satisfaction.

Risk Management: In finance, insurance, and other industries, analytics is used to assess and manage risks, including credit risk, market risk, and fraud detection.

Healthcare Improvement: Analytics is applied in healthcare to improve patient outcomes, optimize hospital operations, and support disease management and prevention.

Public Policy and Governance: In the public sector, analytics helps government agencies and policymakers make data-driven decisions, optimize resource allocation, and improve public services.

Manufacturing and Operations: Analytics are utilized in manufacturing to promote productivity, decrease downtime, and boost overall efficiency.

Environmental Sustainability: Analytics aids in monitoring and managing environmental factors like climate change, pollution levels, and natural resource usage.

Transportation and Logistics: Analytics is applied in transportation and logistics to optimize route planning, reduce fuel consumption, and enhance supply chain efficiency.

Social Media and Marketing: Analytics is used to track and analyze social media data, enabling businesses to understand customer sentiment, track brand reputation, and identify market trends.

Energy Management: Analytics helps in optimizing energy consumption, predicting energy demand, and increasing energy efficiency.

Education and Learning: In the education sector, analytics is used to personalize learning experiences, identify students at risk, and optimize educational programs.

DIFFERENT ROLES IN ANALYTICS

In the field of analytics, there are various roles and positions that require different skill sets and responsibilities. These roles play a crucial part in leveraging data to gain insights and support decision-making. Here are some of the key roles in analytics:

Data Analyst: Data analysts are responsible for collecting, cleaning, and analyzing data to provide actionable insights. They use statistical methods and data visualization tools to present findings in a clear and understandable manner.

Business Analyst: Business analysts focus on understanding business processes, identifying business needs, and recommending solutions based on data analysis. They bridge the gap between business stakeholders and data analysts.

Data Scientist: Data scientists are skilled in statistical modeling, machine learning, and programming. They develop predictive models, create algorithms, and conduct in-depth data exploration to extract meaningful insights.

Data Engineer: Data engineers are responsible for designing and maintaining data pipelines and databases to ensure data availability and reliability for analysis. They work on data integration, transformation, and storage.

Machine Learning Engineer: ML engineers specialize in building and deploying ML models and algorithms. They work closely with data scientists to operationalize and scale machine learning solutions.

Business Intelligence (BI) Developer: BI developers design and implement dashboards, reports, and data visualizations using BI tools to facilitate business reporting and decision-making.

Data Architect: Data architects design the overall structure and architecture of databases and data systems. They ensure data integrity, security, and scalability.

Data Analyst Manager: Data analyst managers lead and oversee a team of data analysts. They set project priorities, provide guidance, and ensure data analysis meets business objectives.

Data Science Manager: Data science managers are responsible for managing data science teams and projects. They collaborate with stakeholders to identify business problems and oversee the development of data-driven solutions.

Data Quality Analyst: Data quality analysts focus on ensuring data accuracy, consistency, and completeness. They develop data quality checks and processes to maintain data integrity.

Data Visualization Specialist: Data visualization specialists are skilled in creating impactful visualizations and interactive dashboards to communicate complex insights effectively.

Research Analyst: Research analysts conduct industry and market research, gathering data and providing insights to support strategic planning and decision-making.

Each role in analytics contributes to the overall data-driven decision-making process within an organization. Collaborating effectively between these roles is essential to leveraging data to gain valuable insights and drive business success. As businesses increasingly understand the value of data in their operations and decision-making processes, the need for people in these areas is expected to increase.

TOOLS AND TECHNIQUES IN ANALYTICS

Analytics is a broad field that involves the systematic analysis of data to extract valuable insights and make informed decisions. There are various tools and techniques used in analytics to process and interpret data effectively. Here are some of the key ones:

Statistical Analysis Software (SAS): A popular software package for multivariate analysis, corporate intelligence, and data management is called SAS. It is well known for its powerful statistical abilities.

R: For statistical computing and graphics, R is a potent open-source programming language and software environment. It is commonly used in ML, data analysis, and data visualization.

Python: Numerous libraries for data manipulation, analysis, and ML, including NumPy, Pandas, SciPy, and Scikit-learn, are available in the flexible programming language Python.

SQL (Structured Query Language): SQL is essential for working with relational databases. It allows analysts to extract, manipulate, and manage data, making it a fundamental tool for data preparation and exploration.

Excel: Excel is a common tool for basic data analysis, data visualization, and creating charts and graphs. While not as powerful as specialized software, it is widely accessible and easy to use for simple tasks.

Data Visualization Tools (Tableau, Power BI, etc.): These tools help analysts create interactive and visually appealing dashboards and reports to communicate insights effectively to stakeholders.

Machine Learning Libraries (TensorFlow, PyTorch, etc.): For advanced predictive modeling and pattern recognition, machine learning libraries provide the necessary algorithms and tools.

Predictive Analytics Tools: These tools focus on forecasting future trends and behaviors based on historical data, enabling organizations to make proactive decisions.

Text Analytics Tools: Unstructured text data, such as social media posts, client reviews, and news articles, can be analyzed and valuable information extracted using text analytics techniques.

Data Mining Software: Data mining tools are used to discover patterns, associations, and relationships within large datasets.

Descriptive Analytics: This technique involves analyzing historical data to understand what happened and why it happened, often presented through reports and dashboards.

Diagnostic Analytics: Diagnostic analytics focuses on understanding why certain events occurred by delving deeper into the data to identify root causes.

Predictive Analytics: Utilizing previous data, predictive analytics creates models and forecasts future events.

Prescriptive Analytics: This advanced technique combines historical data, predictive modeling, and optimization to provide recommendations for the best course of action.

Data Cleaning and Data Preparation: Techniques for cleaning and preparing data, such as handling missing values, outlier detection, and feature engineering, are critical for accurate analysis.

Data Storytelling: The art of presenting data and insights in a compelling and easy-to-understand narrative, using visualizations, storytelling, and context to convey the message effectively.

Big Data Technologies: Tools like Hadoop, Spark, and Hive are used for processing and analyzing large-scale datasets that traditional systems cannot handle efficiently.

A/B Testing: This method compares two or more versions of a process, design, or user experience side by side in controlled studies to see which one performs better.

Time Series Analysis: A specialized technique for analyzing data that is ordered chronologically, commonly used in forecasting and trend analysis.

Data Integration and ETL (Extract, Transform, Load): Techniques for combining data from various sources and transforming it into a usable format for analysis.

Depending on the particular needs of the analytics project and the type of data being examined, these tools and methodologies can be combined and adapted. Keeping up with the most recent developments and trends in the field is also necessary to maintain a competitive edge in the analytics sector.

CRISP MODELING FRAMEWORK

For the purpose of directing data mining and analytics initiatives, the CRISP-DM (Cross-Industry Standard Process for Data Mining) framework is a commonly used technique. It offers an organized method for addressing challenging data analysis issues, and data scientists and analysts frequently use it. There are six primary phases in the CRISP-DM system:

Business Understanding: It focuses on comprehending the project's goals and demands from a commercial standpoint. Determining the issue, setting objectives, and comprehending how the outcomes will be put to use to generate corporate value are all necessary.

Data Understanding: In this phase, data exploration and analysis take place. Data sources are identified, collected, and evaluated to understand their structure and quality. Exploratory data analysis techniques may be used to gain insights into the data.

Data Preparation: Data cleansing, integration, and transformation are all part of this step. Data is produced in a modeling-friendly format. To enhance model performance, this may involve resolving missing values, addressing outliers, and developing additional features.

Modeling: During this stage, different modeling methods are chosen and used on the prepared dataset. To determine the model that best solves the business challenge, many techniques and methods are tested. The effectiveness of models is assessed using the right metrics.

Evaluation: The selected models are rigorously evaluated to determine their effectiveness in solving the business problem. This involves validating the models against a holdout dataset or using cross-validation techniques to ensure generalizability.

Deployment: Once a satisfactory model is obtained, it is deployed into the production environment. This phase includes integrating the model into the existing business processes, making it accessible to end-users, and providing documentation and training as needed.

It's essential to note that the CRISP-DM framework is iterative, meaning that there is a feedback loop that allows for revisiting and refining previous stages based on the evaluation results or changing business requirements. The process may go through several iterations before reaching the final solution.

The CRISP-DM framework provides a structured and systematic way to manage complex analytics projects, enabling organizations to effectively use data-driven insights for making informed business decisions.

SCALES OF MEASUREMENTS

In statistics and data analysis, there are four commonly recognized scales of measurements, also known as levels of measurement or data types. These scales categorize data based on the nature and characteristics of the data being measured. The four scales of measurement are:

Nominal Scale: The nominal scale is the simplest level of measurement. It involves categorizing data into distinct categories or groups with no inherent order or numerical value. Examples of nominal data include categories like gender (male/female), colors (red/blue/green), or types of fruits (apple/banana/orange).

Ordinal Scale: The ordinal scale includes data that has a natural order but lacks a consistent interval between the categories. It allows us to rank or order the data, but the differences between the ranks are not uniform. Examples of ordinal data include rankings in a competition (1st place, 2nd place, 3rd place), educational grades (A, B, C), or survey response options (strongly agree, agree, neutral, disagree, strongly disagree).

Interval Scale: The interval scale has ordered categories with consistent intervals between them, but it does not have a true zero point. In this scale, the absence of a value (a zero) does not indicate a lack of the attribute being measured. Examples of interval data include temperatures measured in Celsius or Fahrenheit. A difference of 10 degrees on this scale means the same in any part of the scale.

Ratio Scale: The ratio scale is the most comprehensive and informative level of measurement. It has ordered categories with consistent intervals and a true zero point, where zero represents the complete absence of the attribute being measured. Ratios between values on this scale are meaningful. Examples of ratio data include height, weight, time, age, and income.

It's important to choose the appropriate scale of measurement for data analysis as it affects the type of statistical methods that can be applied. Generally, more advanced statistical analyses can be performed on data with higher levels of measurement, while more limited analyses are applicable to data with lower levels of measurement.

REVIEW QUESTIONS

Multiple Choice Questions

Q.1. What is data analytics?

(*a*) The process of collecting data
(*b*) The process of analyzing and interpreting data to extract insights
(*c*) The process of visualizing data
(*d*) The process of storing data

Q.2. Which of the following is NOT a common step in the data analytics process?

(*a*) Data collection (*b*) Data visualization
(*c*) Data transformation (*d*) Data encryption

Q.3. What is exploratory data analysis (EDA)?

(*a*) The process of visualizing data
(*b*) The process of summarizing data using descriptive statistics
(*c*) The process of cleaning and preprocessing data
(*d*) The process of analyzing data to understand its key characteristics

Q.4. Which data analytics technique is used to identify patterns or relationships in the data?

(*a*) Descriptive analytics (*b*) Predictive analytics
(*c*) Diagnostic analytics (*d*) Prescriptive analytics

Q.5. What is the primary goal of descriptive analytics?

(*a*) To predict future outcomes (*b*) To understand historical data
(*c*) To identify patterns or relationships in the data
(*d*) To prescribe actions based on data insights

Q.6. Which data analytics technique is used to understand why a certain event occurred?

(*a*) Descriptive analytics (*b*) Predictive analytics
(*c*) Diagnostic analytics (*d*) Prescriptive analytics

Q.7. What is the primary goal of prescriptive analytics?

(*a*) To predict future outcomes (*b*) To understand historical data
(*c*) To identify patterns or relationships in the data
(*d*) To prescribe actions based on data insights

Q.8. Which of the following is NOT a common type of data analytics?

(*a*) Text analytics (*b*) Social analytics (*c*) Spatial analytics (*d*) Time analytics

Q.9. What is the purpose of data visualization in data analytics?

(*a*) To summarize data using descriptive statistics
(*b*) To encode additional information or variables
(*c*) To transform the data into a different format
(*d*) To communicate insights and findings effectively

Q.10. Which of the following is a characteristic of predictive analytics?

(*a*) Understanding historical data
(*b*) Identifying patterns or relationships in the data
(*c*) Predicting future outcomes
(*d*) Prescribing actions based on data insights

Q.11. What is the primary goal of diagnostic analytics?

(*a*) To predict future outcomes
(*b*) To understand why a certain event occurred
(*c*) To identify patterns or relationships in the data
(*d*) To prescribe actions based on data insights

Q.12. Which data analytics technique is used to understand what will happen in the future?

(*a*) Descriptive analytics
(*b*) Predictive analytics
(*c*) Diagnostic analytics
(*d*) Prescriptive analytics

Q.13. What is the purpose of data preprocessing in data analytics?

(*a*) To collect data
(*b*) To analyze and interpret data
(*c*) To visualize data
(*d*) To clean and transform data

Q.14. Which of the following is a common step in data preprocessing?

(*a*) Data collection (*b*) Data visualization (*c*) Data transformation(*d*)Data encryption

Q.15. What is the primary goal of prescriptive analytics?

(*a*) To predict future outcomes
(*b*) To understand historical data
(*c*) To identify patterns or relationships in the data
(*d*) To prescribe actions based on data insights

Q.16. Which data analytics technique is used to understand why a certain event occurred?

(*a*) Descriptive analytics
(*b*) Predictive analytics
(*c*) Diagnostic analytics
(*d*) Prescriptive analytics

Q.17. What is the purpose of data visualization in data analytics?

(*a*) To summarize data using descriptive statistics
(*b*) To encode additional information or variables
(*c*) To transform the data into a different format
(*d*) To communicate insights and findings effectively

Q.18. Which of the following is a characteristic of predictive analytics?

(*a*) Understanding historical data
(*b*) Identifying patterns or relationships in the data
(*c*) Predicting future outcomes
(*d*) Prescribing actions based on data insights

Q.19. What is the primary goal of diagnostic analytics?

(*a*) To predict future outcomes
(*b*) To understand why a certain event occurred
(*c*) To identify patterns or relationships in the data
(*d*) To prescribe actions based on data insights

Q.20. Which data analytics technique is used to understand what will happen in the future?

(*a*) Descriptive analytics (*b*) Predictive analytics

(*c*) Diagnostic analytics (*d*) Prescriptive analytics

Answer to Multiple Choice Questions

1. (*b*) **2.** (*d*) **3.** (*d*) **4.** (*b*) **5.** (*b*) **6.** (*c*) **7.** (*d*) **8.** (*d*) **9.** (*d*)
10. (*c*) **11.** (*b*) **12.** (*b*) **13.** (*d*) **14.** (*c*) **15.** (*d*) **16.** (*c*) **17.** (*d*) **18.** (*c*)
19. (*b*) **20.** (*b*)

❑❑❑

9

PRE PROCESSING

PRE PROCESS & DESCRIPTIVE SUMMARY

Pre-processing and descriptive summary are essential steps in data analysis, helping to clean and explore data to gain insights and prepare it for further analysis. Let's look at each step:

1. **Data Pre-processing:** Cleaning, converting, and preparing raw data for analysis are all parts of data pre-processing. It makes sure that the data is accurate and that any potential problems are fixed before moving on to further in-depth research. Several typical steps in data pre-processing include:

   Data Cleaning: Handling missing data, removing duplicates, and dealing with outliers to ensure data integrity.

   Data Transformation: Transforming data to a more appropriate scale or distribution, such as logarithmic or normalization transformations.

   Data Integration: Combining data from multiple sources into a single dataset.

   Feature Engineering: Combining current traits to produce new ones that offer more insightful analysis.

   Data Reduction: PCA or feature selection can be used to reduce the dimensionality of the data, which can expedite analysis and lessen complexity.

   Data Sampling: If the dataset is large, sampling techniques can be used to work with a smaller representative subset.

2. **Descriptive Summary:** Descriptive summary involves the exploration and summarization of the main characteristics and patterns present in the data. It offers a summary of the data distribution and aids in comprehending the salient points and insights. The following are typical methods for producing a descriptive summary:

   Summary Statistics: Calculating measures like mean, median, mode, standard deviation, minimum, and maximum to describe the central tendency and spread of the data.

   Data Visualization: Creating charts, graphs, and plots to visually represent the data distribution, relationships, and patterns. Common visualizations include histograms, box plots, scatter plots, and bar charts.

   Frequency Analysis: Analyzing the frequency distribution of categorical variables to understand the occurrence of different categories.

Correlation Analysis: Examining the relationships between variables to identify correlations and dependencies.

Cross-Tabulation: Creating contingency tables to analyze the association between two or more categorical variables.

Exploratory Data Analysis (EDA): Conducting a thorough exploration of the data to uncover interesting patterns and relationships.

By performing data pre-processing and generating a descriptive summary, data analysts gain a better understanding of the dataset, identify potential issues, and lay the groundwork for more advanced analyses and modeling. This process helps ensure that the data used for decision-making is reliable and meaningful.

PRE PROCESSING DATA

Data preprocessing is an essential stage in both data analysis and machine learning. To prepare the raw data for additional analysis or model training, it entails cleaning, converting, and arranging it. The accuracy and efficiency of your models can be greatly enhanced by careful data preprocessing. The typical steps in data preparation are listed below:

Data Cleaning: Handling missing values: dealing with missing values Make a decision for how to handle missing data (delete columns or rows, fill with the median or average, etc.). Outlier recognition Find any outliers that can bias your analysis or model, and deal with them.

Data Transformation: Feature scaling: Scaling features is a technique used to avoid the dominance of one characteristic over another in numerical features. Adding a code for category variables: the one-hot encoding method) to express categorical variables numerically.

Feature engineering: Create new features that might be more informative for the problem at hand.

Data Reduction: Dimensionality reduction: Reduce the amount of features while retaining critical information by using methods like PCA.

Data Normalization: Ensure all numerical data falls within a similar scale (e.g., between 0 and 1) to prevent any particular feature from dominating the model.

Data Splitting: Create training, validation, and testing sets from the data. The validation set is used to fine-tune hyperparameters, the testing set is used to assess the model's performance, and the training set is used to train the model.

Feature Selection: Choose the most relevant features to use for training the model. Removing irrelevant features can help reduce noise and improve model efficiency.

Handling Imbalanced Data: Use strategies like oversampling, undersampling, or employing class weights during training to overcome class imbalances in classification difficulties.

Handling Text Data: Tokenization: Break down text into individual words or tokens. Text cleaning: Remove punctuation, special characters, and unnecessary spaces. Stopword removal: Eliminate common words that carry little meaning (e.g., "the," "is," "and").

Lemmatization or stemming: Reduce words to their root forms to consolidate similar words.

Normalization and Standardization: Depending on the requirements of the algorithm, you might need to normalize or standardize numerical features to have a mean of 0 and standard deviation of 1.

Remember that the precise preprocessing techniques you choose will depend on the type of data you have and the issue you are trying to solve. Always analyze your data carefully and choose the appropriate preprocessing techniques accordingly. Additionally, data preprocessing is often an iterative process, and you may need to revisit and adjust the steps based on your model's performance.

ROUP SUMMARIES

Group summaries, also known as group aggregations, involve computing summary statistics or aggregations on data grouped by specific categories or groups. It is useful for understanding patterns and trends within different subsets of the data. Here's how you can compute group summaries:

Consider that you wish to construct summary statistics based on one or more categorical categories in a dataset having a variety of columns. For example, you might have a dataset of sales transactions with columns like "Product Category," "Sales Region," "Sales Amount," and "Date."

Grouping the Data: First, you need to group the data based on one or more categorical columns. For instance, if you want to compute summaries based on "Product Category," you would group the data by that column.

Applying Aggregations: After the data is grouped, you can apply different aggregation functions to compute summary statistics for each group. Common aggregation functions include:

Sum: Calculates the total sum of a numerical column within each group.

Mean/Average: Computes the average value of a numerical column within each group.

Median: Calculates the middle value of a numerical column within each group.

Count: Counts the number of occurrences of each group.

Min/Max: Determines a numerical column's lowest and maximum values for each category.

Getting the Results: Once the aggregations are applied, you will have a new dataset or summary table with the computed statistics for each group.

For example, using Python's pandas library, you can compute group summaries as follows:

Group summaries are valuable for gaining insights from your data, identifying trends, making comparisons between different groups, and making data-driven decisions in various domains such as business, marketing, and research.

CROSSTAB, PIVOT AND RESHAPE DATA

Performing crosstab, pivot, and reshape operations on your data using the pandas package. These processes are frequently used to analyze data and transform it into a format that is better suited for study or visualization. Let's examine each of these procedures using examples:

1. **Crosstab:** With the use of two or more categorical columns, the pd.crosstab() method creates a cross-tabulation, sometimes referred to as a contingency table, that displays the frequency distribution of variables. It offers a practical method to look at how several category variables relate to one another.

```
In [3]:   import pandas as pd

          # Sample DataFrame
          data = {
              'Category': ['A', 'B', 'A', 'B', 'A'],
              'Region': ['Delhi', 'Mumbai', 'Delhi', 'Mumbai', 'Delhi'],
              'Count': [14, 19, 11, 16, 9]
          }
```

```
df = pd.DataFrame(data)

# Computing a cross-tabulation between 'Category' and 'Region'
cross_tab = pd.crosstab(df['Category'], df['Region'])
print(cross_tab)

Region    Delhi   Mumbai
Category
A           3       0
B           0       2
```

2. **Pivot:** The pd.pivot_table() function allows you to create a pivot table from your data, which is a useful way to summarize and aggregate data based on one or more columns.

```
# Using the same DataFrame 'df' from the previous example

# Creating a pivot table with 'Category' as rows and 'Region' as columns, aggregating using 'Count'

In [4]:   pivot_table = pd.pivot_table(df, values='Count', index='Category', columns='Region',
          aggfunc='sum', fill_value=0)
          print(pivot_table)

          Region    Delhi   Mumbai
          Category
          A           34      0
          B           0       35
```

3. **Reshape Data:** For altering data, Pandas has a number of operations including pd.melt() and pd.stack(). These features facilitate the conversion of data between wide and long formats.

```
# Using the same DataFrame 'df' from the previous examples

# Reshaping the data from wide to long format using 'pd.melt()'

In [5]:   melted_df = pd.melt(df, id_vars=['Category', 'Region'], value_vars='Count', var_
          name='Metric', value_name='Value')
          print(melted_df)

            Category   Region   Metric   Value
          0    A       Delhi    Count    14
          1    B       Mumbai   Count    19
          2    A       Delhi    Count    11
          3    B       Mumbai   Count    16
          4    A       Delhi    Count    9
```

These examples demonstrate how you can use pandas in Python to perform crosstab, pivot, and reshape operations to analyze and transform your data efficiently. Remember to customize the functions based on your specific data and analysis requirements.

MANAGING MISSING VALUES

In data preprocessing and analysis, managing missing values is a crucial step. Missing values may arise due to a number of factors, including incorrect data entry, sensor issues, or respondents' decisions to withhold their responses to certain questions. By handling missing data properly, you can prevent them from impairing the caliber of your study or the effectiveness of machine learning models. These common methods for handling missing values are listed below:

Identify Missing Values: Finding and comprehending the level of missing data in your dataset is the first step. The isnull() and notnull() functions in the Python Pandas package allow users to check for missing values in a DataFrame.

Remove Rows with Missing Values: If the missing values are not significant in number, you may choose to remove rows that contain missing data. However, be cautious with this approach, as it may lead to the loss of valuable information.

```
import pandas as pd
# Assuming 'df' is your DataFrame
# Drop rows with missing values
df_cleaned = df.dropna()
```

Impute Missing Values: Instead of removing rows, you can impute missing values with estimated values. Some common imputation methods include:

- Filling with a constant value (e.g., zero or the mean/median of the column).
- Filling with the most frequent value (mode) for categorical data.
- Filling with values estimated from other related variables using regression or machine learning models.

```
# Impute missing values with the mean of the column
df_filled = df.fillna(df.mean())
```

Forward or Backward Fill (ffill/bfill): With either a forward fill or a backward fill along the same column, you can fill in missing data with the most recent value that is known.

```
# Forward fill missing values in DataFrame 'df'
df_ffill = df.fillna(method='ffill')
# Backward fill missing values in DataFrame 'df'
df_bfill = df.fillna(method='bfill')
```

Interpolation: A technique for guessing missing values using already collected data points is interpolation. Time series data can benefit most from it.

```
# Interpolate missing values in DataFrame 'df'
df_interpolated = df.interpolate()
```

Indicator/Dummy Variables: In some cases, you might want to create a new binary column that indicates whether a value was missing in the original column.

```
# Create a new column 'is_missing' that indicates whether 'SomeColumn' has missing values
df['SomeColumn_is_missing'] = df['SomeColumn'].isnull().astype(int)
```

Handling Categorical Data: For categorical columns, you can treat missing values as a separate category if it makes sense in the context of your analysis.

Keep in mind that the approach you choose to handle missing values will depend on the type of data you have, the degree of missingness, and the particular specifications of your analytic or modeling assignment. It's crucial to carefully weigh the ramifications of each strategy and determine how it might affect the reliability of your data and the accuracy of your analysis.

OUTLIERS DETECTION

Data points known as outliers differ dramatically from the rest of the data in a dataset. They may be brought on by a number of things, including incorrect data entry, sensor issues, or uncommon occurrences. Machine learning and statistical analysis models can be significantly impacted by outliers, which can result in skewed results and poorer model performance. Therefore, detecting and handling outliers is an essential step in data preprocessing. Here are some common methods for outlier detection:

Visual Inspection: Visualizing the data with plots like scatter plots, box plots, or histograms is one of the simplest techniques to find outliers. Outliers frequently show up as data points that are dispersed from the main cluster or have odd patterns.

Z-Score or Standard Deviation Method: A data point's Z-score indicates how far from the mean it is in terms of standard deviations. Outliers are points that have a Z-score over a threshold, which is often set at approximately 2 or 3.

IQR (Interquartile Range) Method: The interval between the 25th and 75th percentiles of the data, or the middle 50%, is known as the IQR. Outliers are data points that deviate from the median beyond a predetermined threshold (often 1.5 times the IQR).

Box Plots: Box plots can visually highlight potential outliers. Data points lying beyond the whiskers of the box plot can be considered outliers.

Distance-Based Methods: In order to identify outliers based on their proximity to other data points, techniques like k-nearest neighbors (KNN) and DBSCAN (Density-Based Spatial Clustering of Applications with Noise) can be utilized.

ML Models: One-Class SVM and Isolation Forest are two ML methods that can be utilized for outlier detection. These models are trained to recognize the normal patterns in the data and identify anomalies as outliers.

Local Outlier Factor (LOF): A data point's local density in relation to its neighbors is determined by the LOF method. Outliers are places where the density is much lower than its surroundings.

It's essential to exercise caution while detecting and handling outliers. Not all data points that appear to be outliers are necessarily erroneous; they could represent legitimate rare events or genuine extreme values. Deciding whether to remove, adjust, or keep outliers depends on the specific domain and context of the data analysis or modeling task. It's advisable to consult domain experts if you are uncertain about how to handle outliers in your particular application. Additionally, outlier detection can be an iterative process, where you evaluate the impact of removing or keeping outliers on your analysis or model performance.

VARIOUS TYPES OF JOINS, MERGE

In the context of relational databases and data manipulation using pandas in Python, there are several types of joins and merge operations. These operations allow you to combine data from multiple tables or DataFrames based on common columns. Here are the main types of joins and merges:

Inner Join: Only the rows with matching values across both tables or DataFrames are returned by an inner join. Rows that don't match aren't included in the outcome.

```
# Using pandas in Python for inner join
import pandas as pd
# Assuming 'df1' and 'df2' are two DataFrames to be joined
inner_merged = pd.merge(df1, df2, on='common_column')
```

Left Join (Left Outer Join): All of the rows from the left table or DataFrame and the matching rows from the right table or DataFrame are returned by a left join. The result will include NaN (null) values for the right-side columns if there is no match in the right table..

```
# Using pandas in Python for left join
left_merged = pd.merge(df1, df2, on='common_column', how='left')
```

Right Join (Right Outer Join): All of the rows from the right table or DataFrame are returned along with any matching rows from the left table or DataFrame in a right join. The result will have NaN (null) values for the left-side columns if there is no match in the left table.

```
# Using pandas in Python for right join
right_merged = pd.merge(df1, df2, on='common_column', how='right')
```

Full Join (Full Outer Join): A full join returns all the rows from both tables or DataFrames. If there's no match in either table, the result will contain NaN (null) values for the columns without matching values.

```
# Using pandas in Python for full join
full_merged = pd.merge(df1, df2, on='common_column', how='outer')
```

Concatenation: Concatenation is not a join, but it is used to combine DataFrames along a particular axis (row-wise or column-wise) without regard to common columns.

```
# Using pandas in Python for concatenation
concatenated = pd.concat([df1, df2], axis=0)  # Row-wise concatenation
concatenated = pd.concat([df1, df2], axis=1)  # Column-wise concatenation
```

The appropriate choice of join or merge depends on the relationship between the datasets and the desired output. It's essential to understand the data and the requirements of the analysis to select the right method. Additionally, keep in mind that some data may have missing values after joining, depending on the type of merge and the data's structure.

MANAGING INDEXES IN PANDAS

In pandas, indexes play a crucial role in data manipulation and analysis. They provide a way to uniquely identify and access rows in a DataFrame. Managing indexes involves various operations, such as setting, resetting, reordering, and using indexes effectively. Here are some common operations for managing indexes in pandas:

Setting an Index: The set_index() method allows you to change a DataFrame's index to a specific column..

```
import pandas as pd
# Assuming 'df' is your DataFrame and 'column_name' is the column you want to set as the index
df.set_index('column_name', inplace=True)
```

Resetting the Index: Use the reset_index() method to return the index to its initial integer-based state.

```
# Reset the index and create a new default integer-based index
df.reset_index(drop=True, inplace=True)
```

Reordering the Index: You can change the order of the index using the reindex() method.

```
# Reorder the index based on a specific order or a list of new index labels
new_order = ['label1', 'label2', 'label3']
df = df.reindex(new_order)
```

Multi-level Index: Pandas allows you to create multi-level indexes (hierarchical indexes) to represent data with multiple dimensions. You can set multiple columns as the index to achieve this.

```
# Creating a multi-level index based on two columns
df.set_index(['column1', 'column2'], inplace=True)
```

Using Index for Selection and Slicing: Indexes are useful for selecting specific rows and slicing data.

```
# Selecting rows based on index label
row_data = df.loc['index_label']
# Slicing data based on index range
sliced_data = df.loc['start_index':'end_index']
```

Removing Index Name: If the index has a name, you can remove it using the rename_axis() method.

```
# Assuming 'df' has an index with the name 'index_name'
df.rename_axis(None, inplace=True)
```

Setting Numeric Index: You can set a numeric index for the DataFrame by using RangeIndex or pd.Index.

```
# Set a numeric index starting from 0 to (number_of_rows - 1)
df.index = pd.RangeIndex(start=0, stop=len(df))
# Alternatively, you can directly create a numeric index using pd.Index
df.index – pd.Index(rangc(lcn(df)))
```

Properly managing indexes can improve the efficiency of data access and manipulation in pandas. It's essential to choose appropriate index columns based on the nature of your data & analysis tasks you want to perform. Additionally, be mindful of the impact of in-place operations (e.g., inplace=True) on your DataFrame and consider making a copy of the data before performing any significant changes to avoid unintended consequences.

PARTITIONING DATA INTO TRAIN AND TEST SET

In order to effectively assess a model's performance, machine learning practitioners frequently divide data into training and test sets. The test set is used to gauge how effectively the model generalizes to fresh, untested data, whereas the training set is used to train the model. Here's how, using Python and the scikit-learn module, you can divide your data into train and test sets:

```
import pandas as pd
from sklearn.model_selection import train_test_split
```

```
# Assuming 'data' is your DataFrame and 'target_column' is the column you want to predict
X = data.drop(columns=['target_column']) # Features (input variables)
y = data['target_column'] # Target variable (output variable)

# Split the data into train and test sets (by default, 75% train and 25% test)
X_train, X_test, y_train, y_test = train_test_split(X, y, test_size=0.25, random_state=42)
```

The characteristics (X) and the target variable (y) are first segregated in the code above. The data is then divided into training and testing sets using the scikit-learn train_test_split() function. The test set's data inclusion percentage (in this case, 25%) is specified by the test_size option. The data is divided consistently by using the random_state parameter.

Your ML model can be trained using X_train and y_train after the data has been split, and its performance can then be assessed using X_test and y_test. This will allow you to determine how effectively your model generalizes to fresh, untested data. Remember that the test size and random_state values you choose will have an impact on your results, so you must experiment to find the ones that work best for your particular dataset and analysis needs.

SCALING OF DATA (USEFUL FOR CLUSTERING)

When working with clustering algorithms or other machine learning models that are sensitive to the scale of input features, scaling of data is an essential preprocessing step. Scaling prevents the dominance of features with bigger scales by ensuring that all characteristics contribute equally to the clustering process. Two popular techniques for scaling data are: Standardization and Min-Max Scaling (Normalization).

Min-Max Scaling (Normalization): The data are scaled using min-max to a defined range, usually between 0 and 1. It operates by altering each characteristic according to its minimum and maximum values.

x_scaled = (x - min(x)) / (max(x) - min(x))

Where x is the original feature value, min(x) is the minimum value of the feature, and max(x) is the maximum value of the feature.

```
from sklearn.preprocessing import MinMaxScaler

# Assuming 'X' is your data matrix (numpy array or DataFrame)
scaler = MinMaxScaler()
X_scaled = scaler.fit_transform(X)
```

Standardization: Data that has undergone standardization is scaled to have a mean of 0 and a standard deviation of 1. When the characteristics have several scales or different units, it is helpful. Data that has undergone standardization will have a normal distribution with a standard mean and variance.

x_standardized = (x - mean(x)) / std(x)

Where x is the original feature value, mean(x) is the mean value of the feature, and std(x) is the standard deviation of the feature.

```
from sklearn.preprocessing import StandardScaler

# Assuming 'X' is your data matrix (numpy array or DataFrame)
scaler = StandardScaler()
X_standardized = scaler.fit_transform(X)
```

The needs of your particular clustering technique and the characteristics of your data will determine which scaling strategy to choose. Both approaches have their uses, therefore it's always a good idea to test both and compare the outcomes to see whether scaling is more effective for your clustering task. To prevent data leaking, keep in mind that scaling should only be done to the training data before being transmitted to the test data.

REVIEW QUESTIONS

Multiple Choice Questions

Q.1. What is data preprocessing?

(*a*) The process of analyzing and interpreting data
(*b*) The process of summarizing data using descriptive statistics
(*c*) The process of cleaning and transforming data before analysis
(*d*) The process of visualizing data

Q.2. Which of the following is NOT a common step in data preprocessing?

(*a*) Data collection (*b*) Data visualization
(*c*) Data transformation (*d*) Data encoding

Q.3. What is the purpose of data cleaning in data preprocessing?

(*a*) To collect data from various sources
(*b*) To remove errors and inconsistencies from the data
(*c*) To transform data into a different format
(*d*) To visualize data

Q.4. Which of the following is a common technique used for data cleaning?

(*a*) Mean imputation (*b*) Data aggregation
(*c*) Dimensionality reduction (*d*) Hypothesis testing

Q.5. What is the purpose of data transformation in data preprocessing?

(*a*) To remove outliers from the data (*b*) To convert data into a different format
(*c*) To summarize data using descriptive statistics
(*d*) To encode categorical variables

Q.6. Which of the following is a common technique used for data transformation?

(*a*) Standardization (*b*) Mean imputation (*c*) One-hot encoding (*d*) Hypothesis testing

Q.7. What is the purpose of feature scaling in data preprocessing?

(*a*) To remove outliers from the data
(*b*) To convert categorical variables into numerical format
(*c*) To transform data into a different format
(*d*) To normalize the range of numerical variables

Q.8. Which of the following is a common technique used for feature scaling?

(*a*) Mean imputation (*b*) Standardization
(*c*) One-hot encoding (*d*) Dimensionality reduction

Q.9. What is the purpose of handling missing values in data preprocessing?

(*a*) To remove outliers from the data
(*b*) To convert categorical variables into numerical format
(*c*) To replace missing values with appropriate values
(*d*) To normalize the range of numerical variables

Q.10. Which of the following is a common technique used for handling missing values?

(*a*) Standardization
(*b*) Mean imputation
(*c*) One-hot encoding
(*d*) Dimensionality reduction

Q.11. What is the purpose of data encoding in data preprocessing?

(*a*) To remove outliers from the data
(*b*) To convert categorical variables into numerical format
(*c*) To replace missing values with appropriate values
(*d*) To normalize the range of numerical variables

Q.12. Which of the following is a common technique used for data encoding?

(*a*) Standardization
(*b*) Mean imputation
(*c*) One-hot encoding
(*d*) Dimensionality reduction

Q.13. What is the purpose of outlier detection in data preprocessing?

(*a*) To remove missing values from the data
(*b*) To convert categorical variables into numerical format
(*c*) To identify and remove outliers from the data
(*d*) To normalize the range of numerical variables

Q.14. Which of the following is a common technique used for outlier detection?

(*a*) Standardization
(*b*) Mean imputation
(*c*) Z-score
(*d*) Dimensionality reduction

Q.15. What is the purpose of dimensionality reduction in data preprocessing?

(*a*) To remove missing values from the data
(*b*) To convert categorical variables into numerical format
(*c*) To reduce the number of features in the data
(*d*) To normalize the range of numerical variables

Q.16. Which of the following is a common technique used for dimensionality reduction?

(*a*) Principal Component Analysis (PCA)
(*b*) Mean imputation
(*c*) One-hot encoding
(*d*) Z-score normalization

Q.17. What is the purpose of data transformation in data preprocessing?

(*a*) To remove missing values from the data
(*b*) To convert categorical variables into numerical format
(*c*) To transform data into a different format
(*d*) To normalize the range of numerical variables

Q.18. Which of the following is a common technique used for data transformation?

(*a*) Standardization
(*b*) Mean imputation
(*c*) One-hot encoding
(*d*) Z-score normalization

Q.19. What is the purpose of data aggregation in data preprocessing?

(*a*) To remove missing values from the data
(*b*) To summarize data using descriptive statistics
(*c*) To identify and remove outliers from the data
(*d*) To normalize the range of numerical variables

Q.20. Which of the following is a common technique used for data aggregation?

(*a*) Standardization
(*b*) Mean imputation
(*c*) Grouping and summarizing data
(*d*) Z-score normalization

Answer to Multiple Choice Questions

1. (*c*) **2.** (*a*) **3.** (*b*) **4.** (*a*) **5.** (*b*) **6.** (*a*) **7.** (*d*) **8.** (*b*) **9.** (*c*)
10. (*b*) **11.** (*b*) **12.** (*c*) **13.** (*c*) **14.** (*c*) **15.** (*c*) **16.** (*a*) **17.** (*c*) **18.** (*d*)
19. (*b*) **20.** (*c*)

❑❑❑

10

STASTICS OF DATA ANALYTICS

STATISTICS

Data collection, analysis, interpretation, presentation, and organization are all topics covered in the mathematic discipline known as statistics. Inferences can be drawn from samples, decisions can be made based on the data, and forecasts can be made using the methods and tools that are provided. Statistics is used to draw meaningful conclusions and patterns from data in a variety of sectors, including science, the social sciences, business, engineering, and more.

Key Concepts and Terminology in Statistics

Population and Sample: The term "population" refers to the total group or collection of people, things, or events that are being studied. A sample is a portion of the population that serves as a proxy for the entire population in a study.

Descriptive Statistics: Methods that enumerate and describe a dataset's key characteristics are included in descriptive statistics. Common descriptive statistics include measurements of dispersion (range, variance, standard deviation), measures of central tendency (mean, median, and mode), and graphical representations (histograms, box plots, etc.).

Inferential Statistics: Inferential statistics use sample data to make inferences or predictions about the population. It involves hypothesis testing, confidence intervals, and regression analysis, among others.

Hypothesis Testing: A statistical technique known as hypothesis testing is used to draw conclusions about a population from sample data. Making a null hypothesis and an alternative hypothesis, gathering data, and assessing whether there is sufficient evidence to reject or fail to reject the null hypothesis are all part of the process.

Confidence Interval: It is a range of values around a sample statistic (e.g., mean or proportion) within which the true population parameter is estimated to lie with a certain level of confidence.

Regression Analysis: Modeling the link between a dependent variable and one or more independent variables is done using regression analysis. Making predictions using the model and comprehending how the independent variables affect the dependent variable are both aided by this.

Statistical Software: Statistical software, such as R, Python (with libraries like NumPy, pandas, and statsmodels), SPSS, SAS, and others, are used to perform various statistical analyses efficiently.

A strong tool for making data-driven decisions, drawing inferences from observations, and confirming or refuting hypotheses is statistics. It helps researchers, analysts, and decision-makers make sense of complex data and gain valuable insights from it. However, it's crucial to apply statistical methods correctly and interpret the results appropriately to avoid potential pitfalls or misinterpretations.

BASIC STATISTICS (MEAN, MEDIAN, MODE)

Fundamental metrics are used to summarize and define a dataset using basic statistics. They give important information about the central tendency and data dispersion. The mean, median, and mode are the three primary basic statistics:

Mean: The mean is a dataset's mean value. By adding together all the data points and dividing the total by the number of data points, it is calculated.

Mean = (Sum of all data points) / (Number of data points)

Extreme values have a considerable impact on the mean's value, hence the mean is sensitive to them.

Median: In an ordered dataset, the median is the midpoint. The median is the midway value when the dataset has an odd number of data points. The median is the average of the two middle values when the number of data points in the dataset is even. Determine the middle value(s) before sorting the dataset in ascending order to determine the median.

The median is more robust to outliers compared to the mean, as it is not affected by extreme values.

Mode: The value that appears most frequently in a dataset is the mode. One mode (unimodal), several modes (bimodal, trimodal, etc.), or no mode (if all values have the same frequency) can exist in a dataset.

When working with categorical or discrete data, the mode can be helpful, but it can also be used to continuous data.

```
import numpy as np
import pandas as pd

data = [10, 20, 30, 40, 40, 50]

# Calculate the mean using NumPy
mean = np.mean(data)

# Calculate the median using NumPy
median = np.median(data)

# Calculate the mode using pandas
series_data = pd.Series(data)
mode = series_data.mode().values

print("Mean:", mean)
print("Median:", median)
print("Mode:", mode)
```

In [6]:
```
import numpy as np
import pandas as pd
data = [10, 20, 30, 40, 40, 50]

# Calculate the mean using NumPy
mean = np.mean(data)

# Calculate the median using NumPy
median = np.median(data)

# Calculate the mode using pandas
series_data = pd.Series(data)
mode = series_data.mode().values

print("Mean:", mean)
print("Median:", median)
print("Mode:", mode)

Mean: 31.666666666666668
Median: 35.0
Mode: [40]
```

Output:

Mean: 31.666666666666668

Median: 35.0

Mode: [40]

Understanding the central tendency and distribution of the data requires the use of these fundamental statistics. One or more of these measures may be more informative in revealing insights into the dataset depending on the nature of the data and the analytic task.

OTHER STATISTICS (SD, VAR, QUANTILE, SKEWNESS, KURTOSIS)

Other significant statistics offer extra information on the composition and distribution of a dataset. Let's look at a few of them:

Standard Deviation (SD): The spread or dispersion of data points around the mean is measured by the standard deviation. It calculates the average deviation from the mean that data points have on average.

SD = sqrt((Sum of (data points - mean)^2) / (Number of data points))

```
import numpy as np
data = [10, 20, 30, 40, 40, 50]

# Calculate the standard deviation using NumPy
sd = np.std(data)
```

```
print("Standard Deviation:", sd)
In [7]:  import numpy as np
         data = [10, 20, 30, 40, 40, 50]

         # Calculate the standard deviation using NumPy
         sd = np.std(data)

         print("Standard Deviation:", sd)

         Standard Deviation: 13.43709624716425
```

Output:

Standard Deviation: 13.43709624716425

Variance: The dispersion of data points around the mean is also measured by the variance. It is the standard deviation squared.

Variance = (Sum of (data points - mean)^2) / (Number of data points)

```
import numpy as np
data = [10, 20, 30, 40, 40, 50]

# Calculate the variance using NumPy
variance = np.var(data)
print("Variance:", variance)

In [8]:  import numpy as np
         data = [10, 20, 30, 40, 40, 50]

         # Calculate the variance using NumPy
         variance = np.var(data)
         print("Variance:", variance)

         Variance: 180.55555555555557
```

Output:

Variance: 180.55555555555557

Quantile: Quantiles are values that divide a dataset into equal parts. The median is the 50th percentile, dividing the data into two equal halves. Other common quantiles include the quartiles (25th and 75th percentiles) and deciles (10th, 20th, ..., 90th percentiles).

```
import numpy as np
data = [10, 20, 30, 40, 40, 50]

# Calculate the median (50th percentile) using NumPy
median = np.median(data)
```

```
# Calculate the 25th and 75th percentiles (1st and 3rd quartiles) using NumPy
quartiles = np.percentile(data, [25, 75])

print("Median:", median)
print("1st Quartile:", quartiles[0])
print("3rd Quartile:", quartiles[1])
```

```
In [9]:   import numpy as np
          data = [10, 20, 30, 40, 40, 50]

          # Calculate the median (50th percentile) using NumPy
          median = np.median(data)

          # Calculate the 25th and 75th percentiles (1st and 3rd quartiles) using NumPy
          quartiles = np.percentile(data, [25, 75])

          print("Median:", median)
          print("1st Quartile:", quartiles[0])
          print("3rd Quartile:", quartiles[1])

          Median: 35.0
          1st Quartile: 22.5
          3rd Quartile: 40.0
```

Output:

Median: 35.0
1st Quartile: 22.5
3rd Quartile: 40.0

Skewness: Skewness measures the asymmetry of the distribution of data points. A longer tail on the right side of the distribution is indicated by positive skewness, whereas a longer tail on the left is indicated by negative skewness.

```
from scipy.stats import skew
data = [10, 20, 30, 40, 40, 50]

# Calculate skewness using SciPy
skewness = skew(data)
print("Skewness:", skewness)
```

```
In [10]:  from scipy.stats import skew
          data = [10, 20, 30, 40, 40, 50]

          # Calculate skewness using SciPy
          skewness = skew(data)
          print("Skewness:", skewness)
```

```
C:\ProgramData\Anaconda3\lib\site-packages\for this version of SciPy (detected version
warning.warn(f"A NumPy version >=(np_min

Skewness: -0.3053162697580519
```

Output:

Skewness: -0.3053162697580519

Kurtosis: Kurtosis evaluates how peaked or flat the data point distribution is in comparison to a normal distribution. Low kurtosis denotes a flatter peak, while high kurtosis denotes a sharper peak (more outliers).

```
from scipy.stats import kurtosis
data = [10, 20, 30, 40, 40, 50]

# Calculate kurtosis using SciPy
kurt = kurtosis(data)

print("Kurtosis:", kurt)
```

```
In [11]:  from scipy.stats import kurtosis
          data = [10, 20, 30, 40, 40, 50]

          # Calculate kurtosis using SciPy
          kurt = kurtosis(data)

          print("Kurtosis:", kurt)

          Kurtosis: -1.151715976331361
```

Output:

Kurtosis: -1.151715976331361

These additional statistics provide valuable information about the spread, distribution, and shape of data. Understanding these measures helps in making more informed decisions and selecting appropriate statistical methods for data analysis and modeling.

HYPOTHESIS TESTS (T-TEST, CHI-SQ TESTS, ETC)

Statistical tests called hypothesis tests let us draw conclusions about the population from a sample of data. These tests aid in determining whether there is sufficient data to accept or reject a specific hypothesis on a population parameter. Some typical tests for hypotheses include:

T-Test: When comparing the means of two groups to see if they differ substantially from one another, the t-test is utilized. When the sample size is small and the population standard deviation is unknown, it is frequently utilized. T-tests can be divided into two categories:

- **Independent Samples T-Test:** used to compare the means of two separate groups.
- **Paired Samples T-Test:** When comparing the means of two related groups (for instance, pre- and post-test measures of the same subjects), this term is used.

Chi-Square Test: To evaluate the independence of two category variables, apply the chi-square test. It is used to examine whether the variables are significantly associated.

ANOVA (Analysis of Variance): The means of three or more groups are compared using an ANOVA to see if there are any appreciable differences between them. It is frequently employed when there are several groups involved.

Wilcoxon Rank-Sum Test (Mann-Whitney U Test): When the data is not normally distributed, the Wilcoxon rank-sum test is a non-parametric test used to compare two independent groups.

Kruskal-Wallis H Test: When the data is not normally distributed, a non-parametric alternative to ANOVA called the Kruskal-Wallis test is used to compare the medians of three or more independent groups.

Chi-Square Goodness of Fit Test: This test evaluates if a categorical sample fits an assumed distribution or anticipated frequencies.

Fisher's Exact Test: When assessing a 2x2 contingency table with tiny sample numbers, Fisher's exact test is utilized.

Z-Test: When the population standard deviation is known and the sample size is large, the population mean is tested using the z-test.

These are merely a few illustrations of typical statistical hypothesis testing. The type of data, the research question, and the data assumptions that might be made all influence the selection of the proper test. To properly evaluate the results and make meaningful inferences from the data, it is crucial to select the appropriate test.

PROBABILITY DISTRIBUTIONS (NORMAL, BINOMIAL, ETC)

The possibility of various outcomes in a random experiment or data-generating process is described by probability distributions. They play a crucial role in statistical modeling and inference. Here are some common probability distributions:

Normal Distribution (Gaussian Distribution): One of the most often used distributions in statistics is the normal distribution. Its symmetric, bell-shaped curve serves as a defining feature. The distribution of many natural occurrences and measurement errors tends to be typical. The normal distribution's probability density function (PDF) is given by:

$$f(x \mid \mu, \sigma) = (1 / (\sigma * sqrt(2 * \pi))) * exp(-((x - \mu)^2 / (2 * \sigma^2)))$$

where μ is the mean and σ is the standard deviation.

Binomial Distribution: The number of successes in a certain number of independent Bernoulli trials with a constant probability of success (p) are modeled by the binomial distribution. The binomial distribution's probability mass function (PMF) is given by:

$$P(X = k) = C(n, k) * p^k * (1 - p)^(n - k)$$

where X is the random variable representing the number of successes, n is the number of trials, k is the number of successes, and C(n, k) is the binomial coefficient.

Poisson Distribution: The Poisson distribution simulates the number of occurrences occuring at a steady rate over a certain period of time or space. The Poisson distribution's probability mass function (PMF) is given by:

$$P(X = k) = (\lambda^k * exp(-\lambda)) / k!$$

where X is the random variable representing the number of events, and λ is the average rate of events per interval.

Exponential Distribution: A Poisson process, in which events happen at a constant rate, describes the interval between successive occurrences using an exponential distribution. The exponential distribution's probability density function (PDF) is given by:

$$f(x \mid \lambda) = \lambda * \exp(-\lambda * x)$$

where x is the random variable representing the time between events, and λ is the rate parameter.

Uniform Distribution: When all possible outcomes within a range are equally likely, the uniform distribution is utilized. The uniform distribution's probability density function (PDF) is given by:

$$f(x \mid a, b) = 1 / (b - a) \text{ for } a \leq x \leq b$$

where a and b are the lower and upper bounds of the distribution.

These are just a few examples of probability distributions commonly used in statistics and probability theory. Each distribution has its own characteristics and applications, making them valuable tools in various fields, including physics, engineering, finance, and machine learning.

SAMPLING TECHNIQUES

Sampling techniques are methods used to select a subset from larger population for purpose of data analysis or statistical inference. Sampling is essential when studying large populations, as it is often impractical or costly to collect data from the entire population. Different sampling techniques are employed based on the characteristics of the population and the research objectives. Here are some common sampling techniques:

Simple Random Sampling: Every person or thing in the population has an equal probability of being chosen for the sample in a basic random selection. With this approach, any potential sample of the appropriate size has an equal chance of being selected.

Stratified Sampling: Stratified sampling involves dividing the population into non-overlapping subgroups called strata based on certain characteristics (e.g., age, gender, location). A random sample is then taken from each stratum. This method ensures that each subgroup is adequately represented in the sample.

Systematic Sampling: In systematic sampling, a random starting point is selected, and then every nth individual or item is chosen to be part of the sample. This method is useful when the population is ordered in some way, and a random start is needed.

Cluster Sampling: Cluster sampling involves dividing the population into clusters or groups, and then randomly selecting entire clusters to be part of the sample. This method is useful when it is difficult or costly to sample individuals directly.

Convenience Sampling: Convenience sampling involves selecting individuals or items that are readily available and easy to access. While it is easy to implement, convenience sampling may lead to biased results, as it may not accurately represent the entire population.

Snowball Sampling: Snowball sampling is used when the population is hard to reach or hidden. The researcher starts with one or a few individuals, and then those individuals refer other participants, creating a "snowball" effect.

Each sampling technique has its advantages and limitations, and optimal of the appropriate method depends on the research objectives, available resources, and the characteristics of the population being studied. It is crucial to use proper sampling techniques to ensure that sample is illustrative of larger population and that the results can be generalized with confidence. Additionally, appropriate statistical methods should be applied to draw valid conclusions from the sample data.

REVIEW QUESTIONS

Multiple Choice Questions

Q.1. What is descriptive statistics?

(*a*) A branch of mathematics that deals with uncertainty and randomness
(*b*) Statistical methods used for making predictions about future outcomes
(*c*) Methods used to summarize and describe features of a dataset
(*d*) Techniques used to test hypotheses about population parameters

Q.2. Which measure of central tendency is affected the most by outliers?

(*a*) Mean (*b*) Median (*c*) Mode (*d*) Range

Q.3. What does the standard deviation measure?

(*a*) The spread of the data around the median
(*b*) The spread of the data around the mean
(*c*) The frequency of each value in the dataset
(*d*) The difference between the largest and smallest values in the dataset

Q.4. What is a quartile?

(*a*) The difference between the largest and smallest values in the dataset
(*b*) A value that divides a dataset into four equal parts
(*c*) The most frequently occurring value in the dataset
(*d*) The spread of the data around the mean

Q.5. What is the interquartile range (IQR)?

(*a*) The difference between the largest and smallest values in the dataset
(*b*) The range covered by the middle 50% of the data
(*c*) The spread of the data around the mean
(*d*) The standard deviation of the dataset

Q.6. In a normal distribution, where is the mean, median, and mode located?

(*a*) They are all located at the center of the distribution
(*b*) They are all located at the tails of the distribution
(*c*) The mean is at the center, while the median and mode are at the tails
(*d*) The median is at the center, while the mean and mode are at the tails

Q.7. What does skewness measure in a distribution?

(*a*) The symmetry of the distribution (*b*) The kurtosis of the distribution
(*c*) The spread of the distribution (*d*) The asymmetry of the distribution

Q.8. In a positively skewed distribution, where are the mean, median, and mode located?

(*a*) Mean > Median > Mode (*b*) Mean < Median < Mode
(*c*) Mean = Median = Mode (*d*) Mean < Median > Mode

Q.9. What does kurtosis measure in a distribution?

(*a*) The symmetry of the distribution (*b*) The spread of the distribution

(*c*) The peakedness or flatness of the distribution

(*d*) The tails of the distribution

Q.10. Which type of distribution has a kurtosis value greater than 3?

(*a*) Mesokurtic (*b*) Leptokurtic (*c*) Platykurtic (*d*) Normal

Q.11. What is a z-score?

(*a*) A measure of spread in a dataset (*b*) A measure of skewness in a distribution

(*c*) A standardized score representing the number of standard deviations a data point is from the mean

(*d*) A measure of central tendency

Q.12. What is correlation?

(*a*) A measure of association between two variables

(*b*) A measure of spread in a dataset (*c*) A measure of skewness in a distribution

(*d*) A measure of central tendency

Q.13. What does a correlation coefficient of -1 indicate?

(*a*) No correlation between variables

(*b*) A strong positive correlation between variables

(*c*) A strong negative correlation between variables

(*d*) Perfect correlation between variables

Q.14. What does a correlation coefficient of 0 indicate?

(*a*) No correlation between variables

(*b*) A strong positive correlation between variables

(*c*) A strong negative correlation between variables

(*d*) Perfect correlation between variables

Q.15. What does a positive correlation coefficient indicate?

(*a*) A strong positive correlation between variables

(*b*) A strong negative correlation between variables

(*c*) No correlation between variables

(*d*) Perfect correlation between variables

Q.16. What is covariance?

(*a*) A measure of association between two variables

(*b*) A measure of spread in a dataset (*c*) A measure of skewness in a distribution

(*d*) A measure of central tendency

Q.17. What is the range of values for the covariance?

(*a*) $[-1, 1]$ (*b*) $(-\infty, \infty)$ (*c*) $[0, \infty)$ (*d*) $(-1, 1)$

Q.18. What does a positive covariance indicate?

(*a*) A strong positive correlation between variables
(*b*) A strong negative correlation between variables
(*c*) No correlation between variables
(*d*) Perfect correlation between variables

Q.19. What does a negative covariance indicate?

(*a*) A strong positive correlation between variables
(*b*) A strong negative correlation between variables
(*c*) No correlation between variables
(*d*) Perfect correlation between variables

Q.20. Which of the following is NOT a measure of variability in a dataset?

(*a*) Standard deviation (*b*) Variance
(*c*) Median (*d*) Range

Answer to Multiple Choice Questions

1. (*c*) **2.** (*a*) **3.** (*b*) **4.** (*b*) **5.** (*b*) **6.** (*a*) **7.** (*d*) **8.** (*a*) **9.** (*c*)
10. (*b*) **11.** (*c*) **12.** (*a*) **13.** (*c*) **14.** (*a*) **15.** (*a*) **16.** (*a*) **17.** (*b*) **18.** (*a*)
19. (*b*) **20.** (*c*)

❑❑❑

11

REGRESSION

LOGISTIC REGRESSION

When doing binary classification tasks, the result variable (response) is binary or dichotomous (i.e., it can only take one of two potential values, such as 0 or 1, Yes or No, True or False, etc.). This statistical technique is known as logistic regression. Numerous disciplines, including machine learning, epidemiology, social sciences, and medicine, frequently employ logistic regression. Contrary to linear regression, which forecasts continuous numeric values, logistic regression forecasts the likelihood that an observation will fall into one of two classes, either 0 or 1. It converts the linear combination of input information to a probability value between 0 and 1 using the logistic or sigmoid function. The definition of the logistic function is:

$$p(x) = 1 / (1 + \exp(-z))$$

where p(x) is the probability of the positive class (class 1), exp() is the exponential function, and z is the linear combination of input features (also known as the logit):

$$z = \beta 0 + \beta 1 * x1 + \beta 2 * x2 + ... + \beta n * xn$$

Here, β0, β1, β2, ..., βn are the coefficients (parameters) of the logistic regression model, and x1, x2, ..., xn are the input features.

By maximizing the likelihood of the observed data given the model, the model calculates the values of the coefficients during the training phase. The maximum likelihood estimate technique is the most often utilized technique for estimating these factors.

The logistic regression model can be used to forecast the likelihood that an observation will belong to the positive class after the coefficients have been computed. The observation is categorized as belonging to the positive class (1) if the probability exceeds a predetermined threshold (often 0.5), and as belonging to the negative class (0) otherwise. A straightforward and understandable approach, logistic regression can be expanded to tackle multi-class classification jobs using methods like one-vs-rest or softmax regression. Additionally, it frequently serves as a foundation for more intricate machine learning models and algorithms.

LINEAR V/S LOGISTIC

Both logistic regression and linear regression are statistical techniques used for various objectives:

Table 2: Linear v/s Logistic Regression

Features	Linear	Logistic
Target	Interval variable	Discrete variable
Predicted value	Mean of the target variable at given values of input variable	Probability of the particular levels of the given values of the input variable
Graph	Straight line 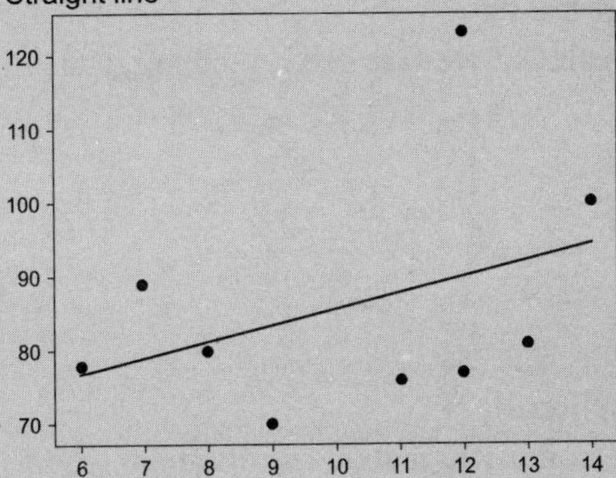	Curve type 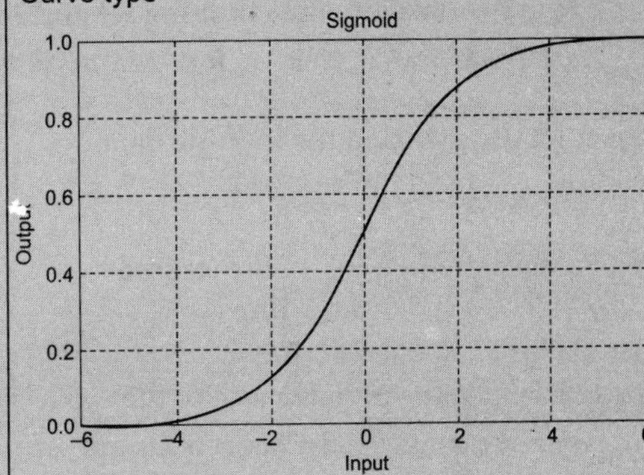
Problem focus	Regression	Classification
Accuracy measure use	Least square estimation	Maximum likelihood estimation
Example	What is temperature? Relationship of my work hour in office and my salary	Gender classification: person is male or female
Application	Forecasting stocks, business domain	Classification, image processing

In conclusion, the primary distinction between logistic regression and linear regression rests in the tasks they are used for and the characteristics of the outcome variable. While logistic regression is used for binary classification problems with binary outcomes, linear regression is utilized for regression tasks with continuous numerical output. Both approaches can be effective tools for data analysis and modeling and each has its own unique applications.

LOGISTIC REGRESSION

You will require a dataset with the input features (independent variables) and the desired binary outcome (dependent variable) to execute logistic regression. To execute logistic regression in Python, you can use libraries like numpy and scikit-learn. Here is a tutorial on how to calculate logistic regression:

Step 1: Import necessary libraries and load the dataset.

```
import numpy as np
from sklearn.linear_model import LogisticRegression

# Assuming 'X' is a numpy array or pandas DataFrame containing the input features
# and 'y' is a numpy array or pandas Series containing the binary outcome (0 or 1)
```

Step 2: Create an instance of the logistic regression model.

```
model = LogisticRegression()
```

Step 3: Split the dataset into training and test sets (optional but recommended).

```
from sklearn.model_selection import train_test_split

# Split the data into 80% training set and 20% test set
X_train, X_test, y_train, y_test = train_test_split(X, y, test_size=0.2, random_state=42)
```

Step 4: Fit the model to the training data.

```
model.fit(X_train, y_train)
```

Step 5: Make predictions on the test set.

```
y_pred = model.predict(X_test)
```

Step 6: Evaluate the performance of the model (optional).

```
from sklearn.metrics import accuracy_score, confusion_matrix, classification_report

# Calculate accuracy
accuracy = accuracy_score(y_test, y_pred)
print("Accuracy:", accuracy)

# Create confusion matrix
conf_matrix = confusion_matrix(y_test, y_pred)
print("Confusion Matrix:")
print(conf_matrix)

# Generate classification report
class_report = classification_report(y_test, y_pred)
print("Classification Report:")
print(class_report)
```

However, logistic regression can be expanded to handle multi-class classification jobs as well. In our example, we assumed a binary result (0 or 1). To further prepare the data for logistic regression, feature engineering and data pretreatment may be required. Don't forget to modify the code to your unique dataset and analysis needs.

METRICS OF LOGISTIC REGRESSION (CONFUSION MATRIX, ROC CURVE)

The effectiveness of the model in binary classification tasks can be evaluated using a variety of assessment criteria in logistic regression. The ROC curve, the confusion matrix, and the Area Under the ROC Curve (AUC-ROC) are some typical metrics. Let's examine each one separately:

Confusion Matrix: A table comparing expected class labels to actual class labels is called a confusion matrix. Truly positives (TP), Truly Negatives (TN), False Positives (FP), and False Negatives (FN) make up this component.

	Predicted Positive	Predicted Negative
Actual Positive	TP	FN
Actual Negative	FP	TN

True Positives (TP): how many instances of a class were correctly predicted to be positive.

True Negatives (TN): the number of instances of the correctly predicted negative class.

False Positives (FP): The amount of negative class occurrences that were mistakenly forecasted as positive.

False Negatives (FN): The amount of positive class instances that were mistakenly classified as negative.

ROC Curve: A visual representation of the model's performance at different categorization thresholds is the Receiver Operating Characteristic (ROC) curve. It demonstrates the trade-off that occurs as the classification threshold is changed between the true positive rate (sensitivity or recall) and the false positive rate (1-specificity). Sensitivity (TPR) and 1-specificity (FPR) are plotted on the ROC curve's y-axis and x-axis, respectively.

Area Under the ROC Curve (AUC-ROC): The total performance of the model is quantified by the Area Under the ROC Curve (AUC-ROC), a single scalar statistic. It indicates the likelihood that the model will give a randomly selected positive instance a higher ranking than a randomly selected negative instance.

The range of AUC-ROC values is 0 to 1, with 1 denoting the best possible model and 0.5 denoting a model that performs no better than random guessing. Scikit-learn can be used in Python to calculate these metrics:

```
from sklearn.metrics import confusion_matrix, roc_curve, roc_auc_score

# Assuming 'y_test' contains the true class labels and 'y_pred' contains the predicted class labels


# Confusion Matrix
conf_matrix = confusion_matrix(y_test, y_pred)
print("Confusion Matrix:")
print(conf_matrix)


# ROC Curve
fpr, tpr, thresholds = roc_curve(y_test, y_pred_proba) # y_pred_proba is the predicted probabilities of positive class


# Plot ROC Curve (optional)
import matplotlib.pyplot as plt
plt.plot(fpr, tpr)
plt.xlabel('False Positive Rate (1 - Specificity)')
```

```
plt.ylabel('True Positive Rate (Sensitivity)')
plt.title('ROC Curve')
plt.show()

# AUC-ROC
auc_roc = roc_auc_score(y_test, y_pred_proba)
print("AUC-ROC:", auc_roc)
```

You may evaluate how well your logistic regression model is doing in the binary classification problem by looking at these metrics. The confusion matrix offers a thorough look at how the model performs for each class, while the ROC curve and AUC-ROC provide a comprehensive evaluation of the model's discrimination power.

PREDICT THE PROBABILITY OF DV ON IV

Using logistic regression, you must first fit the model to your training set of data before applying it to new data to predict the probabilities of the dependent variable (DV) on the independent variable (IV). Using scikit-learn, here's how to accomplish it in Python:

```
import numpy as np
from sklearn.linear_model import LogisticRegression

# Assuming 'X' is a numpy array or pandas DataFrame containing the input features
# and 'y' is a numpy array or pandas Series containing the binary outcome (0 or 1)

# Step 1: Create an instance of the logistic regression model
model = LogisticRegression()

# Step 2: Fit the model to the training data
model.fit(X, y)

# Step 3: Predict the probabilities on new data
# Assuming 'new_data' is a numpy array or pandas DataFrame containing the new data
predicted_probabilities = model.predict_proba(new_data)

# The predicted_probabilities will be a 2D array with each row containing the probabilities
# of the sample belonging to class 0 and class 1, respectively.

# To get the probability of class 1 (positive class), you can access the second column:
probabilities_class_1 = predicted_probabilities[:, 1]
```

In the code above, model.predict_proba(new_data) will give you the predicted probabilities of the positive class (class 1) for each sample in new_data. The predicted probabilities are in the second column of the 2D array, accessed using predicted_probabilities[:, 1].

It's important to keep in mind that the projected probabilities, which range from 0 to 1, represent the possibility that each sample belongs to the positive class. Use the predict method as opposed to predict_proba if you wish to make binary predictions (0 or 1) based on a given threshold. For instance:

```
# Make binary predictions (0 or 1) based on a threshold of 0.5
predicted_labels = (predicted_probabilities[:, 1] >= 0.5).astype(int)
```

APPLICATIONS OF LOGISTIC REGRESSION

Logistic regression has various applications in different fields due to its ability to handle binary classification tasks and predict probabilities. Some common applications of logistic regression include:

Medical and Healthcare: Predicting the likelihood of a patient having a disease based on medical test results.

Identifying the risk of readmission to the hospital for patients with specific conditions.

Assessing the probability of a patient responding positively to a particular treatment.

Marketing and Business: Predicting customer churn (likelihood of customers stopping using a service or product).

Analyzing the probability of a customer making a purchase or responding to a marketing campaign.

Credit risk assessment to determine the probability of default for loan applicants.

Social Sciences: Predicting the probability of a voter supporting a particular candidate in elections.

Identifying factors influencing customer satisfaction or brand loyalty.

Analyzing the probability of success in educational programs or interventions.

Natural Language Processing (NLP): Determine the sentiment (positive/negative) of a piece of text using sentiment analysis.

Text classification tasks, such as spam detection, topic categorization, or sentiment classification.

Image and Object Recognition: Object detection, where logistic regression can be used as a classifier for identifying objects in images.

Psychology and Behavioral Sciences: Predicting the likelihood of individuals engaging in specific behaviors or actions.

Analyzing the probability of patient adherence to treatment plans.

Environmental Studies: Predicting the presence or absence of specific species based on environmental variables.

It's crucial to remember that while logistic regression is a strong and understandable model, it works best for jobs requiring binary classification. Using methods like one-vs-rest or softmax regression, logistic regression can be expanded for multi-class classification applications. Additionally, logistic regression makes the assumption that there is a linear relationship between the input features and the outcome's log-odds, which may not always be the case. In such cases, more complex models like decision trees, random forests, or deep learning models might be more appropriate. Nonetheless, logistic regression remains a fundamental and widely used tool in data analysis and predictive modeling.

REVIEW QUESTIONS

Multiple Choice Questions

Q.1. What is regression analysis used for?

(*a*) Describing the relationship between two or more variables
(*b*) Classifying data points into different categories
(*c*) Identifying outliers in a dataset
(*d*) Calculating summary statistics for a dataset

Q.2. Which type of regression is used when the dependent variable is categorical?

(*a*) Linear regression (*b*) Logistic regression
(*c*) Polynomial regression (*d*) Ridge regression

Q.3. In linear regression, what is the role of the dependent variable?

(*a*) To predict the values of the independent variables
(*b*) To be predicted based on the values of the independent variables
(*c*) To classify data points into different categories
(*d*) To identify outliers in the dataset

Q.4. What is the goal of multiple linear regression?

(*a*) To predict a categorical variable
(*b*) To predict a continuous variable using multiple independent variables
(*c*) To fit a line to the data points
(*d*) To identify outliers in the dataset

Q.5. What is the primary assumption of linear regression?

(*a*) The relationship between the variables is linear
(*b*) The dependent variable is categorical (*c*) The data points are not correlated
(*d*) The independent variables are normally distributed

Q.6. Which of the following is NOT a method to assess the goodness of fit in linear regression?

(*a*) R-squared (*b*) Adjusted R-squared
(*c*) F-test (*d*) Chi-square test

Q.7. In logistic regression, what type of function is used to model the relationship between the independent variables and the probability of a categorical outcome?

(*a*) Linear function (*b*) Exponential function
(*c*) Sigmoid function (*d*) Polynomial function

Q.8. What does the odds ratio represent in logistic regression?

(*a*) The probability of the dependent variable being in a certain category
(*b*) The change in the dependent variable for a one-unit change in the independent variable

(c) The likelihood of the dependent variable occurring in one group compared to another
(d) The standard error of the coefficient estimates

Q.9. What is multicollinearity in regression analysis?
(a) The presence of outliers in the dataset
(b) The relationship between the dependent and independent variables
(c) The correlation between independent variables
(d) The distribution of the residuals

Q.10. What is heteroscedasticity in regression analysis?
(a) The presence of outliers in the dataset
(b) The relationship between the dependent and independent variables
(c) The non-linear relationship between variables
(d) The unequal spread of residuals across the range of predictor variables

Q.11. What is ridge regression used for?
(a) Handling multicollinearity in regression analysis
(b) Modeling the relationship between variables with polynomial functions
(c) Addressing heteroscedasticity in regression analysis
(d) Predicting a categorical outcome variable

Q.12. What is the penalty term added to the cost function in ridge regression?
(a) L1 regularization (b) L2 regularization
(c) Lasso regularization (d) Elastic Net regularization

Q.13. What is the primary difference between ridge regression and lasso regression?
(a) Ridge regression shrinks the coefficients towards zero, while lasso regression can shrink coefficients to exactly zero.
(b) Lasso regression is used for handling multicollinearity, while ridge regression is used for feature selection.
(c) Ridge regression uses L1 regularization, while lasso regression uses L2 regularization.
(d) Ridge regression is more computationally efficient than lasso regression.

Q.14. What is the goal of polynomial regression?
(a) To model the relationship between variables with exponential functions
(b) To handle multicollinearity in regression analysis
(c) To model non-linear relationships between variables
(d) To predict a categorical outcome variable

Q.15. What is the degree of a polynomial in polynomial regression?
(a) The number of predictors in the model (b) The number of observations in the dataset
(c) The number of terms in the polynomial equation
(d) The number of categories in the dependent variable

Q.16. What is the purpose of stepwise regression?

(*a*) To select the best subset of predictors for a regression model

(*b*) To handle multicollinearity in regression analysis

(*c*) To reduce overfitting in the model (*d*) To test the assumptions of regression

Q.17. What is residual analysis in regression?

(*a*) The analysis of the relationship between the dependent and independent variables

(*b*) The analysis of the distribution of the residuals to check the assumptions of regression

(*c*) The analysis of outliers in the dataset

(*d*) The analysis of the interaction effects between variables

Q.18. What is the purpose of cross-validation in regression analysis?

(*a*) To test the assumptions of regression (*b*) To handle multicollinearity in the dataset

(*c*) To assess the predictive performance of the regression model

(*d*) To select the best subset of predictors for the model

Q.19. What is the primary goal of residual plots in regression analysis?

(*a*) To visualize the relationship between the dependent and independent variables

(*b*) To identify outliers in the dataset (*c*) To check the assumptions of regression

(*d*) To handle multicollinearity in the dataset

Q.20. What is the Akaike Information Criterion (AI (*c*) used for in regression analysis?

(*a*) To assess the predictive performance of the model

(*b*) To measure the amount of multicollinearity in the dataset

(*c*) To compare the goodness of fit of different models

(*d*) To test the assumptions of regression

Answer to Multiple Choice Questions

1. (*a*)	**2.** (*b*)	**3.** (*b*)	**4.** (*b*)	**5.** (*a*)	**6.** (*d*)	**7.** (*c*)	**8.** (*c*)	**9.** (*c*)
10. (*d*)	**11.** (*a*)	**12.** (*b*)	**13.** (*a*)	**14.** (*c*)	**15.** (*c*)	**16.** (*a*)	**17.** (*b*)	**18.** (*c*)
19. (*c*)	**20.** (*c*)							

❑❑❑

12 CLASSIFICATION

INTRODUCTION

Assigning input data (features) to predetermined groups or classes based on prior observations is the aim of classification, a type of supervised learning in machine learning. In order to create predictions on brand-new, unforeseen data, the procedure entails learning a mapping between the input attributes and the appropriate output labels. The output labels, which indicate various classes or categories, are discrete. Data is separated into two basic categories for categorization tasks:

Input Data (Features): The qualities or traits of each instance (observation) in the dataset are represented by the input data, which is often referred to as features or independent variables. These features serve as the basis for making predictions.

Output Labels (Classes): The output labels, also known as classes or dependent variables, are the predefined categories or classes that the model aims to predict for each instance in the input data.

The process of classification involves the following steps:

Data Collection: Gather a labeled dataset, where each instance in the dataset is associated with a known class label.

Data Preprocessing: To manage missing values, outliers, and normalize the features if necessary, clean and preprocess the data.

Feature Selection/Extraction: Choose relevant features that have the most impact on the classification task or extract new features from the existing ones.

Model Training: The dataset should be divided into training and validation sets. Then, using the training data, train a classification method to discover the relationship between features and class labels, such as logistic regression, decision trees, random forests, support vector machines, or neural networks.

Model Evaluation: Assess the performance of the trained model using the validation set. Accuracy, precision, recall, F1-score, and the confusion matrix are common evaluation criteria for categorization.

Model Prediction: Use the model to make predictions on fresh, unforeseen data to categorize instances into the proper classes after it has been trained and validated.

Numerous applications, including spam detection, sentiment analysis, picture identification, medical diagnosis, customer churn prediction, fraud detection, and many more, use classification extensively. The type of the data and the difficulty of the problem determine which classification algorithm should be used. The quantity and quality of the labeled data, as well as the choice of the best features and methods, all affect how well the classification model performs.

DIFFERENCE BETWEEN CLASSIFICATION AND REGRESSION DECISION TREES FROM CART MODELS

Regression and classifiers The idea of segmenting data based on input features into decision trees and decision trees are two different decision tree models. But they have unique objectives and scenarios:

Classification Decision Trees: The use of categorical or discrete outcome variables in classification decision trees makes them appropriate for classification tasks. They make predictions about an input's class or category based on the feature values. The best feature and threshold for optimally separating the classes are chosen by the decision tree method to recursively divide the data into subsets. It seeks to maximize each resulting subset's homogeneity or purity with regard to the target classes.

Each leaf node in a classification decision tree represents a specific class, and the majority class in a leaf node becomes the predicted class for new instances falling into that leaf's region.

Regression Decision Trees: Regression decision trees are used for continuous outcome variables, making them suitable for regression tasks. They predict a numeric value (real number) based on the input feature values. The algorithm, like classification decision trees, iteratively divides the data into subsets, but instead of increasing purity, it seeks to minimize the variance or sum of squared errors within each resulting subset.

Each leaf node in a regression decision tree represents a specific numeric value (predicted outcome), which is typically the average (mean) of the target variable for instances falling into that leaf's region.

CART (Classification and Regression Trees) is a particular approach used in decision tree modeling that can handle both classification and regression tasks. When using classification or regression, the CART algorithm creates a binary tree structure with each leaf node representing a forecast for a class and each interior node representing a split on a feature.

The main difference between classification and regression decision trees lies in the type of outcome variable they handle. Classification decision trees handle discrete classes, while regression decision trees handle continuous numeric values. Despite this difference, both types of decision trees share the concept of recursively partitioning the data based on feature values to make predictions.

UNDERSTANDING TREE FROM THE PLOT

Understanding a decision tree from its plot can deliver valuable intuitions into how the tree makes predictions. Decision tree plots are graphical representations of the tree's structure, showing the decision-making process at each node and the predicted outcomes at the leaf nodes. Let's go through the elements typically present in a decision tree plot:

Root Node: Top node of the tree, representing the entire dataset. It is the first node where the data is split based on a selected feature.

Internal Nodes: In the tree, intermediary nodes signify splits on the input features. Every internal node represents a test on a certain feature. These nodes in the decision tree are used to create subsets of the data based on the values of the features.

Branches: The branches or edges connecting the nodes represent the outcomes of the feature tests. For binary features, there are two branches: one for the condition being true and another for the condition being false.

Leaf Nodes: The terminal nodes of the tree, which do not have any further splits. Each leaf node represents a specific class (in classification) or a predicted value (in regression). The majority class in a leaf node is the predicted class for instances falling into that leaf's region.

Samples: The number of instances from the dataset that pass through each node.

Value: For classification trees, the value indicates the class distribution of the samples passing through the node. For regression trees, it represents the average predicted value for the samples in that node.

Gini/Entropy (For Classification Trees): Gini impurity or entropy is used to measure the homogeneity of the classes in a node. A node with low Gini impurity or entropy means the classes are more pure, while higher values indicate mixed classes.

MSE (For Regression Trees): Mean Squared Error (MSE) is a measure of the variance or uncertainty in the predicted values at a node. Lower MSE values indicate less variation in the predicted values.

By following the path from the root node to a leaf node, you can understand how the decision tree reaches a particular prediction for an instance. The tree makes decisions based on the feature values and the conditions at each node. The final prediction is determined by the class or value associated with the leaf node reached by the instance.

Reading and interpreting a decision tree plot can provide valuable insights into the important features for making predictions, how the data is divided, and how the model makes decisions. Decision trees are particularly useful for interpretability and visualization in machine learning models.

CLASSIFICATION TREE - PREDICT CLASS, PLOT, ACCURACY

To perform classification using a decision tree, you can follow these steps in Python using the scikit-learn library:

Step 1: Import necessary libraries and load the dataset.

```
import numpy as np
import pandas as pd
from sklearn.model_selection import train_test_split
from sklearn.tree import DecisionTreeClassifier
from sklearn.metrics import accuracy_score, confusion_matrix
import matplotlib.pyplot as plt

# Assuming 'X' is a numpy array or pandas DataFrame containing the input features
# and 'y' is a numpy array or pandas Series containing the target classes (labels)
```

Step 2: Split the data into training and test sets.

```
X_train, X_test, y_train, y_test = train_test_split(X, y, test_size=0.2, random_state=42)
```

Step 3: Create and train the Decision Tree Classifier.

```
classifier = DecisionTreeClassifier()
classifier.fit(X_train, y_train)
```

Step 4: Make predictions on the test set.

```
y_pred = classifier.predict(X_test)
```

Step 5: Calculate the accuracy of the model.

```
accuracy = accuracy_score(y_test, y_pred)
print("Accuracy:", accuracy)
```

Step 6: Create a confusion matrix (optional but useful for performance evaluation).

```
conf_matrix = confusion_matrix(y_test, y_pred)
print("Confusion Matrix:")
print(conf_matrix)
```

Step 7: Plot the decision tree (optional but useful for visualization).

```
# You can use graphviz to visualize the decision tree
from sklearn.tree import export_graphviz
import graphviz

# Create a dot file
dot_data = export_graphviz(classifier, out_file=None,
    feature_names=X.columns,
    class_names=np.unique(y).astype(str),
    filled=True, rounded=True, special_characters=True)

# Plot the decision tree
graph = graphviz.Source(dot_data)
graph.render("decision_tree") # Saves the tree as a PDF file
graph.view() # Opens the PDF file for visualization
```

A classification decision tree model is created in this code using DecisionTreeClassifier. The predict approach is used to make predictions on the test data, whereas the fit method is used to train the model on the training data. The accuracy_score function calculates the model's accuracy, and the confusion_matrix function generates a confusion matrix to assess the model's performance.

The decision tree can be visualized using the graphviz library. The tree is saved as a PDF file and can be opened to visualize the nodes, branches, and decisions made by the model. Visualization helps in understanding the model's decision-making process and the important features used for classification.

REGRESSION TREE - PREDICT NUMERICAL VALUE, PLOT, RMSE

Regression problems can be solved using a regression tree, a machine learning approach for forecasting numerical values. To produce predictions, it recursively divides the data into subsets depending on several attributes and builds a structure like a tree.

Let's create a regression tree, make predictions, display the tree, and calculate the Root Mean Squared Error (RMSE) to assess the model's efficacy using Python and Scikit-learn, a well-known machine learning library. The procedures below should be followed assuming that your data is prepared with characteristics (X) and associated goal values (Y).:

Step 1: Import necessary libraries and split the data into training and testing sets.

```
import numpy as np
import matplotlib.pyplot as plt
from sklearn.model_selection import train_test_split
from sklearn.tree import DecisionTreeRegressor
from sklearn.metrics import mean_squared_error
```

```
# Assuming you have your features (X) and target (y) ready
# Split the data into training and testing sets
X_train, X_test, y_train, y_test = train_test_split(X, y, test_size=0.2, random_state=42)
```

Step 2: Train the Regression Tree model.

```
# Initialize the Regression Tree model
regression_tree = DecisionTreeRegressor(random_state=42)

# Train the model on the training data
regression_tree.fit(X_train, y_train)
```

Step 3: Make predictions on the test set.

```
# Predict target values using the trained model
y_pred = regression_tree.predict(X_test)
```

Step 4: Calculate Root Mean Squared Error (RMSE).

```
# Calculate the RMSE
rmse = np.sqrt(mean_squared_error(y_test, y_pred))
print("Root Mean Squared Error (RMSE):", rmse)
```

Step 5: Visualize the regression tree.

```
# Visualize the Regression Tree (plot the tree)
from sklearn.tree import plot_tree

plt.figure(figsize=(12, 8))
plot_tree(regression_tree, filled=True, feature_names=feature_names)
plt.show()
```

Make sure to replace X with your feature data, y with the target values, and feature_names with the names of your features in the plot function. The plot_tree function from Scikit-learn will visualize the constructed regression tree.

Keep in mind that, especially if the tree is quite deep, decision trees might be subject to overfitting. This can be avoided by adjusting the hyperparameters max_depth, min_samples_split, and min_samples_leaf while building the model. You should be able to create a regression tree, generate predictions, plot the tree, and assess its effectiveness using the RMSE metric by following these instructions.

IMPROVING TREE ACCURACY USING RANDOM FORESTS

An ensemble learning technique called Random Forest can raise the precision of individual decision trees. Several decision trees are combined, and predictions are then made based on the average or majority vote of these trees. With this strategy, overfitting is decreased and overall prediction accuracy is increased. These steps can help you increase the accuracy of your model while utilizing Random Forest:

Step 1: Import the necessary libraries.

```
import numpy as np
import matplotlib.pyplot as plt
from sklearn.model_selection import train_test_split
from sklearn.ensemble import RandomForestRegressor
from sklearn.metrics import mean_squared_error
```

Step 2: Split the data into training and testing sets.

```
# Assuming you have your features (X) and target (y) ready
# Split the data into training and testing sets
X_train, X_test, y_train, y_test = train_test_split(X, y, test_size=0.2, random_state=42)
```

Step 3: Initialize and train the Random Forest model.

```
# Initialize the Random Forest model
random_forest = RandomForestRegressor(n_estimators=100, random_state=42)

# Train the model on the training data
random_forest.fit(X_train, y_train)
```

Step 4: Make predictions on the test set.

```
# Predict target values using the trained model
y_pred = random_forest.predict(X_test)
```

Step 5: Calculate Root Mean Squared Error (RMSE) to evaluate the model's performance.

```
# Calculate the RMSE
rmse = np.sqrt(mean_squared_error(y_test, y_pred))
print("Random Forest Root Mean Squared Error (RMSE):", rmse)
```

Step 6: (Optional) Tune hyper parameters to optimize performance.

Random Forest has several hyper parameters that you can tune to get better results. Some important hyper parameters are:

n_estimators: how many decision trees there are in the forest. While increasing this parameter might result in better results, it would also lengthen training. Your data and computational resources will determine how to find the ideal value.

max_depth: the deepest decision tree in the forest can go. Overfitting is avoided by setting a limit. To discover the ideal value, try various values or utilize cross-validation.

min_samples_split and min_samples_leaf: The minimal number of samples needed to divide an internal node or be a leaf node is controlled by these parameters. By raising these numbers, overfitting can be avoided.

To explore various hyperparameter combinations and determine the ideal setting for your Random Forest model, employ approaches like Grid Search or Randomized Search. You may use Random Forests to dramatically increase the accuracy of your regression model by following these steps and fine-tuning the hyperparameters.

BAGGING AND BOOSTING

Two well-liked ensemble learning techniques, bagging and boosting, are applied to enhance the performance of machine learning models. Both approaches combine several base models to produce a better, more reliable predictive model.

Bagging (Bootstrap Aggregating): Bagging is the process of independently training several base models on various subsets of the training data. It operates as follows:

Data Sampling: Through bootstrapping, random subsets of the training data are produced. By selecting data points with replacement, a sampling approach called bootstrapping creates datasets of the same size as the originals, but with some data points repeated and some left out.

Model Training: One of these bootstrapped datasets is used to separately train each base model, which are frequently decision trees.

Prediction Aggregation: The final prediction is generated during prediction by combining the predictions of all the underlying models. This aggregate for regression problems is often the mean of the individual predictions. The base models' majority vote may be used for categorization tasks.

Random Forest, a collection of bagging-trained decision trees, is the most often used algorithm. Bagging enhances model generalization and lowers overfitting.

Boosting: Boosting, on the other hand, is an iterative technique where base models are trained sequentially, and each model tries to correct the mistakes of its predecessors. It works as follows:

Data Weights: Initially, all data points are assigned equal weights.

Model Training: The first base model is trained on the original dataset. The subsequent models give more emphasis to the misclassified data points from the previous models.

Weight Update: After each model, the weights of the misclassified data points are increased, so the next model focuses more on getting them right.

Prediction Aggregation: During prediction, each base model's contribution is weighted based on its performance, and final prediction is weighted sum of the individual base models' predictions.

Popular algorithms using boosting are AdaBoost (Adaptive Boosting) and Gradient Boosting Machines (GBM). Boosting can be more powerful than bagging, as it can create highly accurate models by iteratively focusing on hard-to-predict instances in the dataset.

Key Differences

Bagging: On random portions of the data, base models are independently trained. Variance and overfitting are diminished.

Boosting: Base models are trained sequentially, and each model corrects its predecessors' mistakes. It reduces bias and aims to improve accuracy.

Bagging focuses on parallel training of base models, while Boosting focuses on sequential training and assigns weights to each base model based on its performance.

In summary, both Bagging and Boosting are powerful techniques in ensemble learning. Bagging reduces variance and improves stability, while Boosting tries to improve the model's accuracy by focusing on difficult-to-predict instances. Choosing between them depends on the specific problem and the characteristics of the dataset.

APPLICATIONS OF DECISION TREE

Due to their simplicity, interpretability, and ability to handle both classification and regression tasks, decision trees are flexible machine learning models that find applications in a variety of disciplines. Here are a few typical uses for decision trees:

Classification Problems: In classification problems where the objective is to predict a categorical or discrete target variable, decision trees are frequently utilized. Several instances include:

Email Spam Detection: the ability to categorize emails as spam or not spam based on the content and metadata.

Customer Churn Prediction: To predict whether a customer is likely to churn (cancel a subscription or service) or not.

Disease Diagnosis: To diagnose diseases based on symptoms, medical history, and test results.

Regression Problems: Decision trees can also handle regression tasks, where the goal is to predict a continuous numerical value. Applications include:

House Price Prediction: To determine a home's cost based on attributes like size, location, and amenities.

Demand Forecasting: To predict the demand for products or services in the future.

Financial Risk Assessment: To assess the risk associated with investments or loans.

Feature Selection: Decision trees can be used for feature selection tasks, where they help identify the most important features that contribute to the prediction. This can be valuable for simplifying models and reducing overfitting.

Anomaly Detection: Decision trees can be used to detect anomalies or outliers in data, which can be useful for fraud detection, fault detection, or error identification.

Segmentation: Decision trees are often used for data segmentation, where they divide the data into subsets based on specific features. This can be helpful in marketing to identify different customer segments.

Imputation of Missing Data: Decision trees can be utilized to predict missing values in a dataset by using the available features to make an informed estimation.

Recommendation Systems: In collaborative filtering, decision trees can be part of the recommendation algorithm to provide personalized suggestions to users based on their preferences and behavior.

Multi-output Tasks: When many target variables must be forecasted simultaneously, decision trees can handle multi-output jobs.

Ensemble Methods: The predictive performance of ensemble approaches like Random Forest and Gradient Boosting, which frequently use decision trees as basic models, is greatly enhanced.

Natural Language Processing (NLP): Decision trees can be employed in NLP applications for things like sentiment analysis and text categorization.

It's important to note that while decision trees are powerful and interpretable, they can suffer from overfitting, especially when the tree becomes too deep. Ensemble methods like Random Forest & Gradient Boosting help mitigate this issue and are often preferred in practice. Additionally, large and complex datasets might require more sophisticated algorithms to achieve better performance.

KNN (K-NEAREST NEIGHBORS)

A straightforward and efficient machine learning approach called K-Nearest Neighbors (KNN) is utilized for both classification and regression problems. In this kind of instance-based learning, the model predicts outcomes based on how closely input data points (instances) resemble data points in the training dataset.

Here's how the KNN algorithm works:

Training: KNN stores all the available data points and their matching labels (for classification) or target values (for regression) during the training phase.

Prediction (Classification): The technique locates the K closest data points in the feature space to the input data point, depending on a distance metric (for example, Euclidean distance), in order to predict the class of a new data point. The predicted class for the new data point is determined to be the most prevalent among these K nearest neighbors.

Prediction (Regression): The algorithm locates the K closest data points and determines the average (or weighted average) of those data points' target values to predict a numerical value for a new data point. This average is used as the new data point's expected value.

Key hyper parameter of KNN:

K: The number of nearest neighbors to consider for making predictions. It's an important hyperparameter that can significantly influence the model's performance. A small K can lead to a noisy prediction, while a large K can cause the model to be overly generalized.

Some considerations and properties of KNN:

KNN does not involve a training phase, as it simply stores the data points during the training process. The real computation occurs during prediction.

KNN's prediction time complexity is relatively high, especially when dealing with large datasets, as it requires computing distances for each test instance with all training instances.

The choice of distance metric is essential for KNN's performance, and it can be customized based on the nature of the data.

KNN works well for data with simple decision boundaries and when the dataset is not very large.

It is crucial to normalize or scale the features before using KNN to ensure that features with larger scales do not dominate the distance calculation.

KNN can be a good starting point for simple classification and regression tasks. However, for more complex problems and large datasets, other algorithms like Random Forest, Gradient Boosting, or Deep Learning models may yield better results.

NEURAL NETWORKS

The structure and operation of the human brain served as the inspiration for the class of machine learning algorithms known as neural networks (NNs). Due to their ability to recognize and learn complicated patterns in data, they are strong models that can solve challenging issues. As a result, they are becoming increasingly popular in a variety of industries. Neural networks are used for a variety of machine learning tasks, including speech and picture recognition, natural language processing, and many others.

Key components of a Neural Network:

Neurons (Nodes): The basic building blocks of a neural network. Neurons receive inputs, process them, and produce an output. In a neural network, neurons are organized into layers.

Layers: A neural network typically consists of multiple layers, arranged in a specific sequence. The three main types of layers are:

Input Layer: Receives the raw input data and passes it to the next layer.

Hidden Layers: Intermediate layers between the input and output layers. They process the data and learn representations.

Output Layer: creates the neural network's ultimate output. Depending on the specific issue, such as binary classification (one neuron) or multiclass classification (many neurons), the number of neurons in the output layer may vary.

Weights and Biases: Each connection between neurons in adjacent layers has a weight associated with it. During training, these weights are updated to learn the patterns and features in the data. Additionally, each neuron has a bias term that adjusts the neuron's output.

Activation Function: Each neuron's output is subjected to an activation function. By adding non-linearity to the model, it enables the network to understand intricate data correlations. Sigmoid, tanh, and ReLU (Rectified Linear Unit) are frequently used activation functions.

Training a Neural Network: Training a neural network involves a process called backpropagation, where the network learns from the data and updates its weights to minimize the error (difference between predicted and actual output). The most common optimization algorithm used during training is Gradient Descent or its variants.

Deep Learning: Deep neural networks are neural networks with numerous hidden layers. Deep Learning, often known as Deep Learning models, is a branch of machine learning that focuses on training deep neural networks. Deep Learning has transformed a wide range of fields, particularly computer vision and natural language processing, reaching cutting-edge outcomes in tasks like image classification, object recognition, machine translation, etc.

While deep neural networks are powerful, they also require large amounts of data and computational resources for training, making them more suitable for complex tasks with sufficient data. Popular deep learning frameworks include TensorFlow and PyTorch, which provide tools for building and training complex neural network architectures.

GRADIENT DESCENT

During the training phase of a machine learning model, the gradient descent optimization algorithm is often used to update the parameters in order to minimize or maximize a function. It is widely used in various machine learning algorithms, especially in training neural networks and other models that involve optimizing a cost or loss function. Gradient Descent's primary principle is to iteratively alter the model's parameters in the direction of the cost function's sharpest ascent or descent. The gradient is a vector that indicates the direction of the function's greatest rate of growth. When a cost function is being minimized, the gradient points in the direction of the steepest reduction, enabling the algorithm to locate the function's minimum.

Here's how Gradient Descent works:

Initialization: The procedure begins by randomly choosing or setting the model's parameters' values.

Compute Gradient: The gradient of the cost function with respect to each parameter is then calculated. In the case of neural networks and other sophisticated models, this is often carried out via the chain rule of calculus.

Update Parameters: Using the obtained gradients scaled by a learning rate (denoted by), the parameters are updated. The step size or rate at which the parameters are updated is determined by the learning rate, a hyperparameter. Slower convergence is caused by a lower learning rate, whereas overshooting the ideal solution is possible with a higher learning rate.

Repeat: Until the convergence conditions are satisfied or for a predetermined number of repetitions (epochs), steps 2 and 3 are repeated. When the change in the cost function or the parameters is less than a predetermined threshold, convergence is attained.

There are different variants of Gradient Descent, such as:

Batch Gradient Descent: Each time an update is made, the gradient is calculated using the whole training dataset, which can be computationally expensive for big datasets but yields a more precise estimate of the gradient.

Stochastic Gradient Descent (SGD): It computes the gradient using only one training data point (or a mini-batch) for each update. This reduces computation time but introduces more noise in the updates.

Mini-batch Gradient Descent: A compromise between Batch and SGD, where the gradient is computed using a small batch of data points. This approach strikes a balance between accuracy and computational efficiency.

Momentum: An extension of Gradient Descent that adds a momentum term to the updates, helping the algorithm to navigate through areas with high curvature or noise.

Gradient Descent is a foundational optimization algorithm in machine learning and plays a critical role in training various models by iteratively updating their parameters to find the optimal solution that minimizes the cost function and improves the model's performance.

SVM (SUPPORT VECTOR MACHINE)

Support Vector Machine (SVM) is a powerful supervised machine learning algorithm used for both classification and regression tasks. SVM is particularly effective in solving problems with complex decision boundaries and is widely used in various domains, including image classification, text classification, and bioinformatics.

1. **SVM for Binary Classification:** SVM searches for the best hyperplane to divide the two classes in the feature space when it comes to binary classification. The support vectors, or nearest data points of each class to the hyperplane, are chosen so that the margin (distance) between them is maximized. The most important data points are the support vectors since they establish the decision boundary.
2. **SVM for Multi-Class Classification:** Multiple methods can be used to extend SVM to multi-class classification issues. One common approach is the one-vs-one (OvO) strategy, where SVM trains one classifier for each pair of classes and combines their decisions through voting. Another approach is the one-vs-all (OvA) strategy, where SVM trains one classifier for each class to distinguish it from all other classes.
3. **SVM for Regression**: In order to create a hyperplane that best matches the data points while taking into account a tolerance (epsilon) around the hyperplane, SVM can also be used for regression tasks. Reduce the number of data points that are outside of this tolerance region as much as possible.

Key Concepts and Features of SVM

Kernel Trick: By utilizing the kernel method, SVM can effectively handle non-linear decision boundaries. The data points are implicitly mapped to a higher-dimensional space where they might be linearly separable. The radial basis function (RBF) kernel, polynomial kernel, and linear kernel are popular types of kernel functions.

C Parameter: In SVM, the C parameter is used for regularization. It manages the compromise between increasing margin and reducing categorization mistake. A greater C will prioritize decreasing misclassifications, which may result in a narrower margin, whereas a smaller C would prefer a broader margin but may result in more misclassifications.

Margin: The distance between the support vectors and the hyperplane is known as the margin in SVM. Since SVM offers a more reliable and generally applicable decision boundary, it seeks to maximize this margin.

Outlier Robustness: Due to its emphasis on support vectors, which are the data points that are closest to the decision boundary, SVM is relatively resistant to outliers.

SVM has been widely used for a variety of applications, but its main shortcomings are that it can be computationally expensive for large datasets and that it is sensitive to the choice of hyperparameters, such as the kernel and C parameter. Due to its efficiency and adaptability, SVM continues to be a preferred option for many classification and regression applications in spite of these difficulties.

REVIEW QUESTIONS

Multiple Choice Questions

Q.1. What is classification in machine learning?

(*a*) A technique for predicting continuous values
(*b*) A technique for categorizing data points into predefined classes or categories
(*c*) A technique for clustering similar data points together
(*d*) A technique for reducing the dimensionality of data

Q.2. Which of the following algorithms is commonly used for binary classification?

(*a*) K-means
(*b*) Decision Trees
(*c*) K-nearest neighbors
(*d*) Linear Regression

Q.3. What is the output of a classification model?

(*a*) Continuous values
(*b*) Categorical labels or classes
(*c*) Clusters of data points
(*d*) Reduced dimensionality representation

Q.4. What is the difference between binary and multiclass classification?

(*a*) Binary classification has two classes, while multiclass classification has more than two classes
(*b*) Binary classification deals with continuous values, while multiclass classification deals with categorical values
(*c*) Binary classification predicts probabilities, while multiclass classification predicts discrete values
(*d*) Binary classification is supervised learning, while multiclass classification is unsupervised learning

Q.5. What is a confusion matrix used for in classification?

(*a*) To measure the accuracy of a classification model
(*b*) To visualize the distribution of data points
(*c*) To evaluate the performance of a classification model
(*d*) To identify outliers in the dataset

Q.6. What does precision measure in a classification context?

(*a*) The ratio of correctly predicted positive observations to the total number of positive observations
(*b*) The ratio of correctly predicted positive observations to the total number of predicted positive observations
(*c*) The ratio of correctly predicted observations to the total number of observations
(*d*) The ratio of true positive predictions to the total number of predictions

Q.7. What does recall measure in a classification context?

(*a*) The ratio of correctly predicted positive observations to the total number of positive observations
(*b*) The ratio of correctly predicted positive observations to the total number of predicted positive observations

(c) The ratio of correctly predicted observations to the total number of observations
(d) The ratio of true positive predictions to the total number of predictions

Q.8. What is the F1-score?
(a) The harmonic mean of precision and recall (b) The arithmetic mean of precision and recall
(c) The geometric mean of precision and recall (d) The ratio of precision to recall

Q.9. Which evaluation metric is more important when the cost of false positives is high?
(a) Precision (b) Recall (c) F1-score (d) Accuracy

Q.10. Which algorithm is specifically designed for handling imbalanced datasets in classification?
(a) Decision Trees (b) Logistic Regression
(c) K-means (d) Random Forests

Q.11. What is overfitting in the context of classification?
(a) The model performs well on unseen data (b) The model captures noise in the training data
(c) The model generalizes well to new data
(d) The model is too simple to capture the underlying patterns

Q.12. Which of the following techniques can help prevent overfitting in classification?
(a) Increasing model complexity (b) Adding more features to the model
(c) Regularization (d) Using a smaller training dataset

Q.13. What is ensemble learning in classification?
(a) Training multiple models independently and combining their predictions
(b) Training a single complex model on the entire dataset
(c) Using a single decision tree to make predictions
(d) Classifying data points into clusters

Q.14. Which algorithm is used to make predictions based on the weighted average of predictions from multiple models in ensemble learning?
(a) Decision Trees (b) K-means (c) Gradient Boosting (d) K-nearest neighbors

Q.15. What is bagging in ensemble learning?
(a) Training multiple models sequentially and combining their predictions
(b) Training multiple models independently and combining their predictions
(c) Using a single decision tree to make predictions
(d) Classifying data points into clusters

Q.16. What is boosting in ensemble learning?
(a) Training multiple models sequentially and combining their predictions
(b) Training multiple models independently and combining their predictions
(c) Using a single decision tree to make predictions
(d) Classifying data points into clusters

Q.17. Which of the following algorithms is a popular choice for boosting in ensemble learning?
(a) Random Forests (b) Decision Trees (c) AdaBoost (d) K-means

Q.18. Which of the following techniques is used to handle missing values in classification?

(*a*) Removing rows with missing values

(*b*) Replacing missing values with the mean of the column

(*c*) Imputing missing values using a predictive model

(*d*) Ignoring missing values during training

Q.19. Which evaluation metric should be used when the classes in the dataset are imbalanced?

(*a*) Accuracy (*b*) Precision (*c*) Recall (*d*) F1-score

Q.20. Which algorithm is known for its interpretability and is often used in classification tasks where model transparency is important?

(*a*) Support Vector Machines (SVM) (*b*) Random Forests

(*c*) Logistic Regression (*d*) K-nearest neighbors

Answer to Multiple Choice Questions

1. (*b*) **2.** (*b*) **3.** (*b*) **4.** (*a*) **5.** (*c*) **6.** (*b*) **7.** (*a*) **8.** (*a*) **9.** (*a*)
10. (*d*) **11.** (*b*) **12.** (*c*) **13.** (*a*) **14.** (*c*) **15.** (*b*) **16.** (*a*) **17.** (*c*) **18.** (*c*)
19. (*d*) **20.** (*c*

❑❑❑